The Strategy Handbook

Michael Hay and Peter Williamson

BLACKWELL
Business

Copyright © Michael Hay and Peter Williamson 1991

Michael Hay and Peter Williamson are hereby identified as authors of this work in accordance with Section 77 of the Copyright, Designs and Patents Act 1988.

First published 1991
Reprinted 1993

Blackwell Publishers
108 Cowley Road, Oxford, OX4 1JF, UK

238 Main Street, Suite 501
Cambridge, Massachusetts 02142, USA

Library of Congress Cataloging in Publication Data
Hay, Michael.
  The strategy handbook/Michael Hay and Peter Williamson.
    p. cm.
  Includes bibliographical references.
  ISBN 0–631–16475–8 (hb)   ISBN 0–631–18208–X (pb)
  1. Management—Dictionaries.   2. Strategic planning—Dictionaries.
I. Williamson, Peter.   II. Title
HD30.15.H39   1991
658.4′012—dc20

British Library Cataloguing in Publication Data
A CIP catalogue record for this book is available from the British Library

Typeset in 11 on 13pt Sabon by Wearside Tradespools, Fulwell, Sunderland
Printed in Great Britain by TJ Press Ltd, Padstow, Cornwall.

This book is printed on acid-free paper.

PREFACE

We are all strategists now. Some have chosen this rocky path to Eldorado. A growing number have, in one way or another, had strategy thrust upon them. In an era of the devolution of responsibility and head office slimming, more and more line managers and functional chiefs are being called upon to think and act strategically. They are also being asked to justify their actions and plans in the language of strategy and strategic planning and learning.

This book is therefore dedicated to those men and women who have just been asked by their bosses to develop 'a strategy'. We hope it will also be useful to those who have suffered a six-hour strategy presentation at a two-day strategy conference in bewildered silence. To those whose interest has been sparked by such events, the book offers an opportunity to explore some of the concepts further.

We trust it will be an aid to some of the strategy converts too. Having seen the light, your problem is to help the uninitiated understand what on earth you are on about. To this end, we have sought to explain each topic with minimal use of jargon, of which there is plenty enough in the titles themselves.

For the manager and business student getting to grips with any new language and way of thinking, time is the enemy. We have therefore chosen the A to Z format, not with the aim of producing a dictionary, but to allow readers to dive straight into the problem at hand. If your problem is cost, for example, you can start by looking at what we have to say on *cost advantage*. This might lead on to *cost analysis*, *cost structure*, *cost leadership* or even *costs of complexity*. By following a cross-reference you could find yourself considering *buyer power*, *competitive advantage*, *differentiation*, *pre-emption* or *value chain*. Before too long the bones of a strategy emerge and you are looking at a *supply side strategy* and a *strategic staircase*, as well as the role of *responsibility accounting*, *acquisition*, and *purchasing strategy* in helping you to achieve it.

Instead of presenting a cold definition, each entry tries to provide a gateway into the subject and a viewpoint on how that concept might play a role in improving thinking about strategy, which issues to look out for in that area, and the practical action which should result. The rest is up to you.

A

Acquisition. Countless acquisitions are consummated each year, yet research has shown that after the event more than 50 per cent of the management involved are disappointed with the results. Even so, acquisition is often heralded as the fastest way to gain a position in a market where greenfield entry would require time-consuming and uncertain building of teams, business systems, customer and supplier relationships, technological competence and CORPORATE CULTURE. Studies of the impact on shareholders show that in the majority of public bids the acquiree's owners enjoy most of the gains in the form of bid premiums, with slim pickings for the shareholders of the acquiror. The key point here is that, having paid a premium (commonly around 30 per cent of the pre-bid price or more), the acquiror has to increase earnings substantially before breaking even.

Reaping the benefits of an acquisition is in reality a long process requiring considerable persistence. It begins with the acquiror setting its own strategy: the goal the acquisition will help to achieve and the critical resources a candidate should bring to further it. Just as in looking to buy an existing house rather than building anew, the available candidates on the market never seem to be ideal in every respect. In particular the potential targets come with their own strategies and corporate cultures that won't exactly fit the acquiror's purpose. (See figure 1.)

Some companies, ostrich-like, try to ignore the deficiencies of their target or fail to appreciate fully the nature of the animal they are buying. Since acquiring a company means buying an existing strategy which may account for much of the company's existing profit and worth, it is essential to take the time to understand how your new strategy for the firm might affect its performance. The greatest acquisition debacles have regularly occurred when the acquiree's strategy was a fragile flower: dependent on a few key individuals, low overhead costs, a specialist market image, customer or dealer

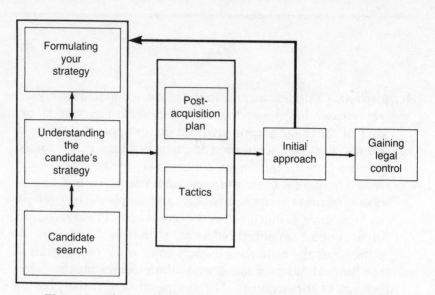

Figure 1   The Acquisition Process Prior to Gaining Legal Control

loyalty to previous owners, or a 'small group', easy-going style. The introduction of a new strategy, designed with the parent's objectives in mind, has undermined these key sources of advantage, leaving a near-worthless shell.

Having found a target with a potentially good FIT, the thrill of the chase follows and the deal is done. It is then, just when top management often finds itself losing interest and looking for the next deal, that the real challenges begin. (See figure 2.)

It is an unfortunate fact of life that the day after a new company is acquired, the existing management still runs it. After gaining legal control, therefore, it remains for the new owner to get true organizational control over the business. This doesn't happen by accident: some companies which have changed hands numerous times are still run by the same bemused management. The ownership waves simply pass them by. Four ingredients have been found to lie behind gaining effective organizational control in successful acquisitions: acting quickly and decisively, even in the face of inadequate information; establishing a clear vision of the future in the minds of staff; communicating the buyer's contribution to the seller (what problem are you solving for

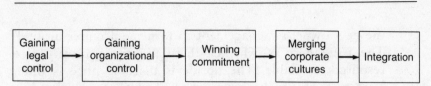

Figure 2 Post-acquisition Management

them?); and being consistent in the negotiating stance (assisted by a single 'face'). Guarantees of autonomy for a limited period generally end in disaster: the existing management has power without responsibility.

The next problem faced by post-acquisition management is merging different corporate cultures. Many successful companies have strong cultures which have emerged from long experience in their businesses. Supplanting an old culture by a substitute risks destroying one of the key ASSETS which have been acquired. Some of the important elements of culture must be examined in the acquisition process including: the driving force of the business (is it in marketing, production, technology, or an entrepreneurial individual?); the margin environment (people from an acquiror who make their money out of high margins have destroyed low-margin businesses who profit from volume by 'correcting the problem' after acquisition); the time horizon (for example, fashion goods versus investment in oil refineries); and the reward structure (the rewards for taking risks and the penalties for failure, for example). The acquiror's culture is unlikely to be a perfect fit with the new business. Post-acquisition management is therefore about merging cultures, not simply substituting them.

Finally, acquisitions are about SYNERGY (remember that bid premium?). Synergy doesn't just 'happen' through ownership. It requires catalysts which might include shared physical facilities, some forum for formal exchange, incentive on both sides (write the synergies into managers' budgets), and champions. It also often needs acceptance and involvement from the market: the benefits need to be sold to the customer as well as the employees.

Buying a business in poor health clearly puts pressure on

the new owner's management to turn the acquiree around. The issue here is whether there are the necessary free resources available. The upside is that the price is often attractive. This makes sense where the business is related to that of the potential acquiror, with consequent opportunities to draw on its experience, management skills, and existing market position. Acquiring an unrelated business in poor health, however, raises a different question: are you out of your mind?

Acquisition screen. A framework is required for determining which acquisition candidates are worth pursuing further, given the company's objectives and resources. A common screen involves looking at the relatedness of the candidate to the core business as well as its health. (See figure 3.)

Acquisition candidates which are both highly related to your core business (a potentially good FIT) and running profitably with strong market positions are clearly attractive. They are also likely to be expensive. The problem revolves around what an acquiror can add to the business to improve its profitability and justify the price premium often associated with the acquisition route. This is likely to be more difficult where the acquisition is unrelated to the core business, in

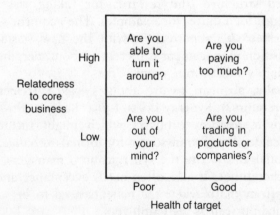

Figure 3   The Acquisition Screen

which case the relevant question is: 'am I trading in products or companies?'
See also ACQUISITION.

Added value. When one asks a business-unit line manager what value is added by his corporate centre his answer is often unflattering. Yet where there is a cost in an organization, the activity which generates that cost must have more than offsetting added value if it is to add to profits. Strategy is essentially about designing activities so that they add more value than they add cost. All activities in the VALUE CHAIN must pass this acid test, otherwise they should be dropped. A classic strategy of cost leaders is to reverse engineer the product or service bundle so as to eliminate those elements which the customer would gladly forego for a reduction in price because their added value is insufficient (*see* COST LEADERSHIP).

While simple in concept, the problem with added value is that traditional measurement systems inside a company often studiously avoid measuring it. Good strategy, however, needs a workable feel for which activities within the firm are pulling their weight through added value to the customers and ultimately the shareholders.

Agency problem. In public companies the directors act as agents on behalf of the shareholders. They are charged with the responsibility of promoting the shareholders' best interests. They, in turn, delegate much of this responsibility to other agents, in the form of management, right down the line. One of the problems with agents is that they have other, often competing, pressures upon them. These may emanate from employees, the press and public arena, as well as their own personal goals. Given these pressures, the chances are that not everything they do will, in fact, be to the long-run benefit of their principals. This proclivity to stray from the single-minded pursuit of their principal's interests is known as the agency problem.

There are many opportunities for the agency problem to surface in the context of strategy. Firms have been known to make acquisitions or diversify into new businesses in pursuit of growth which has more to do with the career prospects and personal standing of the top management than the benefit to shareholders. Nor is it always clear that luxurious offices in the most prestigious locations are designed to satisfy the needs of the shareholders rather than their agents. More generally, the failure to drive costs out of the business through a continued squeeze on inefficiency may be traced to the agency problem. Maybe it also has something to do with the fact that many managers prefer to promote strategies which emphasize building DIFFERENTIATION as opposed to COST LEADERSHIP.

In practice, managers often have wide bounds of discretion to act as agents of their shareholders. When they deviate too much from the path, however, a change in control of the company commonly results. This may take the form of an Extraordinary General Meeting – at which shareholders force a change in the management – or, more often, the launch of a takeover of the company by another, which claims it can make changes to narrow the gap between current policies and shareholder interests. The increasingly popular 'management buy-in' is another powerful way that the agency problem is attacked. The new managers, because they are also major shareholders, are likely to suffer less agency slippage than the old.

MANAGEMENT BUY-OUTS are a particularly interesting phenomenon when viewed in terms of the agency problem. It leads one to ask why the managers who believe they can improve the company's profitability substantially once they own it, did not take these same actions before, while they were still agents of the previous shareholders.

Alliance. Historically, alliances took the form of JOINT VENTURES. Most common were the joint companies formed to manufacture and/or distribute a product in a new region where one party provided the product experience and the other expertise in the local, often developing country, market. These alliances generally involved relatively simple horizontal or vertical relationships between two non-competitors. Less frequently, joint ventures were formed to develop, produce and market a new product, with personnel, skills and technology contributed by the parents. In some cases these became free-standing companies; Unilever is a good example, an Anglo-Dutch joint venture that soon grew larger than either parent.

More recently, there have been a growing number of strategic alliances between competitors. The object of these is often to fill some gaps in the resources required by each party to pursue their chosen strategies. It is hoped that the alliance will allow access to the strengths of the other party which can be used to increase the competitiveness of each firm in the global market. Thus AT&T sought to gain access to marketing and distribution skills through an alliance with Olivetti, who saw benefit in obtaining access to AT&T's base technologies. In other cases, the partners were co-operating to develop expensive, high-risk new technology, thus spreading their exposure.

These new-style alliances tend not to be all-encompassing. The parties co-operate in some areas while competing in others. They often involve complex combinations of capabilities, personnel and assets, rather than simple, vertical relationships. Their intended life is commonly shorter than traditional joint ventures. These features, especially when an 'aggressive' element such as the desire to extract new skills is present, make them inherently difficult to manage.

Experience of these competitor alliances shows that the partner with the less easily transferable capabilities tends to gain the upper hand. Thus partners with complex skills embodied in people and systems tend to gain more and lose less from the alliance compared with firms that have explicit technology, especially where this is embodied in equipment. Many firms, however, fail to gain fully from an alliance as a result of their own unreceptiveness to the new ideas and skills made available from the partner; the 'not invented here' problem. Those most satisfied with alliances tend to be

companies with prior experience of absorbing outside technology or of managing complex relationships with distributors or suppliers. Especially successful were those who explicitly set up organizational structures designed to smooth the
flow of positive spillovers from the alliance into their core
business, who targeted specific skills they wished the alliance
to provide, and who monitored the process of transfer and
'encroachment' by the partner.

When considering the creation of a strategic alliance there
are six key questions that should be borne in mind.

1 'What specific problem are we trying to solve?' Essential
   to the success of an alliance is a clear FIT between the
   strategic need, the problem to be solved, and the alliance
   itself. Understanding precisely the nature of the problem
   is of immeasurable help in determining whether or not it
   is one that an alliance is best suited to resolve.

2 'How will we capture the benefits accruing from the
   alliance?' Being able to answer this question implies that
   we are clear about the nature of the benefits that we are
   trying to obtain. For example, are they scale benefits
   derived from joining forces in, say, production, or are
   they less tangible benefits in the form of transferred skills
   and expertise?

3 'Is our organization sufficiently receptive to gain from the
   intended transfers?' Many alliances fail simply because of
   a reluctance on the part of one party to recognize just
   how much it can learn from the other. Jealously guarding
   one's own way of doing things, and being quick to
   dismiss those things 'not invented here', sets up a resistance within an organization that prevents it from deriving
   the full benefit from an alliance.

4 'How can we control "encroachment" by our partner in
   the alliance?' Both parties are typically pursuing the same
   objective, to maximize their own gains from the alliance.
   Care must be taken however to ensure that our partner
   learns only those things that we intend sharing. One way
   of dealing with this is to set up limited points of contact
   between the two organizations, to control the exchange

of information and to monitor carefully what is being transferred. If participation in the alliance is thrown open to a large number of individuals, and contact between the two organizations is unregulated, there is a real risk that expertise, knowhow and skills will simply leak out of the organization, as through a sieve.

5 'How will we exit from the alliance and realize its value?' Before entering an alliance, thought must be given to its intended life, the likelihood that the other party will want to leave after a certain period, and the scope that exists for extricating oneself in the event that it does not work, or if other, more attractive opportunities present themselves. It is essential to be clear from the outset what form exit might take, and to structure the alliance in such a way that it allows for this.

6 'What form of ORGANIZATION and STRUCTURE should the alliance have?' Alliances come in many forms ranging from a simple gentleman's agreement to more complex cross shareholdings, which may presage an eventual merger. Establishing an appropriate organizational form and determining the right degree of dependence between both parties is essential.

Failure to resolve these questions and attend to the risks inherent in any alliance will usually condemn it to failure. In some instances failure is clear-cut, but in others the alliance may amount to little more than, in the words of a famous Japanese proverb, 'sleeping in the same bed, but dreaming different dreams'.

Ansoff, Igor. In a seminal book entitled *Corporate Strategy* (1965), Ansoff was one of the first writers to emphasize the importance of analysis of the external market environment rather than of a firm's internal needs in arriving at strategic decisions. Underlying many companies' 'strategic decisions' are the internal dynamics of the need to provide growth and career prospects for employees, to secure employment, resolve conflicts over resource availability, and satisfy the personal agenda of top managers. While both inevitable and in many cases appropriate, these influences on strategy can leave the firm isolated from the demands of the market. Since firms ignore market signals at their peril, Ansoff pointed out, strategy must be intimately concerned with the external forces bearing on the selection of 'the product mix a firm will produce and the markets to which it will sell'. This thinking prepared the way for the now classic distinction between CORPORATE STRATEGY (what businesses are we in and how can we achieve SYNERGY between them?) and business strategy (how can we compete most effectively in the businesses we have decided to be in?).

An unfortunate spin-off of the emphasis on external factors in later strategy literature was the distinction between the 'formulation' and 'implementation' of strategy. This tended to leave strategy close to the market and divorced from the day-to-day operation of the firm. More recent views of strategy have sought to close this gap, viewing it as a dynamic process combining both planned and EMERGENT STRATEGY as BOTTOM-UP/TOP-DOWN initiatives merge.

Arbitrage. Strategists borrowed the term from finance to refer to the dealing in bond, currency, and stock markets so as to take advantage of price differences between markets for the same instrument. Thus a quick foreign exchange dealer might buy Deutsche Marks in London and sell them almost instantly in New York at a small profit.

In the strategy context it refers to the deployment of the ASSETS amassed by a company in the course of serving one market to enhance prospects in another. Thus skills in branding or mass-market distribution may be used to give a firm COMPETITIVE ADVANTAGE against its rivals in markets where these skills are scarce. This is particularly important where the requirements for success in a market are changing. Suppose, for example, that the dominant distribution channel is changing from a network of wholesalers to direct selling. Firms with staff knowhow and systems built through experience in direct sales of other products may seek arbitrage advantage from these assets by entering the changing market where they hope to outcompete the incumbents who lack such marketing experience. Other forms of arbitrage include moving technology or products to markets where these are in short supply. As a single European market emerges in the wake of 1992 many believe that opportunities for strategic arbitrage will increase.

Assets. All the things accountants like to write on the balance sheet – land and buildings, plant and equipment, inventories, debtors – are clearly vital to the firm and play an important role in underpinning the execution of a firm's strategy. Without plant of a certain scale some strategies would be unworkable, though often even more important from a strategic perspective are invisible assets such as consumer trust, brand image, control of distribution, CORPORATE CULTURE, and management skill. Since they require conscious and time-consuming efforts to build over an extended period of time, as well as the right environment in which to grow and cannot be bought 'off the shelf' by competitors, they may be the most important and sustainable sources of advantage.

Putting these invisible assets to good use in new ways is a key element of innovative strategy. Having built a reputation for quality in cars and motorcycles, for example, Honda was able to use this invisible asset to launch a campaign to 'Put a Second Honda in Your Garage' in selling lawnmowers. It was also able to use its technology and production experience in building reliable, low-cost petrol engines to move into a range of related products including generators, snowploughs, snowmobiles, and so on. A firm's assets are therefore key in evaluating the FIT of a new product, customer segment, or DIVERSIFICATION opportunity.

Audit. In a strategic context, audit has a much broader meaning than in its accounting sense. The strategist views an audit as an assessment of all of a company's strengths and weaknesses relative to its market. As such, it is useful in defining the core

competences, skills, and resources on which a strategy can be
built. It also helps to identify gaps in a company's resources
relative to its MISSION STATEMENT and strategic GOALS. Decision processes, reward structures, and beliefs identified in the
course of an audit may highlight incompatibilities with the
demands of the strategy (for example, tortuous scheduling
processes in an increasingly fashion-led business, or belief in
entirely in-house, specialist production in a business shifting
to the use of standardized, mass-produced components).

The Latin root of *audit* ('he hears') is an apt description for
the role of an audit in the modern corporation. It is an
opportunity for management to listen systematically to where
the organization stands and to compare this with the requirements of its strategy.

B

Barriers to entry. The threat of entry into an industry by a competitor can be an important determinant of a company's current and future profitability. Entry does not actually have to occur to have an impact. The mere fact that high prices could encourage a flood of new hopefuls may place a ceiling on how much short-term profit a firm is willing to risk making. When entry does take place, be it of newly created firms or diversifying existing ones, it often impairs profitability, causing price reductions and increases in the cost of raw materials, components, or skilled labour as entrants attempt to gain their share.

Barriers to entry are therefore often important in protecting profitable businesses. They raise the ceiling above which entry becomes a real threat and reduce the frequency of actual attempts at breaching the wall. They may arise from many sources including: ECONOMIES OF SCALE, which may mean that entrants face higher costs compared with existing firms with large production; product DIFFERENTIATION, in the form of brand recognition, loyalty of customers or distributors, which it may take entrants a great deal of time or costly advertising to break down; proprietary technology; or product design. Other barriers can arise from high SWITCHING COSTS in moving from one supplier to another (because of re-tooling or resistance from operating staff, for example), difficulties in gaining access to distribution channels (for example, unproven brands often have difficulty competing for shelf space), the control of access to the best locations or raw materials by existing firms, and government restrictions on new entry through licensing laws.

From a strategy standpoint, it is important to recognize that many of these barriers can be built or increased by the established firms. Increased investment in brand image or building tight relationships with distributors often pays dividends in the form of higher entry barriers. Investment in new capacity may be used to pre-empt markets, achieving cost reductions through scale or experience which entrants will find it difficult to match (*see* EXPERIENCE CURVE). Rapid expansion to tie up scarce sites in the early stages of an industry's life can be an important means of building barriers which protect future profit – witness the development of discount, 'out of town' retailing.

Barriers to exit. When a new substitute causes demand to go into terminal decline, massive excess capacity keeps driving prices lower, or a business unit seems to be unnecessarily diverting the attention of management from its core purpose because it lacks strategic FIT with the rest of the business, firms usually begin to think about exit.

Purists would argue that they should approach this decision as if starting with a clean slate: continuing the business either earns an acceptable rate of return on the assets tied up or it doesn't. Anything that went before is a 'sunk cost' – the cash is gone whether you write it off in the books or not. Facing substantial write-offs on book value, paying compensation on long-term supply contracts, trying to forget all that past advertising expenditure, or meeting the cost of employee redundancy, however, businessmen often have a different view. The barriers to exit are substantial.

The existence of barriers to exit, actual or perceived, has important influences on strategy. If you are deciding on investment in a new plant with modern technology and capable of a big increase in market share, it clearly matters how difficult it will be to force other competitors' capacity to exit so as to make room. If they have old, fully depreciated plant they may be prepared to stay in at prices which only just cover their variable cash costs, reporting losses for years. Worse still, if they are part of a large and generally profitable group, it may 'lose' their poor performance in its accounts and keep them running. While they stay prices may remain artificially low and your new plant, even with lower total costs than your competitors, may never earn its keep.

The height of barriers to exit partly depends on the strength of the 'resale' market for capacity. This tends to be poor where the assets are very specific to the business, therefore of little use elsewhere, or where many of the assets are intangibles like accumulated brand image which may be difficult to resell, especially in a mature or declining market.

Many of the actions a firm takes to build BARRIERS TO ENTRY to protect its profitability during the earlier phases of industry development – such as investment in large-scale plants, advertising, direct-sales distribution networks and other types of VERTICAL STRATEGY, or long-term contracts for sales or materials supply – may subsequently become barriers to exit when an industry loses its attractiveness to the group.

Barriers to mobility. The concept is perhaps best summed up by the Dingle farmer's advice to a lost traveller: 'if you want to go there, I shouldn't start from here.' Analysis may reveal that a particular strategy or STRATEGIC GROUP has the highest growth or profit potential given customer needs and industry structure. A company not following that strategy, but wishing to emulate the firms that are, may, however, face substantial barriers to mobility if it attempts to change its strategic course.

Barriers to mobility may be external or internal to the firm. External barriers may arise, for example, from the difficulty in gaining shelf space from specialized retailers who already have strong relationships with existing manufacturers, or from lack of brand awareness among customers. Thus a supplier trying to reposition its strategy so as to compete in the specialized, heavily branded end of a market may face high mobility barriers compared with the private-label segment where buyers face lower SWITCHING COSTS and are more willing to take on a firm wishing to redirect its strategy towards this segment.

Internal mobility barriers can be just as potent. A company with technology, systems, CORPORATE CULTURE, and a management style which have grown up in the course of serving one type of customer may face huge problems in changing its internal organization so that it becomes consistent with a strategy designed to compete in a different part of the market.

Firms with a long history of dealing with a relatively few, large, and less price-sensitive customers commonly find it difficult to support a shift in strategy aimed at accessing the mass market. In the video cassette recorder industry, for example, the leading firm in professional video equipment, Ampex, failed to make a successful transition to serving the consumer mass market, despite a technological lead and early recognition of the market potential. Barriers to mobility in terms of lack of experience with mass production, distribution, and consumer marketing, proved too great.

Barriers to mobility have important implications for the best choice of market segment for a particular firm. It is not simply a matter of identifying the most attractive segment in terms of profit potential. Proper consideration of the difficulties of repositioning existing strategy so as to serve that segment may lead the company to concentrate elsewhere.

BCG. *See* BOSTON CONSULTING GROUP.

Benchmarking. Strategy emphasizes the position of a company relative to its competitors as the key to success (*see* COMPETITIVE ADVANTAGE). Yet the measurement systems in most companies, including the budget process, compare a company's present performance relative to its own past. Competitive advantage, although much discussed, is rarely measured.

Comparison of key performance indicators such as stock turns, lead times, costs, prices, employee productivity, advertising-to-sales ratios, expenditure on R&D, and customer service relative to sales, against the benchmarks of other firms in the industry offers an important chance to make the concept of competitive advantage (or disadvantage) real.

The first issue presented by benchmarking is that of which companies to include in the comparison. The appropriate use of different competitor comparisons depends on the degree of segment overlap and strategic similarity. (See figure 4.)

Companies with a similar strategy, operating in essentially the same segments ('clones') are the most closely comparable

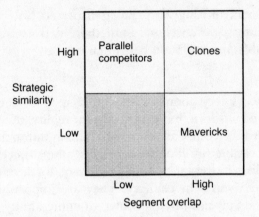

Figure 4   Types of Benchmark Competitors

benchmarks. Success relative to these firms largely depends on the quality of strategy execution, therefore they provide a useful benchmark as to how well your strategy is being implemented. Currently non-competing firms pursuing a similar strategy, but in a different segment of the market (for example, regional brewers), are useful 'parallel competitors' against which to compare key indicators. Differences in approach may offer valuable lessons or improve strategy by questioning conventional wisdom. Such firms are also potential entrants should they decide to stray outside their segment into yours. 'Maverick' competitors are potentially the most dangerous. When the market begins to change in a way which plays to their strengths (in the last example, say, the shift toward supermarket distribution of beer and wine) they may become powerful competitors against which it is difficult to respond because of BARRIERS TO MOBILITY. Knowing how the performance of these firms differs is the first stage in preparing a defence. Again, benchmarking against these competitors may also result in conventional wisdoms being questioned, with resulting improvements in strategy.

A second key issue in benchmarking is getting the data. Many managers wrongly believe that this is impossible. Experience shows that in addition to published sources a large amount of competitor intelligence already resides with a company's own staff down the line, as well as with joint customers and suppliers. Being dispersed, however, it fails to enter strategic decisions until there is a conscious push to assemble and maintain benchmarks.

Blind spots. Every company has blind spots in the form of the received wisdom that denies current reality, the 'sacred cows' that reduce competitiveness yet remain untouched. They are an inevitable result of the firm's learning a successful formula and, like individuals, being reluctant to deviate from it as their environment changes. They are important to strategy because they are often a source of vulnerability as well as an important determinant of how a competitor will respond to a particular move. They may well lead to the neglect of certain customer segments (which are 'known' to be small or unprofitable), LOOSE BRICKS in the product line or existing customer base, or unwillingness to adopt innovations in the production, distribution, marketing, or service processes.

Blind spots are not always associated with ignorance or irrationality among managers. Individuals may be well aware of the problem, but existing measurement systems, incentive structures, or MIXED MOTIVES may effectively result in a blind spot because they discourage managers from acting in the appropriate way.

Boston Consulting Group (BCG). Founded by Bruce Henderson in 1963, it has pioneered a number of strategy frameworks which have since entered the 'standard toolbox' of strategy formulation throughout the world. These include the GROWTH–SHARE MATRIX and the ENVIRONMENTS MATRIX.

Early in its history BCG popularized the EXPERIENCE CURVE. At a time of rapid and consistent market expansion this helped many of its clients develop competitive advantage through the lower unit-costs scale and learning benefits coming from larger market share and more rapid accumulation of volume than their competitors. The growth–share matrix helped to conceptualize the problems of capital budgeting and cash redeployment across the ever more complex portfolios of businesses which had been built by many firms in the early 1970s. The 'environments matrix' proved a potent framework within which firms could analyse the implications of industry structure and competitive dynamics and develop the kind of strategies which would offer sustainable competitive advantage as the industry evolved. This reflected the experience among many leading firms in the early 1980s that getting ahead of the competition was no guarantee of staying ahead as many new and often foreign firms mounted powerful attacks on traditional industry leaders. More recently, BCG's work has emphasized TIME-BASED COMPETITION, a framework designed to deal with the increased pressure for more responsive service, wider variety, and reduced lead times faced by many firms as we move into the 1990s.

Although BCG's frameworks have been criticized by many as unduly simplistic or even misleading, there can be little doubt that they have made a contribution to strategy thinking, and that, when introduced, each was well attuned to the key business problems of its time.

Bottom up/top down. Given that top management does not enjoy a monopoly on either wisdom or information, it is unlikely that the best strategy will result from army-style 'top down' orders conforming to a grand strategic plan. Effective strategy involves people right through the organizational hierarchy.

One important role of strategy is to provide a framework in which the requirements for achieving competitive advantage in a market can be linked to the way individuals perform their jobs. Clearly a complete definition of what a strategy means for every individual in the company cannot be included in a plan. In any case, the precise application of the strategy will lead to different actions for each situation or point in time. The details of a strategy and what it means to a particular person in a specific situation must result from interpretation and adaptation right down the line. In this sense, purely top-down strategy is a nonsense.

The broad principles of a strategy may also be strongly influenced by initiatives moving through an organization from the 'bottom up'. When unexpected developments take place, new skills, capabilities, and options often arise within the organization – often in the form of 'necessity is the mother of invention'. Good strategy involves recognizing the market patterns and new capabilities arising from these day-to-day actions. Favourable, if unexpected, developments must be promoted through additional resources or incentives so that this EMERGENT STRATEGY adjusts as new information is obtained from the 'front line'. Contrary to the implication of some planning literature, strategy is therefore both a top-down and a bottom-up process.

Brainstorming. This takes place when an unstructured group works together to generate a list of ideas or solutions to a problem. The technique, which has been in use since 1941, works in three stages: firstly, ideas should be freely generated and expressed without regard to their quality or relevance. Then group members should follow up each other's ideas, modifying and combining them in novel ways. No idea should be judged or criticized until all ideas have been expressed. Only then should the third stage of sifting and evaluation take place.

Research into the effectiveness of brainstorming has produced mixed results. For example, individuals working alone, rather than in unstructured groups, typically produce more original, high-quality ideas. Brainstorming groups, in contrast, usually produce *more* ideas, although this may simply be a reflection of the capacity of such groups to work together for a longer period than an individual working alone. Whereas groups can generate ideas indefinitely, individuals 'run dry'. Ironically, the technique is most effective when it comes to evaluating rather than generating ideas. At this stage the process of group interaction proves a particular asset in testing and appraising proposed ideas and solutions.

Branding. With increasing costs of brand creation and maintenance, and high risks (an 'investment' made in the promotion
of a brand failure is simply lost), branding strategies have
come under closer scrutiny. Brands can have a number of
strategic benefits: they can be important in reducing the
BUYER POWER of distributors or retailers by virtually forcing
them to carry the brand because of strong preference for it
among final consumers. They can help to preserve FIRST
MOVER advantages by enabling the pioneering firm to develop
an image of high quality, and they can increase barriers to
mobility for imitators who must overcome established consumer loyalty. Brands can also contribute to increased generic demand for a product where customers would be uncertain
about taking the risk on an unknown supplier's product
(pharmaceuticals are a good example).

The key strategic question is whether the additional profit
stream associated with creating a strong brand justifies the
initial investment and ongoing maintenance (necessary expenditure to prevent brand preference from fading in the face
of competitors' prices or marketing signals). To do so the
brand must be of some actual or perceived value to the
customer. The benefit to the final customer is often in the
form of reducing risk because the brand is an economical way
of reducing the risk of failure or unacceptable quality (chemi-
cally testing every package of washing powder would be
expensive for a customer!). In other cases, the brand may
offer the consumer positive spillovers, such as a status
symbol.

Intermediate buyers, such as wholesalers or retailers, may
also gain from a brand in the form of higher stock turns or
increased customer traffic. The availability of Procter and
Gamble's strong 'Pampers' brand of disposable nappies, for
example, has been shown to influence where young mothers,
wishing to make a single shopping trip, buy all of their
groceries. Where these positive spillovers exist, manufacturers with strong brands can induce distributors to accept
lower margins, enhancing their own profitability.

Break-even analysis. This is a useful method of assessing the viability of strategies involving different levels of fixed costs such as advertising, R&D, or interest on the capital tied up in indivisible facilities (production lines, for example, often come in minimum sizes).

Break-even market share can be calculated as follows:

$$\text{Price} \times \left(\frac{\text{Fixed costs}}{\text{Price} - \text{Variable costs}} \right) \Big/ \text{Total market sales}$$

At the core of the formula is the number of units which must be sold in any period in order to cover fixed costs. Sensitivity analysis can then look at the impact of increased advertisement commitment, for example, on the market share required in order to break-even, as well as different pricing assumptions.

Highlighting the relationship between fixed costs and break-even market share is an important step in strategy formulation. A high break-even market share in a mature industry clearly demonstrates the need to consider and plan for likely strong retaliation from competitors currently supplying the market. A low break-even market share, especially with rapid industry growth, by contrast, confirms a lower likelihood of severe competitor response.

Budgeting. The working lives of most line managers are heavily influenced by the responsibility for achieving their budgets. Far from being a forecast, or even a plan, in many companies the budget is a commitment, virtually a contract between the line manager and his or her superiors. In some others the budget is sacrosanct. The reality, therefore, is that unless a firm's strategy gets linked to operating budgets it has little hope of serious implementation.

Strategy can be linked to budgets in a number of ways. First, the sales forecasts on which most STRATEGIC BUSINESS UNIT budgets are based should reflect a market strategy with allowance for expected competitor moves. Too often, this is not the case: five or ten per cent growth is simply added to last year's sales figures with scant regard to the strategic implications of the increasing share in a market which is growing at, say, three per cent. Second, if the investment or expenditures necessary to pursue a strategy are to be made, they must be incorporated into the operating budget. While many broad strategic initiatives are agreed, their expenditure implications are often nowhere to be seen in the operating budgets. If this is the case, progress is unlikely to be achieved. Finally, certain strategy objectives, such as increased market share or reduced customer lead times, can be monitored as part of the budget review and tracking process. This keeps them continually under the eyes of operating managers along with measures like sales, manufacturing, and overhead variances, ensuring that they are not only examined as part of an annual planning ritual.

Bundling. Many firms market more than one of their products or services bundled together at a single price for the package. A computer lease, for example, commonly represents hardware, software, training, maintenance services, and financing provided as a single bundle. Likewise, large 'turnkey' construction contracts bundle together design, materials, labour, project management, quality control, and so on, each of which could be contracted out separately.

Bundling is attractive to suppliers for a number of reasons. The cost of identifying new customers and building relationships may be high. This investment may only become profitable if it can be spread over the total sales across a bundle. Bundling may help reduce competition for support products, building a BARRIER TO ENTRY. Powerful original equipment suppliers, for example, often bundle spare parts and service into the original contract so as to prevent smaller, focused firms from competing for this business. Bundling might also be a way to reduce the amount of bargaining power the buyer exerts by disguising the true costs of individual elements, making it difficult to compare prices.

On the other hand, bundling can have important advantages for the buyer. It may be convenient to purchase COMPLEMENTARY PRODUCTS as a single bundle. Uncertainty about the co-ordination of different suppliers or the compatibility of their equipment can be avoided. However, if the buyer derives little value from buying a bundled product, or bundling forces the purchase of unwanted extra products or services, or to accept lower quality than could be obtained by drawing on a number of specialist suppliers, the pressures to unbundle will be strong.

Many firms who have traditionally sold bundled products have recently faced competition from new, focused competitors who unbundle the offering. The entrants charge the customer only for the pieces he wants. Alternatively, their strategy may be to specialize in offering exceptional quality or value for an individual element in the bundle. A classic case is the emergence of discount brokerage services following the 'Big Bang' in London and the deregulation of commissions on Wall Street. Traditional brokers bundled together advice, research, and the execution of transactions on the exchange. Discount brokers attacked the market for those who really wanted only the execution of trades. Having avoided all of the costs associated with other activities, they were able to offer a 'transaction only' service at very attractive prices to this segment.

Suppliers with a long history of bundling often find it difficult to respond to this unbundling by very targeted competitors because they have little idea of the real costs and profitability of the individual elements in their bundled product. Analysis often reveals massive CROSS SUBSIDIZATION, with some elements being highly profitable and others making losses. Such a situation offers an open invitation for entrants to CHERRY PICK the profitable activities, thus undermining the economics of existing firms.

Business cycles. Despite considerable controversy about the predictability and frequency of business cycles (ranging from arguments suggesting three- to four-year sequences of boom and bust to the Russian economist N. D. Kondratieff's theory of 50–60-year cycles of economic activity), there is no doubt that economic growth lurches from peak to trough in the course of its general upward trend. This impacts most heavily on industries with a heavy fixed-cost structure, especially where capacity must be added in 'lumps' which have a significant impact on total market supply. Industries with these characteristics are prone to committing themselves to large capacity additions during booms, which result in substantial excess capacity during most of the subsequent business cycle. Because of heavy fixed costs, customers who purchase substantial volumes are able to exert strong BUYER POWER while some excess capacity exists. Any sales volume which more than covers cash costs will offer a contribution to covering the fixed charges. Thus as long as someone in the industry has excess capacity, they will force prices down in an attempt to fill it. Chronic low profitability often results. The metal-can industry is a class example of this process.

Successful strategies in dealing with the business cycle have included the use of subcontractors and outside sourcing of components so as to minimize fixed costs, the importation of products to meet boom demand, DIFFERENTIATION of products or services with the aim of building buyer SWITCHING COSTS, and pre-emptive capacity expansion designed to discourage competitors from adding to their own capacity.

Buyer power. Buyers exert an important squeeze on a firm's profits through the pressure they apply on prices. The extent to which margins are reduced depends on the bargaining power of buyers in the market.

Buyer power is generally high when the company faces a concentrated set of buyers, when the buyer's costs of switching from one supplier to another are low, when buyers are well informed about the merits, availability, and prices of alternative brands or substitutes, or where the buyer could backward integrate – bring supply in-house – with ease. Buyers tend to exert more of their potential power when the product represents a significant part of their total costs (small-cost elements tend to receive less scrutiny), where the buyer is stagnant or unprofitable, or where the buyer himself competes on the basis of low costs.

Isolating the sources of buyer power is only the first stage of developing a strategy towards it. The real question is: how can strategy reduce the buyer power a company faces? The first set of policies is associated with how a company reaches its buyers. Many companies write off small customers on the basis that they are costly to serve, or a poor credit risk, allowing these accounts to be serviced by distributors. Such a policy may make sense, but it needs to be recognized that buyer power is likely to be increased when a large number of small buyers are replaced with a few large distributors. Margins are likely to be impaired as a result. The second set of policies revolves around increasing the buyer's switching costs. Many companies who offer their buyers a comprehensive inventory control and replenishment service have placed those buyers in a situation where they must accept the cost of developing an alternative replenishment system or increased costs if they switch. Likewise, maintenance contracts tend to increase switching costs and reduce buyer power.

Other policies aimed at reducing buyer power include maintaining relationships with multiple decision-makers in the buyer's organization (for example, plant managers as well as purchasing agents), with the object of building allies within the buying firm, educating the buyer about the risk of product failure, or linking the sale to financing or lease arrangements. It is also one of the benefits of successful DIFFERENTIATION that it reduces the bargaining power of buyers.

See also FIVE FORCES, SUPPLIER POWER.

Buyer selection. The group of buyers in a market is generally varied, covering ultimate users, intermediate distributors, service agents, and original equipment manufacturers. Even within these groups buyers differ widely in the volume and frequency of their purchases, the importance of the product in their BUYER VALUE CHAIN, their needs for quality, service, or durability, and the costs involved in selling and distributing to them. Selecting the right group of buyers to target is an important strategy decision because the extent of a company's COMPETITIVE ADVANTAGE will vary between buyer types.

The first goal is to choose buyers whose value chain and consequent needs suit the capabilities of your company to supply in terms of volume, speed of response, and so on. Buyers who are rapidly growing are often attractive. While they make many demands on service and support, they are not only repaying the initial sales investment with higher volumes but are often also less price-sensitive. Buyer selection also needs to take into account the amount of bargaining power the buyer potentially has and the extent to which this is likely to be exercised (*see* BUYER POWER). Buyers with large volumes and standardized needs often exert strong bargaining power, reducing available margins. On the other hand, these buyers may have low costs to serve. They generally won't require special product formulations, innumerable small delivery drops, or impose the high costs of last-minute 'crisis' demands on their suppliers.

Buyer value chain. Many companies' immediate buyers are in fact businessmen themselves. These include distributors, retailers, and industrial and commercial firms. They buy a firm's product because it helps them make profits. The more profitable a product is for them to handle, the more they will be willing to pay for it. Poor strategists encourage these intermediate buyers to handle or use their product by cutting the price and hence their own margins. However, because the product and the way it is supplied influence both the costs and revenues right along the buyer's value chain, there are many more interesting ways to increase the buyer's willingness to purchase it.

Suppose you set up a system to deliver the product on a JUST IN TIME basis, thereby reducing the buyer's inventory and hence his costs. You should be able to share in some of that gain through a higher price. Likewise, by cutting out an unnecessarily wide product line of sizes or varieties, you may improve the buyer's stock turn, again leading to a price premium over competing suppliers. Offering the buyer a high-quality product which improves his image in the market (for example, offering a Rolex dealership to a Hong Kong jeweller) often has a positive spillover on the buyer's other business, improving his total revenues. In this case he will probably be willing to deal in the product at low margins just in order to get the other benefits. Hence the profits of his supplier are increased.

It is sometimes important to recognize conflicts between the needs of the ultimate buyer and the intermediate buyer's value chain. When watches with ultrasonically sealed cases were introduced, for example, they had to be thrown away if they broke down. Defective watches were simply replaced with new ones. The ultimate customer valued this 'no questions' replacement guarantee. The jewellers, however, lost an important source of revenue in the form of watch repairs. Because a key part of the buyer's value chain had been eliminated there was resistance to selling the product, resulting in slow build-up of volume for the manufacturer.

A key part of strategy, including successful DIFFERENTIATION, therefore depends on analysing how the buyer makes money. By working on all of the interactions between your product or service and the buyer's value chain, strategies for increased profitability can be developed.
See also VALUE CHAIN.

C

Cannibalization. Let us imagine that a firm introduces a new product aimed at a market in which it already has other products with essentially similar features. Assuming market size to be relatively static, sales of the new product will almost certainly eat into the sales of the company's existing products. This process of cannibalization occurs in a number of industries; for example, the publisher of a leading textbook in finance may deliberately choose to launch a second, alternative textbook knowing that the latter's success will partly be achieved at the expense of the former. Far from being foolhardy this may represent a perfectly defensible strategy provided that: (a) the combined sales and profitability of both titles substantially outweigh the total sales of the original, single title; and (b) that the new product takes market share away from the offerings of competing publishers, rather than simply away from its predecessor from the same stable.

The anticipated trade-off between losing sales through cannibalization and gaining new sales at the expense of competitors will underlie any decision to launch a new product, either *ab initio* or in response to a move made by a competitor. Often the fear of cannibalizing an established product range will deter a firm from producing new products to counter – or pre-empt – competitors' moves.

Cannibalization thus creates a dilemma. Do we do nothing, and risk losing ground to a competitor, or do we act (that is, by introducing a product), and risk self-inflicted damage in the form of lost sales? Moreover, if we judge that the market is already saturated then does it automatically follow that new product success will only be achieved at the expense of cannibalizing existing products? This question vividly illustrates the problem of MIXED MOTIVES faced by many firms.

Capital budgeting. The process by which capital is allocated between competing investment opportunities available to the company involves important strategic decisions. Financial theory emphasizes the allocation of funds to projects where the marginal return from each extra £1 of capital invested is highest. In an ideal world this magical number would adequately reflect all of the relevant strategic considerations. In practice, however, the strategic aspects are often complex and difficult to quantify. Investment in a particular project, for example, may offer a positive strategic spillover by keeping a competitor out of a business which might otherwise offer a foothold from which he could attack the core market. Other projects, although not profitable in themselves, may allow the firm to maintain its capability in a key technology, thereby preserving its strategic options for the future. Strategic considerations therefore augment the straight financial presentation of the capital-budgeting issues.

Strategy has also offered broad 'rules of thumb' for capital budgeting in the form of portfolio models. One of the best known, the GROWTH–SHARE MATRIX, argues that cash should be transferred from mature CASH COWS to growing businesses which require further rapid investment in order to achieve dominant positions in their markets.

Strategists have also pointed out that capital-budgeting decisions can act as an important market signal to competitors, customers, or suppliers, about the company's long-term commitment to a business and hence its likely reaction to a competitive threat, technical change, or new entry.

Capital intensity. Strategists must adopt a flexible definition of the level of capital tied up in a business relative to its sales. Historically, measures of capital intensity emphasized fixed assets such as plant and equipment. Thus the heavy manufacturing businesses were commonly viewed as the most capital intensive. More recently, however, the importance of stocks, debtors and the value of real estate in increasing capital intensity has been recognized with the consequent drive to ensure the full utilization of this capital. Oil companies, for example, took a harder look at their retail sites on realizing that their petrol stations had in fact become one of the most capital-intensive parts of their businesses with rising property values.

Capital-intensive businesses require a higher sales margin in order to reach the same return on capital employed (ROCE) compared with those that are more labour intensive. However, a number of empirical studies have found that while margins on sales do rise with capital intensity the extra margins are insufficient to compensate fully for the extra capital tied up. On average, therefore, highly capital-intensive businesses have been found to produce relatively low ROCE. One important reason for this is that capital intensity, especially in the form of land, buildings and plant, often increases the proportion of fixed costs in the cost structure. When capacity utilization in the industry falls, competitors seek 'contribution' volume by cutting prices, since this adds to profit even if it fails to cover its full costs. Since this damage to the price structure can be difficult to reverse, particularly where chronic excess capacity exists, returns in capital-intensive industries may remain permanently depressed.

Capital structure. The financing of a firm's assets will typically require a mix of liabilities and shareholders' funds, both in terms of the type of security (for example, debentures, mortgages, trade credit, convertible bonds, preference shares, and ordinary equity) and the mix of maturities between call, short, medium, and long term.

Capital structure can have an important impact on the strategic options available to a company in responding to competitor moves or changing market needs. Companies with high levels of debt relative to equity often lack the flexibility to change strategic direction. They are forced to maintain cash flow to meet interest and debt repayments and thus may be handicapped if a battle for market share ensues. They are often unable to exit quickly from an industry because the necessary write-offs would reduce their equity

and increase the leverage shown in their books to unacceptable levels. They are often constrained in adapting to technological change by lack of borrowing capacity to finance the
new investment required. Similarly, the constraints of debt
covenants may restrict them to lower-risk strategies. Strategy
considerations may therefore argue for a lower debt-to-
equity ratio than the pure optimization of the cost of capital
might suggest in order to preserve the strategic flexibility of
the firm. Conversely, firms with low costs of capital may have
to underpin a cost-leadership advantage.

The maturity aspect of capital structure also influences
strategy. Firms with access to long-term financing may
operate with longer horizons, playing for the END GAME
rather than for early cash flow.

Cascade approach. Much strategy formulation has to do with
the identification, evaluation, and eventual selection of different courses of action open to a firm. This process of search
and selection takes two principal forms. Perhaps the most
commonly used approach is to start by producing a list of all
possible alternatives and then to develop a framework, or
devise a set of criteria, against which these can be evaluated
and progressively eliminated. The cascade approach proceeds
rather differently.

Using this technique you start by formulating a set of
broad objectives or decision rules which are then progressively refined. The following process would therefore apply:

Stage 1   Establish a set of objectives, based on, say, return
          on investment target, growth through diversifica-
          tion, etc.
Stage 2   Identify the gap between the firm's current perform-
          ance or position and these broad objectives.
Stage 3   Formulate one or more courses of action designed
          to bridge this gap.
Stage 4   Try to determine the extent to which the proposed
          courses of action will – or will not – close the gap
          identified in stage 2. If none effectively does this

then clearly new alternatives need to be developed
and the original objectives reconsidered.

Thus the two key characteristics of the cascade approach are:
first, the process allows for feedback, since information
gathered at any stage may be brought to bear upon decisions
made at a previous stage. Secondly, it represents a way of
progressively searching for, or converging upon, the best
solution, with the results of the analysis becoming increasingly refined as each stage of the solution unfolds.

Cash cow. As the name implies, this is a product or business that
generates cash – conceptually, occupying the lower left
quadrant of the BCG GROWTH–SHARE MATRIX. Why have
such products/businesses reached this position? Typically,
cash cow businesses are those that have a relatively high
market share and strong competitive position in markets
which are growing slowly, if at all. But that is only part of the
story.

Given their high market share, the total cumulated output
of these businesses (that is, the total volume of production) is
greater than that of competitors with lower market shares. In
achieving dominance such businesses have accumulated more
experience relative to competitors and their average unit
costs are lower as a result. This combination of high market
share and low unit-costs creates a virtuous circle, the upshot
of which is high levels of profit and cash generation.

Since the market is mature, and the competitive position of
the business is strong, there is little need to reinvest this cash,
for instance in marketing designed to increase share. The
surplus cash can be used to pay dividends, cover debt, finance
R&D and, importantly, finance the development of other
products/businesses within the portfolio for which growth
potential exists; that is, STARS and QUESTION MARKS. This
assumes of course that decision-making in respect of cash and
resource allocation is relatively centralized, since, left to his
own devices, the manager of a cash cow is quite likely to
remain convinced of the need to continue investing in the

business, its strong position notwithstanding. In many instances, such over-investment may be a strategic mistake, but
the reverse is also true.

Indeed, the real danger with this approach to categorizing
businesses within a portfolio is that it can, in the case of cash
cows, encourage management prematurely to write off such
businesses, thereby failing to grasp the need for continual
renewal and refurbishment. Starved of investment, and possibly also of energetic managers for whom the prospect of
'milking out' a business is not challenging, cash cows may
prematurely dry up as they lose ground to aggressive competitors who see the strategic virtue in continuing to invest in
ostensibly 'mature' markets.

Cash flow. The amount of cash generated from the operations of
a business in any period reflects profit before depreciation
plus the cash released by reductions in stock or receivables.

The existence of strong cash-flow generation within a
business reduces the need for management to submit its
strategy for investment directly for capital market approval
in the form of a prospectus to raise funds. This tends to
reduce the impact of capital market pressures on strategic
decisions and increase the scope for strategy which improves
the stability of the firm's position in the product market or
meets the growth needs of the organization, rather than
necessarily maximizing profits.

The desire of companies to utilize cash flow being generated by a business with few new investment opportunities
commonly as the root cause of a DIVERSIFICATION strategy is a
prime example of cash flow allowing organizational needs to
dominate the strategy. Since such a strategy reflects the
internal needs of the firm, rather than those of the market or
a real opportunity to develop competitive advantage, the
chance of failure is often increased.

The availability of strong cash flow also influences competitor interactions. Firms with a 'long purse' tend to wage a
longer war against new entrants, for example, than those
with a more modest cash flow. They are also more likely to

adopt strategies based on technological leadership and capacity pre-emption.

Finally, cash flow plays a key role in determining which strategies are accepted given its primacy in investment decisions based on discounted cash-flow analysis and CAPITAL BUDGETING.

Cash trap. There are some businesses where positive cash flow always seems to be just over the next rise. Whenever you survey the horizon there seems to be a profitable opportunity out there. Such businesses often grow rapidly, absorbing cash into product development, new plant and equipment, inventory, and marketing and advertising to 'educate' potential customers. Yet the day when the investment slows down, and the cash comes flowing back in, never comes. These businesses are known as cash traps.

Cash traps are often associated with businesses where technological change is rapid and the life of each new generation is too short to repay the investment in development and launch plus a reward. Clearly not all businesses of this type are cash traps; it takes another adverse ingredient to create a cash trap. This may be a tendency toward rapid and low-cost imitation by competitors once a product is launched, aggravated by low buyer SWITCHING COSTS. Any price premium on the new product therefore rapidly disappears. Many medical and dental consumables have this problem. Very low rates of customer conversion from one generation to another, necessitating continued high selling costs, are another important potential contributor to cash traps. This is a common cause in products which are purchased infrequently, so that customer loyalty is difficult to carry through time.

Cash traps are not easy to identify since their futures always 'seem to look rosy at the time'. Nonetheless, companies guilty of INCREMENTALISM in their decision-making are more likely to fall foul of cash traps than those who anticipate shifts in their COMPETITIVE ADVANTAGE as competitors adjust and technology moves forward, rather than planning on the basis of *status quo*.

CEO. Chief executive officer. The American acronym is becoming increasingly common in international English-language business usage, replacing equivalent designations such as 'managing director'. Outside the US the word 'officer' is frequently dropped in favour of 'chief executive'. The term is not to be confused with 'chief operating officer', COO, which as the title implies indicates a role biased towards the operational side of the business.

The manner in which CEOs and their successors are appointed has only recently begun to yield its secrets to academic research. Among the most striking findings is the increasing tendency of companies, notably in the US, to appoint outsiders to the top job, where 'outsider' is defined as an individual who has served for less than five years with the company. In large US companies in the 1960s, eight per cent of CEOs were outsiders. By the early 1980s the number had increased to 25 per cent. In the UK by comparison, in 1986 79 per cent of promotions to CEO in large companies were from within; two years later the figure had fallen to 68 per cent. This might account for another startling finding, that ten per cent of newly appointed CEOs of large US companies are fired within five years of getting their feet under the desk.

Further changes in the role of the CEO are revealed by shifts in the prevailing top management structures. Again using US data, the dominant chain of top management command in 1960 was represented by a single executive sitting atop the pile – the so-called 'solo mode'. By 1985 the bias had shifted towards more broadly based team approaches in which three or more executives occupied 'pole positions', that is, CEO plus two vice-chairmen. Between 1960 and the mid-1980s the use of the solo mode decreased from 36 to 21 per cent, while team-based approaches moved from eight to 25 per cent of the total of large US companies. In part, company size is the determinant of structure at the top with the solo mode becoming steadily less common the bigger the company.

A variant of the solo mode in the UK is represented by the concentration of two roles – those of chairman and chief executive – in the hands of a single individual. Guinness under Ernest Saunders, Coloroll under John Ashcroft are but two examples, chosen with care. Why? Because the amalgamation of these roles is a topic of intense debate with advocates claiming there can only be one captain on the bridge (an observation attributed to Robert Maxwell), and critics replying that the price of eliminating ambiguity as to who is in charge is a dangerous concentration of power within one individual. Moreover, the two jobs are in fundamental respects quite different and require different skills. According to Sir Adrian Cadbury (Chairman of ProNed, a Bank of England body concerned with the duties and obligations of non-executive directors), 'the Chairman is responsible for ensuring that the Board makes the necessary decisions and the Chief Executive is responsible for carrying them out.' However, the separation of these roles is the norm, though many company chairmen graduate to that position from that of CEO. In the US at least, CEOs rarely withdraw completely on retirement, they just fade away, with 80 per cent of those who have 'retired' continuing to serve, on a non-executive basis, on the board of the company they once led. Which brings us to the heart of the CEO's role: leadership.

Leadership, as distinct from management, is the essential role of the CEO. Indeed, John Kotter, the Harvard expert on business leadership, has argued that the greatest difficulty facing US companies today are that many of them are over-managed and under-led. What is required is a combination of both strong leadership and strong management.

In strategic terms, central to the leadership role is the capacity of the CEO to provide and articulate a clear vision of where the company is going, what sort of company it will become. For example, within a year of taking over the loss-making SAS, Jan Carlzon defined his vision for it in terms of becoming the preferred airline of the frequent business traveller. Everything that the airline subsequently did, from the planes it purchased and the routes it flew to the food that was served in-flight, was dedicated to accomplishing this aim, to realizing this simple – but not simplistic – ambition (*see* MISSION STATEMENT).

Having defined the vision and direction, the CEO's

strategic priorities are twofold: to communicate that purpose and, less tangibly, to create a CORPORATE CULTURE that will support the strategies put in place to accomplish it. As expressed by Carlzon, for instance, the decisive role of a CEO is 'to create a unique corporate culture which cannot be copied by the competition. That will be our [SAS's] unique strength.'

This implies a shift in that role from being a 'decision-making machine' to what Carlzon calls,

> an enlightened dictator – one who is willing to dissemi-nate the vision and goals but who will not brook active dissent to the underlying ideas. He must be able to present his vision so convincingly that the goals and strategies feel right to everyone within the company.

Channel strategy. Between the production of a good and its final consumption there is a gap. How do we get the good from the point of production to the consumer? In bridging this gap the product in question may pass through a number of different stages or distribution channels. At the simplest level, for example, direct-mail selling by the producer, there will be only one channel. More usually, where customers are widely dispersed and production is concentrated, there will be a number of different channels – for example, agents, wholesalers, retailers, and so on. Effective distribution in these circumstances clearly depends upon co-operation between channel members. Such co-operation will break down where one party is able to exert control over the channel, as, for example, occurs when an intermediary is able to achieve a powerful position in relation to a small number of suppliers servicing a geographically dispersed market. The degree of channel control exercised by any one firm will depend upon factors such as technical complexity, service requirements, and above all the relative costs incurred by either producers or intermediaries in meeting customer demand.

Gaining access to distribution channels constitutes a major BARRIER TO ENTRY in some industries. Incumbents can, moreover, strengthen their position and block access to

existing channels through a variety of means such as negotiating exclusive distribution agreements, heavily price-
discounting products in the channel, saturating the channel
with products, undertaking private-label manufacturing, and
providing good service support. The choice of distribution
channel, the manner in which it is used, and the scope that it
offers for creating value for the consumer (either at the
intermediate level or the final point of consumption) all
constitute key elements in the development of effective
strategy.

But channel strategy is not concerned exclusively with
issues relating to control, to blocking competitor access to a
channel or to creating value for customers. Increasingly,
many firms have come to recognize the potential offered by
different channels to learn about the market and what makes
it tick. The channel serves, in other words, as a listening post
– as a means of feeding information from the market back to
the firm.

Good strategy therefore approaches this issue in terms of a
two-way street. In one direction goods are being delivered to
markets and customers; in the other, information is continuously flowing back through the distribution channel,
educating the firm about those markets and customers. One
test of any channel strategy is therefore this: 'are we establishing and running the channels in such a way as to
maximize our organizational learning?' (*see* LEARNING).

Cherry picking. When buying a new hi-fi system we typically
have two choices. Either we can buy a completely integrated
unit, comprising speakers, amplifiers, CD player, and so on,
or we can individually select each component and put
together the system of our choice. In doing so we may choose
speakers from one maker, amplifiers from another, CD
player from a third. If we go for option one we are buying a
BUNDLED product. Under option two we cherry-pick. That is,
we make each selection the best of a series of alternatives.

Similarly, distributors and other middlemen or agents are
often well placed to take only a selection of products from a
supplier's range. Typically, this selection will reflect the

distributor's assessment of how well established the product is, and the likely sales that it will achieve. Such a selection inevitably makes it that much more difficult to get new, unproven products selected and established.

Responses to cherry picking take a number of forms, the most common of which is to supply a bundle of products which have to be taken in their entirety. For example, for a number of years IBM successfully pursued a strategy of bundling together software, hardware, and service support. Other responses include offering incentives to distributors or agents to take the full line (including new products), rather than select between products in the range, or alternatively, 'penalizing' the consumer for cherry picking. For example, penalties may be applied in the form of higher costs, inconvenience or reduced service support for those consumers who decide to make an individual selection of the most attractive products from competing suppliers.

At the product level cherry picking is an easily observable phenomenon and one to which a firm can respond in specific ways. But there is another dimension to cherry picking that is rather more insidious and difficult for an organization to respond to. Many firms serve a wide range of customers, who may well be dispersed across a number of different market segments. Inevitably, the revenues derived from these customers and the costs of servicing them will vary. In serving certain groups or types of customer the firm will make a profit, while in other segments of the market it may well make losses. Faced with this situation the firm may choose to use the profits generated in one area to cross subsidize the losses incurred elsewhere. Frequently, CROSS SUBSIDIZATION occurs without the firm fully realizing what is happening. Assessing different levels of profit derived from different customers or segments is not always easy, and it is frequently difficult to isolate the specific costs associated with each type of customer. But if the firm is unaware of the problem, or unable to pin it down accurately, it exposes itself to the risk that other competitors, particularly those that are better able to solve the cost/revenue equation by customer group, might move in and pick off the lucrative parts of a firm's own business. And not knowing exactly where the money is being earned, the firm is poorly placed to decide just how much it should spend in defending those of its customers under threat.

To illustrate: an airline operating an extensive network, made up of both long- and short-haul routes, will typically generate good margins on certain routes while it only breaks even or incurs losses on others. Such a situation presents opportunities to MAVERICK competitors who can choose to focus their activity on a limited number of lucrative routes, picking off those that offer the greatest profit potential. This is essentially the strategy adopted by Virgin Atlantic as it competes with British Airways and other trans-Atlantic carriers on the lucrative London–New York route. Much strategy has to do, therefore, with identifying those parts of the business in which we are vulnerable to cherry picking by aggressive competitors.

Chief executive officer. *See* CEO.

Chief operating officer (COO). *See* CEO.

Competence. Most managers have a set of beliefs regarding what their company is 'good at', and a vision, either explicit or implicit, of where lie the bounds of what the firm's financial, human and technical resources can and cannot achieve. These beliefs are sharpened by the quest for COMPETITIVE ADVANTAGE – the realization that being good at something is not enough in an industry where most of the competitors are also expert. The important element is what makes the firm uniquely better than competitors in certain aspects of the business, its distinctive competence (*see also* DIFFERENTIATION).

Distinctive competence may arise from skill in a particular technology, the knowledge of how to run the key systems underpinning distribution or control costs in a specialized manufacturing plant. It may be an approach to the collection of market intelligence, consumer packaging or employee training for instance. An increasingly important source of distinctive competence is the ability of an organization to react to changes in the market. This may be its experience in new product launch, the introduction of new technology in existing plants, or its ability to shift a network of international sources to exploit changes in demand, exchange rates and factor costs.

The perception of a firm's distinctive competence among its top managers has a pervasive influence on CORPORATE STRATEGY, particularly in decisions regarding DIVERSIFICATION and COMPETITIVE SCOPE. The following statements by CEOs of large US and UK firms serve to illustrate: 'new lines of business must be comfortable to our management, in consumer products and in the United States'; 'R&D will allow us to compete in industries where we do not have a strong position, but we must stay out of electronics'; 'advertising is our strength in building brand image, where advertising is out so are we.'

Unrealistic perceptions of distinctive competence have been a common cause of unsuccessful diversifications and acquisitions. Beer manufacturers who had benefited from superior advertising against competitors in their own industry, for example, found the going much tougher when they tried to exploit this 'distinctive competence' against the experience of established firms in soft drinks. Firms therefore often find it useful to become more explicit about where their real distinctive competence lies through rigorous COMPETITOR ANALYSIS.

Competitive advantage. The deceptively simple idea of assessing a company's capabilities and market position by how they give it advantage relative to competitors is one of the central tenets of modern business strategy. Its powerful message is that absolute measures of strengths and weaknesses are a nonsense. A company which prides itself on being 'good at marketing' has a competitive disadvantage in this capability if it faces competitors who are more expert. A firm using a steam engine has a competitive advantage if its competitors are in the age of the treadmill. That strength only remains an advantage, however, until its competitors catch up. Since competitive advantages are relative, they are in a constant state of flux. Almost inevitably, therefore, they are ephemeral and need continual replenishment, improvement, and maintenance.

The second key message of competitive advantage is that strengths and capabilities are worth only as much as the value the market places upon them. Hidden corporate talents or potentials are worth little if the firm fails to recruit them in the battle with competitors to serve the customers or improve its supply, efficiency, or distribution. That the customer 'ought to' value something it offers is no defence.

Competitive advantage is the key to above-average profitability. The capability or flexibility to offer customers a product or service which suits their needs better than the competitive offering opens the way to more sales at a higher price. The ability to supply this at a lower cost than competitors, underpins above-average margins. Again the concept and its relationship to success is simple. Yet how often do we actually measure competitive advantage? Most of the measurement systems in a firm focus on comparing performance with the past. Are our costs up or down on last month? Are our lead times becoming longer or shorter? Are our prices rising or eroding? General Motors' increase in productivity by 15 per cent only added to its disadvantage when Toyota achieved a 30 per cent increase in the same period. Competitive advantage says, 'don't try to beat your personal best time; keep your eye on the other runners in the race.'

Competitive scope. The extent or range of a firm's activity is measured along a number of different dimensions. Traditionally, the most significant of these dimensions involved the distinction between those activities which a firm undertook in-house (for example, production) and those that it acquired or bought in from the external market (for example, distribution). The boundary between these two sets of activities represented a measure of the degree to which the firm was vertically integrated; that is, its vertical scope.

The strategic view of competitive scope incorporates other dimensions; geography – the breadth of a firm's activity by region or country; segment – the extent to which the firm, via its product offerings or range of services or customers, occupies different segments of the market in which it is operating; industry – the number of different industries in which the firm is engaged and across which it is co-ordinating its activities.

Defined in these terms it is clear that competitive scope is measured in relative rather than absolute terms: that is, in relation to the range of activities performed by competitors. Determining the appropriate or optimal degree of competitive scope is a central task of strategy, a task that has to do with a fundamental question: where – in the broadest sense – should the firm be competing? Being clear about the 'where' is an essential element of good strategy. This in turn implies that the firm is equally clear about where it will *not* compete, in terms of geography, product range, degree of integration and so forth.

Strategy is therefore about focusing a firm's resources where the potential benefits are greatest. This requires saying 'no' to opportunities, 'no' to ostensibly attractive markets. But saying 'no' is not something that comes naturally or easily to many firms. Choice of competitive scope therefore lies at the heart of strategy. Achieving the right balance in each of the dimensions of scope often holds the key to competitive success – or failure. The strategic message is therefore this: be clear about where you choose to operate and why your firm's activities are bounded in specific areas.

Competitor analysis. Given strategy's emphasis on a firm's strengths relative to those competing for the same market, competitor analysis plays a key role in the assessment of COMPETITIVE ADVANTAGE and its potential sources through BENCHMARKING. Because the success of any strategic option will depend importantly on the actions and reactions of competitors, their analysis is also critical to choice of strategic initiatives.

Competitor analysis often tends to focus on describing the existing strategy and capabilities of competitors. This kind of information is generally easiest to obtain. Unfortunately it is not the most relevant. The key information is that which illuminates the likely actions of competitors in the future – their assumptions about trends in the market and their future goals.

Many companies claim that their competitors are 'irrational' and are surprised at the policies, such as aggressive pricing, that those competitors adopt in situations where it seems clear to *them* that everyone can only lose. Judged by their own assumptions, which they often impute to the competitor as well, such a policy does indeed seem inconsistent. Yet for a competitor who assumes that customers are price-sensitive and that market share is the key to profitability, attempting to 'buy' extra sales on the basis of price seems perfectly reasonable. Imposing irrationality to competitors is a poor, and unusually incorrect, premise on which to base strategy. By understanding the assumptions which drive a competitor's actions, a firm improves its chance of formulating a strategy to predict and deal with them.

A competitor's future goals are the other key area which competitor analysis must address. These are usually some trade-off between profitability, cash flow, market-share objectives, growth and risk. Competitors, just like your firm, usually can't have everything, and which goals tend to dominate in practice has important implications for likely competitive response. A competitor whose primary objective is growth or market share will react very differently to an expansion of your share, for example, from one which sees itself as a CASH COW.

The nature of a STRATEGIC BUSINESS UNIT's future goals often reflects not only the goals of its managers but those of its parent company. In assessing competitor's goals, therefore, it is often useful to ask, 'what are my counterparts getting most pressured on when they present their budgets?'.

Many believe that it is an almost impossible task to gain a

realistic appreciation of competitors' assumptions and goals. On the contrary, however, a little probing often reveals that a wealth of information about these aspects of the competition actually exists within your own salesforce, your distributors and suppliers or sub-contractors. What is often lacking is simply an adequate system to collect, analyse and act upon it.

Competitor intelligence. Even without his/her own espionage team or a mini 'Watergate' a manager can gather a great deal of useful information on which to base COMPETITOR ANALYSIS. Most public companies choose to brief security analysts about their strategy, capabilities and plans. What a firm releases to, and what appears in the reports of, a single analyst may be uncontroversial; but by watching for significant changes in the same measures she would monitor in her own company – costs, market share, product lines and their distribution and marketing, lead times and stock turns – the competitive manager can piece together the jigsaw to create a powerful picture of the competitor. Likewise, promotional materials, technical seminars, patent lodgements and information provided to shared customers or distributors can be important sources for pieces to complete the puzzle. The PIMS databases of competitors, data collected by trade associations, and even those uncovered by its own sales staff, add crucially to intelligence.

Although obvious, many firms fail to access these sources

Table 1 Tracking your Competitors' Performance Needs to Become as Routine as Tracking your own Performance

Measures	Information sources
• Lead times	• Your sales staff
• Stock turns	• Distributors
• Marketing spend	• Suppliers
• Product line	• Trade associations
• Costs	• PIMS
• Distribution	
• Market share	

systematically because it isn't the responsibility of any individual within the company. Designating an individual to collect, assemble, analyse and disseminate competitor intelligence regularly is commonly found to improve strategic decisions, reduce nasty surprises, and sharpen the managers' focus on their performance relative to competitors in a world where most measurement systems are based on internal performance norms. Tracking competitors' performance needs to become as routine as tracking your own (see table 1).

Complementary products. When two products are used together, with neither having any utility on its own, they are said to be complementary; for example, computer hardware and software, cameras and films. In such cases neither product can be substituted for the other (*see* SUBSTITUTION). Both must be used together and the sale of one, for example personal computers, will boost the sales of the other, software. In other instances complementarity is much less obvious but no less important: a discount electrical goods retailer providing credit facilities, for instance, or a clothing manufacturer providing pre-priced bar-code labels on its garments to a retailer.

The existence of a complementary product raises important strategic questions for a firm. For example, to what extent should, say, a manufacturer of computer hardware, also make and supply the appropriate software? In other words, should the computer manufacturer's product line encompass the full range of complementary products, or should it focus on only one end of the line, leaving other specialists (in this case software suppliers) to complete it? Secondly, if the firm chooses to supply the full range of complementary products should it insist that these are bought together, or should it allow customers to pick and choose (*see* BUNDLING)? The third question concerns the extent to which the firm should price and promote one product in such a way as to promote the sale of its complements, that is, to cross subsidize. So, for example, for many years Kodak heavily promoted the sale of cameras specifically designed to use their proprietary film formats as a way of establishing a huge 'installed base' of Kodak film users who faced the SWITCHING COST of a new camera if they wished to use another brand of film.

Concentration ratio. As the name suggests, the concentration ratio is a measure of the degree to which the VALUE ADDED in an industry is concentrated in the hands of a few firms. The concept of 'industry concentration' encompasses two separate ideas. First, that the total number of firms in an industry can have an important impact on a single firm's profit potential and its ability to exert BUYER or SUPPLIER POWER. The second idea is that profitability will partly depend on whether the competitors are of roughly equal size or a mix of a few giants and many dwarfs.

The feeling that having a monopoly would be quite profitable is familiar. With a small number of relatively equal-sized firms, say three to five, we would expect tacit understanding of likely RETALIATION and mutual dependence to blunt excesses of competition, such as aggressive price cutting, and contribute to favourable profitability. As the number of firms increases and/or the differentials in size increase, the probability that individual firms will have objectives at odds with the group makes competitive stability more fragile. As a very broad generalization, as the concentration falls profits are more likely to be 'competed away'.

In addition to RIVALRY, the level of concentration has potentially important effects on buyer and supplier power. If you and your competitors face a single buyer (termed a 'monopsony') it is fairly clear who has the leverage to bargain your profit away. Similarly, if there are few suppliers of your inputs they are likely to extract a high margin on every unit – after all, if you don't buy it at that price your many competitors probably will.

Firms in industries with many small players facing a high concentration among buyers or suppliers commonly react by forming central buying or marketing organizations to serve the industry as a whole, thereby increasing the *effective* concentration.

Common concentration ratios used in practice include the percentage of industry turnover or value added controlled by the largest four, five or eight firms (often labelled C4, C5 and C8 respectively). C5 is estimated at an average of 46 per cent for UK manufacturing industries while C4 is an average of 34 per cent in the US. Some industry analysts prefer to use the 'Herfindahl Index', which is obtained by taking the square of the market share of each individual competitor expressed as a fraction and summing the results. The index will approach one where there is a clearly dominant industry leader. A small Herfindahl value denotes many, equal-sized firms.

The most difficult problem with measuring the concentration ratio is settling on the appropriate definition of the 'industry'. If you are interested in rivalry, the industry probably includes only the direct competitors in your segment of the market. When looking at potential supplier-power it might include all firms using your raw materials. As a result, no single concentration ratio will be appropriate for all strategic analysis.

Conglomerate. What do the following products have in common? Helicopters, hearing aids, stationery, garden equipment, pens, watch bands, zippers, snowmobiles, hydraulic equipment, stainless steel flatware and solar-energy products. The link is not immediately obvious. Yet all were produced by companies owned, in the 1970s, by Textron, a US corporation that was in many respects the archetypal conglomerate. That is, a highly diversified corporation, that had grown through a process of mergers and acquisitions, in which the parent company had complete ownership of its various subsidiaries.

These multidivisional enterprises, which first emerged in the US in the 1950s, are typically characterized by tight financial control from the centre and an insistence upon standardized accounting, budgeting and reporting procedures, but with considerable strategic and operational autonomy vested in the individual businesses. This immediately raises a fundamental question. Given the inevitable costs incurred in staffing and running a corporate centre, and given the tendency of these costs to increase as the corporation becomes larger and co-ordination more complex and therefore more costly, how is the 'centre' creating value? More specifically, what is the relationship between the value added by the centre and the cost of keeping it going?

Throughout the 1980s, as loose conglomerates fell from favour, the answer to such questions became increasingly jaundiced. The cost/value equation typically cast the corporate centre in an unflattering light, calling into question the reason for its existing at all. Diversified corporations producing heterogeneous products have now given way to a preoccupation with focus – often achieved by unravelling past DIVERSIFICATION.

But this concern with focus should not be taken to mean that product diversity *per se* is symptomatic of a lack of focus or strategic coherence. Take the case of the Sharp Corporation of Japan which produces calculators, portable computers, medical imaging equipment, personal videos, miniature television sets and, currently under development, very large-screen TV sets. What single thing do these different products have in common? A screen. Moreover, it is a screen that works on the basis of the same technology: liquid-crystal display. Sharp originally developed this technology for use in calculators. The same technology then spawned a whole range of other products. Thus Sharp now produces a wide range of items for very different markets. But common to all of these is a core capability or competence which binds together all these activities, imbuing them with a logic and coherence so conspicuously lacking from the loose conglomerates of the 1960s and 1970s such as Textron.

Constituency. The interest groups to which a business is responsible make up its constituencies. Typically, corporations comprise a number of different interest groups: shareholders, employees, suppliers, customers, trade unions, government agencies and, more generally, society at large. In relation to each of these groups the corporation has certain rights and obligations although these are not necessarily well defined. In a sense, any business stands at the vortex of competing – and often conflicting – constituency demands, in much the same way, for example, as an elected Member of Parliament, whose job it is to reconcile and represent the interests of a particular geographically defined sector. But to how many constituencies does a business really have to answer?

The answer is, essentially, three: the capital market – that is, shareholders and all suppliers of debt capital; the product market, consisting of customers, suppliers and the communities within which the organization operates; and the organization itself, made up as it is of managers and employees at all levels. This threefold classification immediately highlights a number of key issues. Each core constituency will have different needs and interests and, moreover, there is no guarantee that interests within a particular constituency will be homogeneous. Over time, the balance of influence will shift from one constituency to another; for example, deteriorating financial performance, escalating debt or a series of strategic mistakes will all serve to strengthen the voice and influence of the capital-market constituency. The conflicting interests of the three constituencies will inevitably act as a constraint on management, thereby limiting its discretion. The success of the business will finally depend upon the co-operation and continued support of all three constituencies. The withdrawal of support, for example by way of limiting the availability of new funds in the case of the capital market, will inevitably be profoundly damaging.

Seen in these terms the task of management is to retain constituency support and, specifically, to reconcile competing demands, thereby ensuring a degree of balance or equilibrium between the constituencies. Sustaining such balance entails making a constant series of choices and trade-offs designed to meet a constituency's needs while limiting its power and influence. Balancing these pressures serves to guarantee the continued survival – and success – of the business while, at the same time, increasing the scope of managerial discretion.

Contribution margin. The difference between the net sales revenue (after discounts) from selling one unit and the variable costs of supplying that unit gives us the margin which that unit contributes towards the fixed costs of the firm. A competitor can be selling products at a loss on a fully costed basis and still be making a contribution to covering fixed costs. Doing so may improve total profits even if it is not possible to sell the additional units at all except at a 'contribution' price – that is, at less than full cost.

The contribution margin is important to strategy because it gives an indication of the price at which competitors may be willing to 'buy' business in an attempt to fill the excess capacity left when demand slackens or in the drive to expand their market share to fill the additional capacity associated with a plant's expansion. Working on such a basis it may be rational to go on cutting the price so long as there is still some contribution margin available.

The danger with offering products to some customers at a contribution price, rather than at a price which reflects full costs, is that these uneconomic prices might spill over to other customers. If the original customers discover they are being disadvantaged relative to the new buyers, a downward price spiral may break out.

Convenience goods. Michael Porter introduced the term into the strategy literature to describe those goods with low unit price, purchased frequently, for which the customer desires an easily accessible outlet and probably requires little or no sales staff assistance in choosing a brand.

The important implication of this type of good, from a strategy standpoint, is that it does not pay the consumer to invest a great deal of time and effort in making objective price and quality comparisons and keeping these up to date. This contrasts with major, infrequent purchases where investment in gathering information has a higher potential pay-off. As a result, convenience goods are often subject to DIFFERENTIATION on the basis of non-objective criteria such as image, advertised perceptions of quality, or packaging.

COO (chief operating officer). *See* CEO.

Corporate culture. Few topics provoke such mixed reactions. From the anonymous US CEO for whom 'the whole culture business is a bunch of bunk; the only culture in this company is in the yogurt in the cafeteria', to an article in *Fortune* magazine which observed that, 'for all the hype, corporate culture is real, powerful and hard to change. If you run up against culture when trying to redirect strategy, attempt to dodge; if you must meddle with culture directly tread carefully and with modest expectations.' Culture is thus viewed with mixed emotions. Testament to *Fortune*'s view is provided in a recent survey of mergers and acquisitions in Europe in which 35 per cent of CEOs questioned identified 'cultural differences' between parties to a merger as constituting the single greatest difficulty in acquisitions. More often than not culture is blamed *after* the event for the failure of a merger (particularly one requiring the close integration of the companies concerned), with rather scant attention being paid to potential cultural clashes *before* the deal is done. So what is corporate culture?

Typically culture is taken to mean the atmosphere, style of 'feel' of the organization; the observable rites, rituals and rules governing how people relate to each other; the explicit values or principles that may find expression in the firm's MISSION STATEMENT; or, more prosaically, culture is simply 'the way we do things around here'. In other words, culture is visible and, by implication, malleable since we can readily observe it. But this is merely the tip of the iceberg. The rules, rituals, behaviour patterns and styles are simply the manifestations of culture, not its essence. The essence of corporate culture is what remains hidden, beneath the surface.

What is it that is beneath the surface? The answer is a set of deep-seated beliefs and assumptions, which give rise to a set of habitual ways of thinking and reacting throughout the organization. Corporate culture comprises a set of beliefs about the central purpose or mission of the firm; the specific GOALS appropriate to that mission; the role of individuals within the firm and the value placed upon their work; how the organization should be structured; what it is distinctively good at doing. In other words, the beliefs or views that constitute a corporate culture provide answers to fundamental questions such as, 'why is the firm in business?', 'how does it define the measure of success?', 'who gets rewarded and why?', 'what does it mean to be "one of us"?' Moreover, the beliefs upon which culture rests are not random, or loosely held. On the contrary, they typically elicit strong emotional attachment, they form a coherent and consistent pattern and, precisely because they *are* taken for granted and therefore barely conscious, they are regarded as being self-evidently 'right' and non-negotiable. Culture is best visualized therefore as an iceberg (see figure 5); what we can see are all the 'ways that we do things round here'. What are

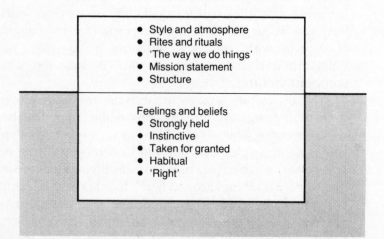

Figure 5   Corporate Culture: an Invisible Barrier to Change

hidden are the feelings and beliefs that give rise to this observable behaviour.

We can appreciate at once that, defined in these terms, culture constitutes an invisible barrier to change. It exerts a decisive influence upon how members of the firm think and react. An influence of which they are barely aware. Unlike other aspects of the organization – its salary system, organizational design or measurement procedures – corporate culture cannot be manipulated and changed at will. It is not so much managers who control culture as culture that controls managers. All of which has profound implications for strategy.

Strategic change that violates fundamental principles of a corporate culture is almost certainly doomed to failure. No matter how impeccable the strategic logic from the point of view of market developments or the firm's competitive situation this will count for little if the fit between strategy and culture is poor. In the process of developing strategy it is therefore essential to pay careful attention to the cultural risks associated with pursuing a particular course of action. This can be done by asking three related questions:

• Which specific elements of the proposed strategy are absolutely critical to its success?
• Upon what core beliefs or assumptions does our culture rest?
• In what specific ways does the intended strategy violate these core beliefs?

In the light of the answers to these questions it may be appropriate to consider ways of adapting your strategy or, failing that, to recognize the cultural risks that you might be running in pursuing it and in being quite specific about those aspects of your culture that you will, over time, have to change. But it is essential constantly to bear in mind that the culture, apart from constituting a barrier to change, also constrains strategy by effectively acting as a filter that screens out 'inappropriate' opportunities, that is, those that don't mesh with the established culture. Culture can therefore narrow your strategic vision and foreshorten your horizons.

Far from being a source of strength it may actually be no longer suited to the competitive environment in which you now operate. It may be outmoded and in need of change. Who can bring about that change? Essentially it is the job of a CEO. The unique and essential function of the CEO is the creation and manipulation of culture.

After these words of caution, a note of encouragement. A well-adapted culture, one that both builds on existing strengths and takes full account of prevailing competitive requirements provides a powerful and sustainable source of competitive advantage. Precisely because culture is difficult to observe and elucidate it proves almost impossible to imitate or replicate elsewhere. If culture cannot be copied it can nonetheless be understood. An essential task of strategy is to try to get to grips with the culture of your competitors. To do so is to gain a real insight into how they work and what they might do in the future. Culture should therefore be taken seriously since there is far more to it than 'what is in the yogurt in the cafeteria'.

Corporate planning. The 1960s and early 1970s were a time of growing demand, requiring companies to bridge the lead time before new manufacturing, distribution and administrative capacity could be brought on stream to meet the demand. Large, diversified organizations of increasing complexity had to attend to the reality of allocating investment resources between their diverse businesses competing internally for funds. These developments led many chief executives to introduce corporate-planning systems aimed at providing the information necessary to make these decisions. The intention was to recognize explicitly the growth prospects of a business and the strength of its competitive position in its market in deciding how it should be managed and further developed.

Initially, many corporate planning systems proved their success; they stimulated fresh thinking and a more market-orientated approach. Over time, however, the books became thicker, the presentation more sophisticated, and the growing planning staffs more divorced from the line management. In many companies the process became a ritual with little impact on line decisions. More and more of the famous 'hockey sticks' emerged – predicted falling profits during the early years followed by dramatic growth further out (when most of the authors would be safely in new jobs). Meaningless long-term projections were substituted for strategic thinking. The development of simplified corporate-planning tools, such as the GROWTH–SHARE MATRIX, helped to 'declutter' portfolios by initiating sensible divestment. However, they commonly led to missed opportunities for growth and innovation as businesses classified as 'mature' or 'cash cows' were unable to throw off their labels and obtain funds for profitable investment.

By the mid-1980s, corporate planning was undergoing a fundamental re-evaluation, paralleling a re-think of the role of the centre and the nature of CORPORATE VALUE-ADDED. This suggests a new, and rather different, role for corporate planning processes focused on:

• exerting continued pressure for improvement of the business-unit plans, now produced by the relevant line managers;
• ensuring that issues which cut across businesses, such as key component technologies, regulatory changes, developments within common third-party distribution, are co-ordinated and addressed;
• recognizing patterns emerging in the individual businesses which, when combined, suggest the need for new directions in the corporation and its investment focus;
• continually re-evaluating the degree of FIT of businesses within the portfolio: posing the question, 'are they better off as part of the corporate group, or are their strategic imperatives opening up a divide between the objectives and needs of the business and its parent?'

Increasingly, corporations are looking to achieve these goals through regular interaction between a small group of top managers, responsible for the separate major divisions as well as their corporate role, who together evaluate the consistency of business-unit plans produced from a corporate perspective by the line management.

Corporate strategy. Consensus about the definition, scope and nature of corporate strategy is in short supply. In part, the debate is about levels of strategy: that is, at what point strategy at, say, the level of the individual business unit gives way to strategy at the corporate level (*see* STRATEGIC BUSINESS UNIT). Underlying this debate is a more fundamental question about what distinguishes the corporation, and the sphere of its activities, from the stand-alone businesses of which the corporation is typically made up. What then are the distinguishing features of strategy at the corporate level?

- Reach – that is, the range of activities that fall within the corporate strategy rubric. At this level, strategy is company wide, encompassing all the different businesses within the corporation. As such, strategy concerns itself with fundamental questions relating to the overall aim or GOALS of the corporation; the policies that it should pursue in accomplishing these goals; the range of businesses in which it should engage, and the manner in which links between parts of the portfolio should be developed.
- Competitive contact – that is, the point at which corporations, as distinct from business units, compete. When we think of competition we typically think of the way in which companies compete for customers; of competition between products or between suppliers. In other words, competition that takes place within the product market, broadly defined. But what are the entities competing at this level? Corporations or business units? Clearly the latter, for corporations as such don't compete directly with each other in the product market. This is not to say that they do not compete at all. Of course they do, but only at certain levels:
finance – raising the finance (for example, from shareholders) required for expansion;
management – recruiting and building a cadre of able managers with long-term potential;

companies – identifying suitable companies for acquisition and incorporation into the corporate portfolio.

We can say therefore that corporations don't compete directly with each other; only business units do. This implies a further difference in what each manages.

• Managing activities or managing business interrelationships – management at a day-to-day level is both about managing activities that are basic to the business – purchasing, production, sales and so on – and managing the links between these often discrete activities. In the domain of corporate strategy, the focus is not so much on the primary activities as on the interrelationships or links between different businesses within the portfolio. This shifts concern from questions such as 'how do we match our distribution strategy to the needs of a product market?', to issues relating to: the transfer of staff (and with them, skills) between businesses; the rules governing trade between constituent businesses; the elimination of unproductive, internal competition; the exploitation of opportunities for collaboration or sharing (for example, sharing sales and fulfilment services); the allocation of financial resources and the resolution of competing claims on these resources. Just as the 'what' of management differs between the SBU and the corporation so does the 'how'.

• Management by intervention or management by reinforcement – within the corporation, responsibility for day-to-day decision-making and performance has to rest with the unit managers. Ceaseless intervention by corporate staff would be both impractical and paralysing. But what can be managed from the corporate level are the processes by which decisions are taken; for example, determining investment criteria, agreeing performance targets, establishing regular reviews and reporting procedures. Such initiatives will have a direct impact on decisions at the day-to-day operating level. Moreover, the process of reinforcement – or persuasion – can be reinforced directly by way of internal staff transfers and promotions (co-ordinated from the centre), the allocation of bonuses, the disbursement of investment funds. At the corporate level, influence or reinforcement rather than direct intervention, with all its attendant problems, has a greater chance of success. Which raises the question, 'how is success judged?'

● Creating value – at the simplest level the FIT or degree of alignment which a firm establishes with its product market (and the relative degree of fit achieved by its competitors) will have a major impact upon its profitability. At a business-unit level, therefore, much of strategy is directed towards matching a business to its market. That is how value is created. But what of the corporate level? Here the challenge is twofold. First, managing the portfolio of businesses in such a way as to maximize their fit with each other, and secondly, managing the resulting interrelationships in a way that adds rather than destroys value; for example, by encouraging the sharing of activities, by transferring staff/skills across the business rather than by creating a corporate centre that simply duplicates functions and accumulates cost.

In summary therefore, the distinction between corporate and business-unit strategy can be expressed as shown in table 2. A summary such as this inevitably runs the risk of implying that between corporate and business-unit strategy there is a hard and fast distinction. That impression is misleading.

Table 2   Corporate Strategy

SBU strategy	Corporate strategy
Competing for ● Products ● Customers ● Suppliers	Competing for ● Finance ● Management ● Companies
Managing ● Activities	Managing ● Process ● Interrelationships
Via intervention	Via reinforcement
Creating value by ● Business-to-market fit	Creating value by ● Business-to-portfolio fit

Although strategy at these two levels is concerned with separate sets of issues, the boundary is often blurred. Overlaps occur, corporate influence often has a profound effect upon the strategy of an individual business unit and, indeed, the business unit itself is, in a sense, the vehicle through which corporate strategy is realized. Decisions made at the centre, at the corporate level, such as those relating to acquisition or divestment, are *de facto* decisions about the positioning of a business in relation to the product market and competitors within that market. Therefore, rather than accentuating the distinction, the most fruitful way of viewing these two dimensions of strategy, about which there is often much confusion, is to see them as being part of a seamless web. A web in which the strategy which is pursued at different levels throughout the corporation is completely coherent and consistent.

Corporate value-added. Recent estimates suggest that the corporate management and co-ordination of large groups cost the equivalent of two per cent of the market value of shareholder equity. That's around three times the fees a fund manager would charge to look after an equity portfolio. With that kind of cost disadvantage, substantial value has to be added by the corporate layer if the group isn't to be justifiably broken up.

How can the CORPORATE STRATEGY add value to its STRATEGIC BUSINESS UNITS? One way is by moving resources around the group, to where they can be most profitably used, more efficiently than an external market. It used to be argued that a prime function here was the allocation of cash. However, with modern capital markets and venture-capital arrangements it isn't clear that this is best done inside the firm. Many SBUs claim they are starved of the capital necessary for expansion by their parents which would be obtainable if they were able to appeal directly to the market. The markets for management, skills and technology are much less perfect so that potentially more can be gained by proper corporate allocation of these assets. Some of the most successful groups draw much of their strength from systems designed to promote this.

A second route is by reaping ECONOMIES OF SCOPE, by promoting the sharing assets such as distribution networks, umbrella brands and salesforces. This almost always involves some degree of compromise for the individual SBU, but may have handsome net benefits if well structured.

A third source of value lies in the establishment of control systems which question, extend and motivate SBU managers to improve strategy and performance continually. Along with its access to 'best practice' information from within the group, corporate management can influence performance in a much more direct way than the external capital market, which has only indirect and 'blunt' instruments like the threat of takeover or bankruptcy to achieve this result – although MANAGEMENT BUY-OUTS suggest that the right external pressures can be a very effective means of eliciting high performance.

Finally, a corporate centre can add value by reducing the transaction costs that each individual SBU would face if they dealt externally. By using group-wide information, better co-ordination should be possible, avoiding unnecessary buffer stocks and risk avoidance. On the other hand, internal transfer-pricing arrangements and other means of transacting internally also impose their own costs and distortions.

Adding real value at the corporate level isn't easy. With continual evaluation of the costs and benefits of central functions in the context of a coherent corporate strategy it can be done, but break-up financiers are increasingly quick to apply a harsh test.

Cost advantage. Firms with lower costs than their competitors don't necessarily have cost advantage; anyone can make a cheaper car, for example, just be leaving out the engine. Cost advantage comes from eliminating costs without materially impairing the buyer's satisfaction. Some of the prime targets for cutting cost without disadvantaging the buyer include:

• inefficiency – this is generally valueless or a nuisance to buyer;

- use of inefficient distribution channels – distributors generally take a margin of between 25 and 35 per cent of product cost, retailers as much as 100 per cent or even more. Are customers really getting value for money from this distribution structure, or would they prefer to bypass it in exchange for lower prices?
- product features the customer hardly ever uses – market research almost always asks what can be added to a product, not what might be taken away to cut costs;
- excessively wide product line – products are often added to satisfy a particular competitive need at a point in time. When that rationale begins to fade away, the product varieties often stay, adding unnecessary COSTS OF COMPLEXITY;
- information and service the buyer would rather not pay for – early in their life cycles, unfamiliar products often require extensive information and service support. As the products become more mature and widely accepted and experienced, customers often require less of this kind of support. Cost advantage can therefore be gained by eliminating it.

Cost advantage results in surplus value which can be shared between the customer, in the form of lower prices, and the supplier, as higher profit.

Cost analysis. Accounting systems seek to allocate costs to time periods (a key task of financial accounting), products (product costing), geographic regions or the individual manager's span of control (as with RESPONSIBILITY ACCOUNTING). Strategy, however, emphasizes the relationship between costs and the activities which create value for the customer. Any cost which is not pulling its weight in terms of ultimately generating extra customer satisfaction is immediately suspect.

The first task of cost analysis in the context of strategy is therefore the allocation of costs to activities along the company's VALUE CHAIN. This often requires a restatement of the available accounting information which is generally collected on some other basis.

The second stage commonly involves a division between 'bought-in' costs and those which are generated within the firm. In the former case, the core issue is how PURCHASING STRATEGY can reduce the costs of *all* inputs (including things like advertising, stationery and sub-contracted services) so as to improve the profitability of the activity to which they contribute.

Finally, strategic cost analysis asks, what is the cost behaviour of each activity? This may differ sharply between activities. Global scale, for example, may be a key source of cost advantage for some activities like basic R&D or component design, while the local customer density may be the primary driver of distribution economics. This understanding of cost behaviour underpins the adoption of strategy to exploit the cost drivers and ensure that every activity is designed to generate a contribution to COMPETITIVE ADVANTAGE and thus long-term profit for the company.

Cost centre. Any department, process, piece of equipment or area of activity for which cost records are kept and against which costs can be allocated is a cost centre. The most obvious example of a productive, direct cost centre is a machine, the costs of which can be allocated to the goods produced by it. Cost centres serve as an effective mechanism for assigning final responsibility for costs incurred to the manager of that centre, in this case, the production department. Thus cost centres sometimes go by the name of 'responsibility' or burden centres (*see* RESPONSIBILITY ACCOUNTING). But in this example, cost allocation is relatively straightforward. It becomes much more difficult of course when the costs of a particular activity (say, running the finance department) have to be allocated to those departments which do not directly incur these costs. Inevitably, the apportioning of costs is a highly contentious issue and one over which many internal battles are fought. And, as with any such battles, the outcome rarely enhances a firm's competitive position. Are such battles therefore necessarily a waste of time? The simple answer is 'no'.

Rigorous cost analysis, and an understanding of exactly where costs are incurred, is a prerequisite of developing effective strategies. Frequently, cost allocation is the result of historical accident, compounded by subsequent inertia. The upshot may well be a massively distorted representation of the apparent 'profitability' of a particular product, activity or range of services. Founding a strategy on such a misrepresentation of reality is clearly dangerous.

To illustrate: for many decades the UK brewing industry was an integrated whole, comprising brewing or beer manufacturing itself, retailing (primarily through public houses) and property management. Failure to assign correctly the costs associated with these three relatively distinct activities, and therefore the failure to recognize the real rates of return afforded by each, resulted in sustained over-investment in brewing (the profitability of which was for many years substantially overstated), and corresponding under-investment in the retailing outlets.

The lessons for strategy are therefore clear. Cost centres are not God-given or self-evident. They require careful definition and analysis, continual re-evaluation in the light of experience, and a willingness on the part of management to analyse the allocation of costs – not on the basis of 'that's how we've always done it', but on the much more challenging premise: 'if we were to start again in this business, how would we allocate the costs associated with it?' In answering this question history is not necessarily a reliable guide.

Cost leadership. A leader is one who has built and can sustain a cost advantage over his competitors in his chosen competitive arena. Cost leadership has often been associated with a single, key source of advantage such as ECONOMIES OF SCALE in manufacturing or in volume-purchasing of key raw materials. In most industries, however, all the important

competitors will quickly learn these basic tricks. They are a
prerequisite for survival, not a source of real COMPETITIVE
ADVANTAGE.

Most of today's successful cost leaders have achieved their
position by shaving costs off every activity through the firm's
VALUE CHAIN. This is not synonymous with 'across the board'
cost-cutting. Instead, it reflects the sensitive elimination of all
costs for which the customer is unwilling to pay. The strategy
of Canon in entering the photocopying market is a good
example. Instead of providing rapid service to all customers,
which would involve holding considerable excess capacity in
order to meet weekly peaks in demand for service, they
offered their customers a choice of three service programmes,
with different maximum service lead times. Large businesses
who had many small photocopiers often chose the longer
lead times at a lower price. This allowed Canon to smooth
out its service workload, and increase capacity utilization,
lowering its costs. The machines were also redesigned to
eliminate features that users of small copiers seldom required.
This meant simpler, hence more reliable, machines. With
fewer components, the parts picking, key assembly steps and
quality control could be automated, contributing to lower
costs. Independent dealers were used to distribute the
machine which sold itself on price and reliability rather than
through heavy promotion, again reducing costs. Cost leadership was thus built up by systematically eliminating costs
which contributed little to customer satisfaction, right
through the chain. The broader the base of cost leadership,
generally the more difficult it is for competitors to copy.

Other cost leaders have exploited the benefits of geographic density. Wal Mart discount stores, well known
because its founder Sam Walton is reputedly the richest man
in the US, achieved cost leadership by its unique 'hub and
spoke' distribution systems, feeding stores in small towns in a
concentrated region from a regional 'mother stock'. It thus
overcame the cost disadvantage of distributing to small, rural
towns while enjoying the cost advantages over its competitors of lower labour costs, cheaper floor space, lower pilfer-
age and cheaper advertising through local papers. The ability

to cut the cost associated with high levels of product variety is becoming an important source of cost leadership with cost leaders attacking the downtime involved in set-up, seeking cheaper sources of variety-specific machine tools, and redesigning products to take advantage of standard base components with variety added at the latest possible stage in assembly. The increased commonality of basic components in products as diverse as motor vehicles, watches and jet engines are examples of this move.

In commodity products, cost leaders have sought to preserve leadership positions based on economies of scale and experience by adding capacity at a faster rate than the growth in market demand. This market pre-emption is aimed at never leaving unserved demand which might offer competitors additional volume to catch up with the cost leader.

Cost leadership is a potentially powerful source of COM-PETITIVE ADVANTAGE. The impact of SUPPLIER POWER is reduced by more efficient use of inputs. BUYER POWER will be mitigated by the floor on prices provided by competitors' higher costs (*see* COST UMBRELLA). Moreover, most competitors find it difficult to pare their expenses in the face of a threat from a cost leader. The inability to separate shared costs across products and customers, organizational resistance to 'cuts' in expenses and jobs, the fact that the cost structure is often deeply embedded in the technology, the design of specialized plants and distribution systems, and management processes, all reduce the flexibility of response. Today's cost leader is therefore often tomorrow's laggard. Cost leadership, as the name suggests, involves continual movement to stay in front.

Cost of complexity. It is an empirical observation that in many industries the overhead per unit of output is higher for companies that produce a greater variety of products or broader line compared with their more focused competitors. This is true even where the companies are of comparable size; and the difference is well beyond that which can be explained by costs and downtime associated with set-up and short run-lengths.

The reason is that the productivity of the personnel who account for a large part of managerial, administrative and factory overheads, tends to decrease as 'complexity' increases. In computer software programming, for example, the Boston Consulting Group found a 140 per cent increase in the time taken to write an instruction each time the total number of lines in a programme doubled. Additional unit cost with increased complexity has been observed in many different areas including: the number of products or product families produced, the number of production steps, the number of operating units, and the number of delivery routes. Significant costs of complexity appear in hand-tool manufacturing (figure 6), construction projects, dairy processing and the manufacture of fork-lifts, to name a few.

Companies often point to the benefits of INTEGRATION and SHARED COSTS (SYNERGY) between operations which are supposed to improve their unit-cost position. It is sometimes suggested that the additional costs of supplying a broad line of 'differentiated' products are low because they share the same plant, distribution or service functions. An alternative justification for launching new products and increasing the variety of what is offered is that, given high, relatively fixed

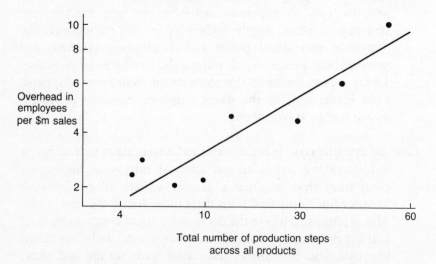

Figure 6   Costs of Complexity in Hand-tool Manufacturing

overhead costs, we need a broader product range across which we can spread our fixed costs, thereby diluting them. But there is another side to this coin. As variety increases, so too does complexity, replete with its own costs. Before it knows what has happened, the firm persuaded of this superficially plausible rationale in support of greater range and variety finds itself caught in a vicious spiral, graphically represented in figure 7.

The lesson for strategy is therefore clear. Analysing the costs of complexity, which are often difficult to detect and isolate, must be an integral part of decisions at many levels of the firm; from plant specialization, product mix and breadth of line, right up to overall corporate DIVERSIFICATION.

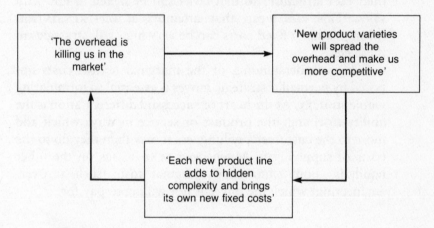

Figure 7   The Complexity Spiral

Cost structure. The distinction between fixed, variable and marginal costs is of especially critical concern to strategists. A company's cost structure affects its viable strategy options. High fixed costs place a premium on strategies which are able to generate a steady volume of throughput. This in turn impacts key strategic choices such as BUYER SELECTION and PURCHASING STRATEGY.

Cost structures are an important indicator of the likely behaviour of competitors, buyers and suppliers. Competitors facing high fixed costs are more prone to cutting price to maintain volume and to retaliating quickly when they lose sales. Buyers with high fixed costs are more willing to accept price increases in a tight market because they cannot allow their throughput to fall. Where fixed costs flow from heavy investment in specialized assets, they represent higher BARRIERS TO EXIT, which means that any strategy which rests on forcing competitors from the market will be more difficult to achieve.

Setting up a business so that its cost structure suits its market is an important aim of strategy. Industries facing erratic demand for raw-material supplies, for example, need strategies which minimize the proportion of fixed costs in their cost structure, so that costs can be flexed in line with sales. This can mean that attempts at DIFFERENTIATION through adding fixed costs can be very high-risk strategies in these fields.

A keen understanding of the marginal (extra) costs imposed by particular strategic moves is essential to formulating viable strategy. At the heart of successful differentiation is the ability to change the product or service in ways which add more to the customer's willingness to pay than they do to the costs of supplying it. Much COST LEADERSHIP, on the other hand, is about eliminating marginal costs (such as over-engineering) which the buyer is not willing to pay for.

Cost umbrella. One of the advantages enjoyed by a cost leader is the fact that, even in the face of strong BUYER POWER, prices cannot be permanently driven down further than the break-even of the less efficient competitors. The existence of high-cost capacity in the industry may therefore provide a cost umbrella which holds up prices and allows more efficient firms to enjoy high profits underneath it.

By acting as a cost umbrella, certain competitors may be valuable to an efficient firm. In the absence of their capacity, others may be encouraged to enter the market, driving down prices. While these high-cost competitors exist, however, new firms may be deterred from entering because exit barriers would make it difficult to force the incumbents to close despite their high costs (*see* BARRIERS TO EXIT).

Care must be taken not to push the cost-umbrella theory too far. Inefficient competitors can also act to depress prices, particularly when their plants are depreciated. If they are suffering from excess capacity, they may be prepared to compete for additional volume while it continues to make some contribution to fixed costs rather than fully covering them (*see* CONTRIBUTION MARGIN). In this case they may be willing to price near to their cash costs to win business, undermining the profitability of their competitors in the process.

Critical-path analysis. This technique was originally developed to solve the scheduling problems of complex construction projects where some activities could occur simultaneously (such as wiring and plumbing) but others had to wait until a prerequisite stage had been completed (walls before windows). Critical-path analysis identifies the slowest sequence of steps in the plan. It then seeks to reduce the total time for project completion by bringing some activities forward and scheduling others in parallel. At the end of this process it is left with a critical path which constrains any further reduction in lead time. This is the set of slow jobs which it is impossible to speed up by resequencing because each relies on the completion of its predecessor. This path is then most tightly monitored since any deviation from plan here would slow the whole project down.

Critical-path analysis is also applied to strategy implementation. It takes a set of activities like product redesign, salesforce retraining, extending plant capacity, and establishing a new distribution network, and minimizes the lead time required for implementation by beginning slow activities early and working on a number simultaneously, again with regard to the prerequisites before any particular one can begin.

Cross parry. Suppose a small firm cuts its price steeply against a key product where you dominate the market. The natural reaction to such an aggressive move may be to respond with a head-on attack. This could, however, be very costly since you lose the profit right across the large volume you sell simply to regain the small percentage of market share it took to fill your competitor's capacity. A better strategy may be, for example, to cut prices in a NICHE segment important to his business, but marginal to yours. This kind of move, where response is made in a second area is termed a cross parry. Such a strategy is viable where competitors meet each other in more than one market (*see* MULTI-POINT COMPETITION).

Cross parrying may be part of a strategy designed to shift the price competition to a side segment and avoid a price war involving a core brand. When a smaller competitor attacked Heublein's 'Smirnoff' vodka brand with a one dollar price cut, for example, Heublein avoided direct RETALIATION. Instead, it raised the price of Smirnoff by one dollar, thus SIGNALLING that it was not prepared to fight on price in the premium segment. However, it simultaneously introduced a new FIGHTING BRAND below its competitor's price enabling it to retaliate on pricing without endangering its core profitability.

Cross subsidization. Products are typically priced so that they make a profit; price is therefore greater than cost. However, in some instances products may be priced at or below actual cost. Were the firm to price all its products in this way it would clearly make an overall loss. But the firm may choose deliberately to price at or below cost and to use profits earned elsewhere in the range as a means of underpinning or subsidizing the 'unprofitable' products. Why should firms cross subsidize in this way? There are a number of reasons.

First, suppose the firm produces two related products that are used together, such as ink-jet printers and ink cartridges. By cutting the cost of the printer the intention would be to increase unit sales of printers and thereby increase the demand for ink cartridges. If the maximum achievable margin on the printer is ten per cent, as against 70 per cent for ink cartridges, this strategy of cross subsidization might well enable the firm to increase its overall profit by increasing the sales of the much more rewarding item, the ink cartridges.

A second rationale might run as follows. Imagine you are in the personal-computer business. First-time buyers are likely to opt for a moderately priced, relatively unsophisticated machine at or near the bottom of the range. Having mastered that, they may decide to go for something more ambitious and expensive. By selling the introductory-level computer at a low or 'subsidized' price, you hope to retain a customer as s/he progresses up the range, buying more expensive and, for your company, more profitable machines. Indeed, the introductory-level PC may be sold at a price at which it makes a 'loss'. The hope is that loss leaders will attract first-time buyers who will then convert to long-term, less price-sensitive purchasers of higher-margin items.

With both the ink-jet printer and the PC, the underlying rationale is identical: to increase total profitability by maximizing sales of the most profitable goods by discounting the price of those that are least profitable. The risks of pursuing such a strategy are immediately apparent. They include:

• the consumer sticks with the loss leader and doesn't trade up to more expensive items, at least in large enough numbers;

• the discounted good introduces the product to the consumer but he then goes on to buy other, similar, but more expensive products from competing suppliers;

• the link between the two goods is insufficiently strong, so that, for example, a customer buys the ink-jet printer from supplier A but purchases the ink cartridge, at a lower price, from supplier B;

• cross subsidization is unintended, rather than deliberate. Ignorance of the real costs of producing a particular product may result in incorrectly underpricing goods which are inadvertently subsidized by those that are profitable;

• as the industry evolves, conditions that originally favoured cross subsidization may disappear.

Customer dominance. Questions of the impact of MARKET SHARE on the profitability figure prominently in many strategy decisions. In analysing these issues the correct definition of the boundaries of the market is always critical. A 'market' can encompass more than one competing industry, or it may be a much narrower buyer, product or geographic segment. Sometimes each individual customer is effectively a separate market.

In many industries, such as those supplying industrial consumables, any individual customer regularly draws the same item from more than one supplier. The idea of spreading purchases in this way is often to promote a degree of direct competition, continually playing off one supplier against another. There is often a major supplier and a number of secondary ones (*see* PURCHASING STRATEGY). The secondary suppliers have to worry about their sales to any particular customer becoming too small because there are usually fixed costs in serving that customer. You might still have to send the delivery van whether he buys a little or a lot; the monthly statement still has to go out, even if it has only one line on the page; the salesman still has to visit; a cash payment has to be collected.

The other problem for the fringe suppliers to a particular customer is that the SWITCHING COST of his moving to a competitor is generally low, so their bargaining position is weak. On the other hand the major supplier is often better off since switching the bulk of his purchases, or even upsetting the smooth flow, is likely to be much more disruptive for the customer.

In these cases the supplier's share of each individual customer's total purchases of the product can matter a great deal. A firm which is always a fringe supplier to its customers will have high unit costs to serve and often will be able to charge only below-average prices. In contrast, a supplier who achieves customer dominance, in other words is the dominant supplier to most of its individual customers, will tend to be much more profitable.

The desire to achieve customer dominance across total sales impacts on a firm's choice of COMPETITIVE SCOPE. A small firm has a much better chance of being dominant supplier to its customers if it adopts a NICHE strategy, rather than competing in the mainstream where it might pick up only fringe shares of each customer's needs.

D

Decentralization. The process whereby decision-making power and authority is diffused throughout the organization. Such diffusion typically devolves part of those levels of management most immediately responsible for implementing decisions. In dispersing such decision-making authority, literally pushing it outwards and downwards from the centre, it is important to be clear about precisely what sort of power is being decentralized; is it the authority to take decisions over operational issues (for example, production planning)? Or is the responsibility for strategic decisions also being devolved?

Operational autonomy is not necessarily accompanied by strategic autonomy. Such an amalgamation is likely to be found only in highly diversified firms in which each business unit or subsidiary manager is given responsibility for both operational and strategic direction. But in many other instances the firm may be decentralized in terms of operating decisions but highly centralized in strategic terms in so far as all operating decisions are taken in the context of a clear, overall strategic framework emanating from the centre. In Unilever, for example, operational decentralization is high while strategic decentralization is limited.

Advocates of decentralization argue that it speeds up managerial decision-making, enabling 'local' management to respond rapidly to changing conditions and emerging problems as they occur. It strengthens managerial commitment to the policies being pursued, it sustains a more dynamic, entrepreneurial managerial climate and it avoids the problem of excessive control residing at the centre. But the process is not without its drawbacks. The corollary of enhanced management commitment may be a degree of myopia, in that divisional managers will pursue strategies and make operational choices that maximize the profitability of their own unit rather than that of the business as a whole. Such a narrow focus makes it more difficult for the corporation to identify areas of intra-firm co-operation and to co-ordinate activities in such a way that the potential benefits of interrelationships *within* the corporation can be exploited. Wherever policies of decentralization are pursued one thing is certain: such policies only work if areas of responsibility and autonomy are precisely defined so that there is little or no room for misunderstanding and uncertainty over who exactly is responsible for what.

Decision tree. Management decision-making typically involves choosing between alternative courses of action and making a series of linked decisions upon which uncertainties and chance events will impinge. In selecting between alternatives, an assessment – either implicit or explicit – will be made of the likelihood of a particular event occurring and the impact that such an event would have upon the value or outcome of the decision itself. The decision tree is one way of diagrammatically representing or explicating that logical sequence of decisions, chance events and probable outcomes. An example is given in figure 8.

The points at which a decision is taken are represented by rectangles, the points at which a chance event occurs, by circles. Between these two points – or 'nodes' as they are termed – runs a straight line representing the logical sequence of choices. In figure 8 the line links a decision node to a chance-event node, although the relationship between these is not necessarily one to one. That is, there may be a series of decision nodes, followed by a series of chance nodes. Whatever the sequence, probability is assigned to each of the branches bearing a chance node. Probability here is an estimate of the likelihood of that chance event occurring. At the end of each branch of the tree there will be a pay-off, usually but not necessarily calculated in financial terms. With all the pay-offs calculated, and probabilities ascribed, a process of elimination is used to identify which particular branch represents the most favourable outcome.

The method therefore provides an effective way of rigorously identifying options and ranking them in terms of (a) the likelihood of their occurrence and (b) the expected benefit or

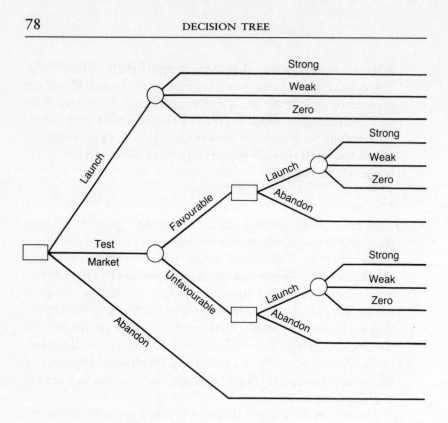

Figure 8 A Decision Tree

pay-off. In using the technique particular care should be taken in assigning probabilities to chance events, particularly where the probability can only be assessed subjectively. Clearly, final decisions will be strongly influenced by the way in which probabilities have been assigned.

One difficulty associated with the decision-tree technique is that the choices available at any one point in the tree are typically represented in somewhat simplified, black-and-white terms, whereas in practice decisions entail selecting between a number of competing alternatives. Representing such alternatives diagrammatically would result in an unmanageable number of branches of the tree. Similarly, the consequences of any particular decision sometimes exceed the two or three outcomes that can be accommodated easily within a decision tree. However, in developing strategy, the technique has a dual value. First, in imposing a degree of rigour on the way in which deciding between choices, uncertainties affecting these choices and their final outcomes are laid out for examination. Secondly, it draws attention to those events or uncertainties which will have the greatest impact upon a decision and therefore merit further consideration.

Declining industries. The identification of irreversible decline is unquestionably the first critical issue associated with so-called declining industries. Implicit in the term is an assumption of a natural contraction of businesses and markets following their growth phase. Yet firms like RCA characterized consumer electronics as a declining industry in the mid-1960s when the US colour-TV market began to show signs of saturation. In response they made ill-fated investments in the computer business. Little more than a decade later they were buying back technology and products to meet an unprecedented boom in demand for VCRs and compact-disc players.

However, when substitution or changing lifestyles does initiate an irreversible decline in demand, firms are often faced with polar opposites as the viable alternative strategies to deal with the END GAME. On one hand, HARVESTING or 'milking' of market positions, raising prices, pruning product lines, cutting advertising and avoiding new investment wherever possible may maximize the firm's NET PRESENT VALUE. Alternatively, it may pay the firm to *invest* in promotion, distribution, product improvement and even capacity, with the aim of attaining market leadership and therefore benefiting from the profitability of the residual, less price-sensitive demand as the market contracts. Paradoxically, investment in a leadership strategy may be more viable when decline is relatively certain. In this case committed rivals will often be more willing to close substantial blocks of their capacity quickly, compared with the situation where demand falls erratically and optimistic forecasts can continue to postpone the liquidation of firms' capacity. Such a strategy, however, is clearly not without risks. Should rivals face higher-than-expected BARRIERS TO EXIT, either actual or emotional, investing with the object of attaining leadership will only aggravate the capacity imbalance created by the industry's decline.

Defensibility. In assessing any COMPETITIVE ADVANTAGE, and the basis upon which it is built, the acid test is this: can the advantage be defended and is it sustainable? Out-performing competitors over the long term entails the building of real advantages that prove enduring and sustainable. But the difficulty with any competitive advantage, from whatever source it derives, is that no advantage lasts forever. Competitors, seeing the benefit associated with performing an activity or configuring a business in a certain way, will, if they possibly can, seek to emulate and imitate. Alternatively, consumers – whose values and perceptions are constantly changing – may cease to value the distinctive benefits derived from using one firm's products or services. Competitive advantage is therefore vulnerable on two fronts: from copying or imitation, and from the erosion of perceived or recognized value. But how can firms guard against this erosion of competitive advantage? There is one golden rule: that is, to multiply the sources of advantage while recognizing that some sources are more robust than others. Some sources may be difficult to replicate, such as proprietary technology or knowhow; scale or the benefits associated with learning; and the timing of competitive moves. Others are hard to fathom out, like interrelationships between the business units that comprise the corporation. In evolving ways of creating competitive advantage always ask yourself this question: 'how sustainable or defensible are our sources of advantage?'

Delphi forecasting. Place a group of six people in a room and ask them to come up with a forecast – for example next year's sales revenue – and a whole variety of pressures or influences will come into play; for example, the vehemence with which a particular forecast is defended, the status or influence of different individuals within the group, peer-group pressure and so forth. The Delphi technique, which takes its name from the ancient Greek oracle at Delphi, revered for its impartiality, is expressly designed to eliminate the influence of group pressures. This is accomplished by simply keeping group members apart and allowing communication solely through a chairman.

Producing a sales forecast using the Delphi method works as follows. The chairman invites each individual to submit his own forecast and, in so doing, to cite the reasons for arriving at a particular figure and the factors that will most significantly affect it. Individual forecasts are then summarized by the chairman, along with a digest of the key factors identified by each individual. The summary, which may include details of the range of the individual forecasts as well as the average figure, is then circulated, and individuals are asked to make a new forecast, this time taking into account the new information with which they have been provided. The process, which remains anonymous in that no-one knows who is making which particular forecast, is repeated until either a consensus emerges or, alternatively, group members are unwilling further to revise their own views. The eventual outcome is the Delphi forecast.

The advantages of this technique are immediately obvious: anonymity encourages individuals to express their genuine views and expectations; the distorting influence of group pressure is minimized; consensus can be developed among a group of far-flung individuals. The method's efficacy has been well tested but the process may be laborious, time-consuming and expensive. Moreover, its success depends in large part upon the quality of chairmanship, the manner in which questions are presented, and the willingness of participants not to play games – for example, by submitting an unrealistic forecast designed to reduce the 'first-round' average. Although Delphi forecasting keeps individuals apart it can provide no absolute guarantee that the distortions associated with group dynamics will be eliminated entirely from the forecasting process.

Differentiation. A firm may endeavour to position its product or service so that it uniquely meets the needs of prospective buyers, providing something that no other offering exactly matches. This requires differentiation of its product or service, developing unique features or attributes: for example, design or brand image, technology, customer service, product quality, distribution network or method of delivery.

Underpinning this strategy is the the recognition that many markets comprise quite discrete segments and that consumer needs will vary between segments, thereby creating opportunities to develop services tailored precisely to meet the specific – and unique – needs of a particular customer group. For example, recent innovations in the design and delivery of UK retail banking services such as electronic or home banking are targeted at a particular group of customers for whom branch banking, with its truncated opening hours, is not well suited. Being able to do all one's banking from home or on the telephone is a service which a particular group of customers values. Moreover, it is something for which they are prepared to pay.

Therein lies the essence of a differentiation strategy: for providing a unique product or service, the firm will expect to charge a price premium. Ostensibly such a strategy is attractive. By differentiating our offering, albeit in small ways, we benefit by being able to charge a higher price and, we hope, thereby earning higher margins than competitors who are providing an undifferentiated product or service at prevailing competitive prices. But beware of the superficial attraction on three counts.

Achieving differentiation invariably costs money. Far from being a licence to ignore costs, differentiation strategies must pay particular attention to the relationship between the cost of differentiation (say, the cost of offering a 24-hour repair service) and the price premium that this will command. Clearly, that price premium must be greater than the cost incurred, but all too often unique products or services are developed with inadequate regard for cost (see figure 9). Moreover, an integral element of any differentiation strategy must be the reduction of all other costs which do not materially contribute to a product's distinctiveness.

Secondly, what we *think* a buyer will value, in terms of unique product features or service attributes, and what the buyer actually values in practice, what creates utility for him/her, may be two quite different things. Ascribing our prejudices or preferences to the prospective customer of this unique service is both easy and dangerous. Moreover, buyers' preferences and expectations are not static: they change over time and, as they do, products with unique features that previously created utility cease to do so.

Thirdly, successful differentiation encourages emulation on the part of competitors. Recognizing the benefits to be gained by differentiating in a certain way, for example, by improved margins, competitors may seek to replicate the 'unique' advantages of a competing product, and to do so at a reduced cost and in some instances at a lower price. In part, this reduced price may be possible by virtue of the fact that those that follow the lead of others can do so without incurring many of the development costs that differentiation entails (*see also* FIRST MOVER).

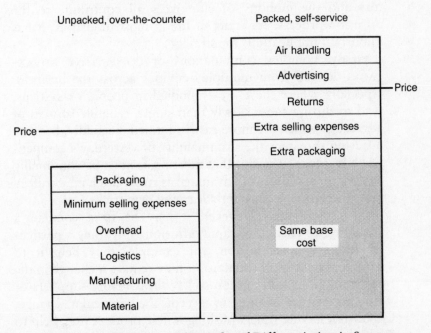

Figure 9 The Costs and Benefits of Differentiation in Sausages

So, if differentiation plays an important part in your strategy, you must ask yourself three questions. First, what is the relationship between the cost of achieving differentiation and the price premium that we can charge for it? Secondly, are we differentiating in a way that consumers genuinely value and are prepared to pay for? Thirdly, can we sustain our unique offering, or is it vulnerable to imitation by competitors and, to add insult to injury, can imitation be accomplished at a lower cost?

Diffusion. Originally applied in a narrow sense to the diffusion of technology, the term can equally apply to sales and service techniques, distribution or purchasing approaches, organizational structures, decision-making processes, and many other areas. It is used to describe the process by which originally unique or proprietary strategies spread between companies to become common industry practice.

Diffusion can occur via many routes, not only through direct imitation by competitors. Buyers, suppliers, distributors and the mobility of employees all contribute to the diffusion process. As a fact of life in most industries, it has important implications for strategy.

Firstly, complex combinations of COMPETITIVE ADVANTAGES derived from multiple activities across the business, especially where these are embodied in people or systems, tend to diffuse more slowly than single, tangible sources of advantage which are more easily imitated. Secondly, because diffusion threatens the sustainability of yesterday's competitive advantage, it means that most firms must be continually creating new sources of advantage as rivals catch up. Strategy must therefore be constantly learning new tricks.

In certain cases, however, it may be to a company's advantage to encourage rapid diffusion. Spreading a particular technical specification, for example, may help it to become the industry standard. It may require a change in the operating policy of a group of key firms before suppliers or distributors are willing to accept the particular change. Likewise, having others pushing a new product may help to generate generic demand for it.

Discretionary policies. In producing a book such as this there are a number of things the publisher must do: the manuscript has to be edited, the result typeset, proof-read, printed, bound, and the book given a dust jacket. These variables are necessary. But within this framework the publisher has considerable choice or discretion over items such as the quality of the editing process, the choice of the paper, the location of the typesetter and printer, whether or not there should be illustrations in the text, the colour of the dust jacket and so on. The choice made for each of these variables plays a significant part in determining the overall cost of the book's production. In making such choices the firm will be guided by an assessment of the cost of expending money so as to differentiate its product, to make it stand out and appear unique; the value that is thereby created, for example, by being able to charge a higher price. In developing strategy it is important to distinguish between those policies that are fixed or 'given', and those over which choice or discretion can be exercised. To ask the question: does the cost of pursuing a particular policy exceed the value or benefit that thereby accrues to the firm?

Which activities the firm engages in, and how it carries these out, play a decisive role in differentiating it from the competition. Achieving uniqueness is in large part discretionary but the cost of pursuing discretionary policies should be constantly borne in mind when analysing current and future strategies.

Diseconomies of scale. In many industries, as output expands unit production costs fall, and the firm reaps the benefits of ECONOMIES OF SCALE. These may result from increased efficiency, dilution of fixed overhead, enhanced purchasing power, and so on. But scale can, in turn, create its own problems. For example, as operations become larger, so they become more complex; greater co-ordination is required; size may be demotivating. The phenomenon is well illustrated in a professional service firm like a design consultancy, where success is critically dependent upon the commitment and responsiveness of highly creative individuals working in

small, close-knit team-based organizations. In such instances the diseconomies of scale – often in the form of intangible costs – may outweigh the more tangible benefits or economies associated with size. As the scale increases the cost curve will typically decline. After some point, however, diseconomies of scale begin to dominate, producing a 'U'-shaped relationship between scale and unit costs.
See also COST OF COMPLEXITY.

Diversification. The strategic gospel of the 1950s, 1960s and 1970s preached the virtues of reducing a company's dependency on a single business or a narrowly defined market in favour of a more broadly based portfolio of activities. The links between these activities was often tenuous in the extreme. For example, the UK company Reed International moved during the 1970s into new areas that encompassed printing, paper, publishing and packaging. The superficial common denominator, paper, in fact masked very different requirements for competitive success. In fact, according to the CEO who inherited this heterogeneous clutch of activities: 'the only thing they have in common is that they all begin with the letter P.' Having divested itself of most of its businesses, Reed International is now left with only one 'P': publishing. But Reed is not an isolated example. Indeed, between 1960 and 1980 the proportion of America's *Fortune* '500' companies which were diversified rose from 50 to 80 per cent. The comparable UK shift was from 40 to 60 per cent.

Various factors influenced this radical restructuring of so many businesses. Among these are principally: the belief that the cyclicality of the economy necessitated the acquisition of counter-cyclical businesses to balance a company's portfolio; the idea that corporations possessed certain core skills which could be transferred across to other businesses; and the apparant efficacy of concepts such as the GROWTH–SHARE MATRIX which justified the inclusion, under a single corporate umbrella, of different kinds of businesses with complementary cash needs, so that the corporation acted as an internal 'bank'.

Underpinning this was a more powerful and possibly more pernicious factor: fashion. In the 1960s and 1970s diversification was the name of the corporate game. And yet by the mid-1980s the trend had gone into sharp reverse. One US study of 33 large diversified companies showed that more than half of the diversifications made by takeover between 1950 and 1980 had been sold off by 1986. In the case of companies acquired in areas unrelated to the core business the divestment rate was 74 per cent. Typical of these divestments is Exxon's withdrawal from electronics and BP's disposal of businesses unrelated to oil, such as coal. In some companies, CBS and RCA for example, more than 80 per cent of a portfolio has been sold off.

In place of corporations diversifying on behalf of their shareholders it is now argued that diversification should be left to the shareholders themselves who can balance risk and reward by diversifying their own share portfolios. Whereas shareholders can accomplish this relatively cheaply, diversifying corporations incur heavy costs, for example, in the form of hefty acquisition premiums or additional costs of co-ordination (*see* COST OF COMPLEXITY). This is not to say that diversification is dead, but where it is pursued it should be done so with careful regard to the scope that exists for sharing activities – like distribution or technology – between businesses, and exploiting such interrelationships as do generally exist. The company should also be mindful of the extent to which it can deploy its specific skills in managing various businesses, and can transfer skills from one business to another. In essence, therefore, strategies of related diversification have a greater chance of success than those that bring together businesses with little more in common than that they all begin with the same letter of the alphabet.

Divestment. The flip side of ACQUISITION, divestment is about selling a business (or part of it), closing the business down entirely or gradually running it down as its residual profitability is harvested (*see* HARVESTING). Whatever route is pursued the outcome is the same: the business no longer forms a part of a company's activities. But getting to this position is often a long, painful process and one that needs just as much thought and planning as the process of acquisition. Deciding to divest is often difficult, particularly if the decision is likely to be interpreted as a sign of failure or of past mistakes. Deferring a decision, in the hope that performance may improve or that the problem will miraculously go away, is easy but rarely right. Too often ailing businesses which no longer fit the company's portfolio are allowed to limp along as management shies away from grasping the divestment nettle. Nettles that are the creation of powerful people near retirement, or those representing businesses that were once central to the organization, prove particularly hard to grasp.

Why then does divestment become necessary? Most commonly because previous DIVERSIFICATION did not work out as expected. Alternatively, the company's very survival may be predicated on its eliminating certain activities; these may range from deleting a product line to selling an entire business. Here divestment represents a relatively quick way of reducing the burden – often represented by high debt or a continuing cash drain – associated with poor performing activities. Thus, as the firm's environment changes, and with it the key strategic objectives, so divestment represents a means of realigning activities and subsidiaries in support of re-defined corporate goals. But, in choosing to divest, careful thought should be given to the best means of accomplishing it; disposal, *franchising*, *spin off*, *management buy-out* and indeed *sub-contracting* are all forms of divestment. In this sense divestment is not exactly the flip side of the acquisition coin, although it may well be necessary to divest yourself of an activity or business before acquiring another.

Divisionalization. The structuring of an organization on the basis of quasi-autonomous divisions gives each responsibility for a particular product market, geographical area or, in the case of vertically integrated firms, one specific dimension of the business – for example, manufacturing or retailing (*see* INTEGRATION). Divisional structures first appeared in the US in the 1920s and their origin is closely associated with two companies in particular: Du Pont and General Motors, to both of whom the structure represented a potential solution to problems resulting from ever-increasing size and complexity. Since then multidivisional structures, or 'M-form' organizations as they have subsequently been termed, have become widespread, with their growth closely tracking that of DIVERSIFICATION strategies which, in the US in particular, represented the dominant strategic thrust from the early 1950s to the 1970s. (See figure 10.)

Advocates of the M form claim a number of advantages for it: divisions can be operated and measured as independent PROFIT CENTRES; the needs and activities of each division can be tailored precisely to the needs of the market that it is serving; the structure facilitates the devolution of general management and profit responsibility, thereby providing central management with a powerful motivational instrument; divestment of a single division can be undertaken without any dislocation to the rest of the organization.

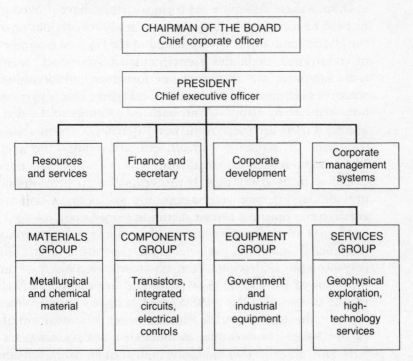

Figure 10   A Multidivisional Structure

But there is inevitably a downside. Drawing precise boundaries between divisional and central management is difficult, for example in terms of who is responsible for determining strategy and defining objectives. The structure encourages rivalry – and conflict is often endemic – over issues relating to the divisional allocation of funds and of the central overhead. The conflict may be interdivisional or with the corporate centre; the employees will typically identify with the division first and the firm as a whole second. Finally, the structure's Achilles' heel is that divisional boundaries may not mirror market boundaries and, as new products emerge – products which cut across the firm's historical divisions – so the firm may find it hard to respond. Developing interdivisional products is notoriously difficult and may entail radical restructuring of the organization to take account of new technological and market developments – developments that pay no heed to the existing divisions around which an organization is structured.

Despite these difficulties M-form structures have proved to be both resilient and highly effective. In studies originating in the US, and subsequently replicated in the UK and a number of countries in mainland Europe, empirical evidence shows that in terms of overall financial performance multidivisional structures out-perform other structural types. This is particularly true in measures of growth (in earnings and sales), although there are much narrower differences in profitability (in terms of return on investment and equity) between M-form and functional structures.

Under ideal conditions the divisional structure should provide an effective mechanism for achieving a balance between the central strategic direction (based upon a longer-term view of the future) and local or divisional autonomy (designed to maximize performance in the shorter term). The corporate centre, having effectively internalized many of the functions of the capital market, should in principle be well placed to optimize the allocation of funds to opportunities offering the highest yield. But achieving this ideal entails clearly defining both the nature and extent of DECENTRALIZA-TION and, allied to this, the development of an overall design for the organization that is internally consistent. Failing this, divisionalization can be a recipe for conflict, which leaves the organization acutely vulnerable to movements of the market – or competitors.

One solution to this problem is to exploit the opportunity that divisional structures afford for moving executives between divisions; for using the divisional structure as a way of giving responsibility and profit accountability to able managers at an early stage in their careers. Exploiting the management-development potential of divisionalization in this way has the added advantage of developing a pool of senior managers who, by virtue of their broader experience, are better able to reconcile corporate and divisional interests, thereby reducing the inherent possibility of conflict between the two poles, the division and the centre.

Downstream. The process of converting raw materials into finished goods, or of producing and delivering a service, goes through a number of distinct phases or stages. Taken together, these stages constitute a chain of linked activities; in each major part of the chain value is added. Every industry comprises a number of different stages which, taken together, combine to form a VALUE CHAIN. At one end of the chain we have the conversion of raw materials; at the other end, the delivery of a product or service that generates customer satisfaction. Typically, firms concentrate their activities on parts of the chain, rather than the whole. Those focusing on the initial stages, for example the conversion of raw materials into commodity products, are described as upstream companies. In contrast, downstream companies focus on adding value by producing and delivering a variety of products or services that meet clearly defined customer needs. A company's 'centre of gravity' may therefore be said to be either upstream or downstream. In electronics, for example, Intel – the major manufacturer of microchips – is engaged in upstream activities the results of which, the microchips, it sells to downstream computer manufacturers.

This difference in focus, or difference in the centre of

gravity, has profound implications for the way in which the company is organized and structured, for its management skills and processes and indeed for its culture. Whereas at the upstream end of the chain emphasis is likely to be given to producing standardized, commodity products at the lowest cost, with a corresponding reliance upon capital-intensive process technologies, those firms operating downstream would typically be more concerned with developing and customizing products, backed by the appropriate marketing, advertising and channels of distribution. Clearly, the skills required in order to succeed upstream are quite different from those needed downstream; the factors that are critical to success are not the same.

This is where the problems arise. In strategic terms there is nothing more difficult than radically changing a firm's centre of gravity and moving it upstream or downstream. To accomplish such a move successfully a firm has to acquire new skills and expertise, create new values and expectations, and install new management systems. Although such a shift may seem a logical or natural extension of a firm's current activities, the risks associated with this shift must be borne in mind. Historic success upstream provides no guarantee of repeating such success downstream, and vice versa.

E

Econometric forecasting. A model of an economy or market embodied in a series of equations (often hundreds or even thousands) may provide the basis on which to predict the behaviour of the key actors and the way their decisions will interact. By feeding in current changes in policy or economic environment (such as a shift in oil price), the impact can be forecast on other key variables such as growth, consumption, investment, pricing, as the original change works its way through the economy. The most common models are of the whole economy (prime examples are those of the Treasury, Data Resources Incorporated, Cambridge Econometrics, and the London Business School), although models of individual markets (such as the world oil or energy market) have also been built. All of these share the problem that the predicted responses of each of the actors in the model (consumers, companies, governments, and so on) are based on their past behaviour which can be notoriously unstable in the face of new environmental conditions. As a result, their forecasts and the associated errors have often been heavily criticized.

Before dismissing econometric forecasting as an input to strategy, however, we should be careful to take a look at the alternatives. The simple extrapolation of a single series or the 'rule of thumb' approach effectively ignores most of the lessons of past behaviour, and often fails to allow for the fundamentals of economic life, such as the fact that higher import prices must be paid for through reduced consumption, extra overseas borrowing, or higher inflows of foreign investment, that extra consumer income must be either spent or saved, or that extra government spending can only be financed by higher taxes, more bond issues, or 'printing money'. For all their inadequacies, econometric models do take into account these basic constraints and feedback loops. Therefore they may be the best available from a poor selection.

Faced with uncertainty as a fact of life, however, strategy

has increasingly shifted its emphasis away from reliance on forecasts and towards ensuring that companies have the ability to respond flexibly to events. This involves tackling both external and internal BARRIERS TO MOBILITY, and ensuring that decision-making processes leave room for the strategy to 'learn' as its environment changes.

Economies of scale. There is a tendency for plants, distribution networks with a large capacity, marketing campaigns with wide reach (for example, national rather than local), or centralized, bulk-purchasing systems to have potentially lower unit costs than their counterparts working on a smaller scale. One of the simplest analogies is that one large building has less wall area than 20 smaller buildings with an equivalent total volume of work space. Economies of scale very often arise from the fact that larger-scale operations can take advantage of different, more efficient, technologies. Continuous manufacturing lines, the use of large trucks or tankers, or national television advertising, would be examples where the fixed costs of using the technology are indivisible. They are often confused, however, with *capacity utilization* effects (spreading fixed costs at any given scale) and EXPERIENCE CURVE effects (lower unit costs resulting from learning and incremental improvements as tasks are repeated in the course of processing a large cumulative volume over subsequent periods).

Opportunities to reap economies of scale are not all straightforward. Because large-scale technologies often introduce higher fixed costs into the operation's cost structure, they make it necessary for the business to utilize capacity more sensitively. Scale economies therefore create the potential for lower unit costs as long as the capacity is heavily utilized. At low utilization, a firm enjoying what seem like scale economies may in fact have much higher actual costs than small competitors. Large-scale operations may also be less flexible in meeting the needs for shifts in strategy when market conditions change. Other activities necessary in order to take advantage of the large scale, such as the ability to co-ordinate and motivate large numbers of staff in a single work place, meanwhile, may be subject to DISECONOMIES OF SCALE and COSTS OF COMPLEXITY which negate much of the original benefit.

Nonetheless, economies of scale have offered substantial advantages to firms with high MARKET SHARES where scale-sensitive technologies for manufacturing, distribution, marketing, or bulk-purchase discounts have been available. In other markets, however, scale has had offsetting disadvantages. Moreover, the emergence of effective 'mini-scale' technologies (such as small breweries or small-scale furnaces for speciality steels) is leading some companies to question the benefits of massive, centralized operations. (See figure 11.)

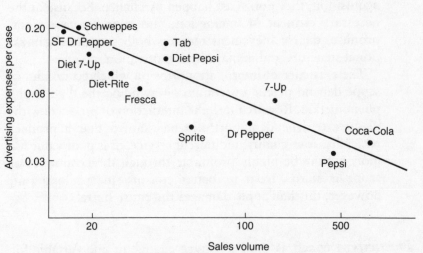

Figure 11 Economies of Scale in Soft-drinks Advertising

Economies of scope. A company that is simultaneously involved in supplying a number of related products may derive benefits in the form of lower unit costs. These economies may flow, for example, from shared distribution facilities, reduced marketing costs through the use of umbrella brands, joint manufacturing plants, or common R&D or central services. Other positive spillovers include favourable consumer experience, with one product encouraging purchase of another. In the industrial and financial services markets, for example, increased demand often comes through a series of cross-sales. 'Trading up' through a range of computers or other machinery is another common instance.

The potential benefits of economies of scope need to be weighed against inevitable costs. Sharing facilities, distribution, brands or services generally means a degree of compromise between the businesses compared with what each would design independently. There may also be substantial COSTS OF COMPLEXITY involved in co-ordination across multiple products or businesses.

Although economies of scope are commonly behind the potential SYNERGIES identified in justifying diversification and acquisition, they don't just happen by chance. Because of the necessary element of interaction, and in many cases compromise, their achievement requires both suitable organizational structure and management motivation.

The existence of interrelationships on which economies of scope depend places a premium on avoiding the 'bad apple' phenomenon. Research into the interaction of products within an interdependent portfolio has shown that a product which has low-quality, indifferent service, or is poor value for money, may be highly profitable through the economies of scope it enjoys from its better cousins. In the long run, however, this bad apple damages the entire barrel.

Elasticity. Defined as the percentage change in one variable for every one per cent change in the other, this is a standardized measure of the responsiveness of one variable to another. Thus the price elasticity of demand is the percentage change in quantity demanded for every one per cent change in the price. Responsiveness is described as elastic if the elasticity is greater than one; that is, the change in the original variable is amplified in the other one. Conversely, an inelastic response (elasticity smaller than one), refers to the case where the original change is muted (less than proportional). Thus when a customer or market segment is described as 'price inelastic', this refers to the fact that a change in price has relatively little impact on the quantity demanded.

Elasticity is an important concept in many strategic contexts. When predicting the response of competitors to a price increase, for example, their ability to expand output given current plant capacity is crucial. If competitors are running at full capacity already, hence their elasticity of supply in the face of increased prices is low, the increase is more likely to be followed. Cross-elasticity – the change in demand for a substitute brand or product when your price changes – is an important measure of the threat of SUBSTITUTION and the SWITCHING COST. Elasticity is also commonly used as a standardized measure of the response of sales or market share to advertising or marketing expenditure.

Emergent industry. In their early stages industries present two main groups of strategic challenges: uncertainty regarding many of the key variables and the changing sources of advantage as the industry develops.

The uncertainty permeates not only the technology, but customer behaviour, potential growth and ultimate market size, and the strategies which competitors will adopt. Strategy must balance the need for flexibility, innovation, and an entrepreneurial approach with the need to invest in development, buyer education, and associated process-technology and distribution. It must also demonstrate the long-term commitment to the market necessary to comfort buyers who are understandably nervous of being caught dependent on technologies or suppliers that subsequently fail or on standards which become obsolete.

Just as problematic is the fact that the skills and resources which offer a company COMPETITIVE ADVANTAGE at one stage of development are unlikely to be those required for success in the next phase. Firms therefore risk getting caught behind BARRIERS TO MOBILITY which impede the adjustment of their strategy to changing market conditions. These barriers include dependence on a single proprietary technology, lack of access to new components or raw materials in high demand as the industry grows, a lack of experience in key areas such as mass production or distribution, and the correct management of alliances designed to win the battle for standards required to succeed as the market develops. ORGANIZATION STRUCTURES and CORPORATE CULTURES which reflect the needs of earlier phases also act as powerful constraints which strategy in emergent industries must overcome.

The following general rules have benefited many companies setting strategy in emergent industries:

- placing low-cost 'bets' on alternative technologies early in the game through the use of cross licensing and parallel research teams;
- seeking out a few sophisticated launch customers with unserved needs who can act as opinion leaders, and focusing on these, even at little profit, rather than seeking to broaden the customer base too quickly;
- getting market reactions relatively early to a new product or process rather than perfecting it based on purely in-house criteria. Even if failures, these launches can provide invaluable market intelligence;
- investing in the development of product technology, the required process technology, and the support products or services in parallel, rather than leaving the problems of how to manufacture and how to provide the necessary user support (for example, in software, training, or service) to catch up once the product is complete;
- recognizing changes in the basis of competition; from base technology to initial customer acceptance, through rivalry over standards to a race to drive down costs, from securing distribution to managing differentiation and product variety as the market emerges. Adjusting the structure of the organization, its relationship with rivals (from co-operative to competitive), and its management process to suit these changing strategic objectives;
- looking towards the END GAME, when the industry settles down, so as to shape the industry and your position in a way that will lead to long-term profitability, rather than simply acting to maximize the company's position in the current

environment. In an emerging industry today's pressures won't be the same as tomorrow's.

Emergent strategy. A salesman visits a customer experiencing problems with the product. They jointly work out some proposals for modifications. The salesman suggests these changes to people within his company. They begin to experiment and after two or three rounds they home in on a satisfactory solution. A new product emerges from this process, opening a new market to the company. The company has altered its strategic course. This is how HENRY MINTZBERG describes the process by which many strategies form in the real world. This view of strategy contrasts with the traditional paradigm where strategies are planned and then implemented, often, by implication, moving from the top down through the organization (*see* BOTTOM UP/TOP DOWN).

In practice, strategy is a mix between this emergent strategy, stemming from the solution to day-to-day problems, and deliberate moves by a business to re-position itself (*see* RE-POSITIONING). Given our notorious inability to *forecast* with accuracy, all effective strategy must learn along the way.

Having recognized the force of emergent strategy, the real question is what a manager should do about it. To harness the potential of the strategy the first requirement is for management to recognize patterns forming in the day-to-day actions which suggest new directions. In the example above, the salesman's solution would not have created a new market if managers in the company were not willing to devote resources to solving it; the new market would never have been found if the company was not alert to the more general applicability of the modified product to the needs of potential customers hitherto untapped. Yet, the ORGANIZATION STRUCTURES and decision-making processes of many companies render them blind to emergent opportunities. Emergent strategy therefore requires a process whereby it can impact the overall direction of the company, rather than being blocked at the first step, just as planned strategy needs channels through which it can flow down to 'doers' within the firm.

Successful companies have the flexibility to adjust the details of their strategy incrementally as new market conditions emerge. Their structures and management processes promote this kind of change. Every now and then, however, a quantum leap in strategy is required. After almost 30 years of producing its famous, reliable, and low-cost 'Beetle', Volkswagen found its product no longer fitted the mass markets in the developed world. So strong was the company's commitment to its core product and the organizational structure, culture and management process which had developed to support it, that a new strategy could not emerge incrementally. A deliberate shift to a new set of more luxurious, more expensive vehicles, championed by a new CEO, was necessary. It is in setting these fundamentally new directions, many of the details of which will subsequently emerge, that many argue a systematic, planned approach to strategy and market analysis comes into its own.

End game. Some industries age gracefully, with the relatively smooth exit or redeployment of capacity as demand declines. Others, however, suffer long periods of chronic excess capacity, price cutting, and intensified competition for a shrinking market which prevents the effective HARVESTING of market positions. The characteristics of the advanced stages of an industry's life and the competitive interactions which take place during this phase are often termed the end game.

The company's forecast of the end game influences the best strategy to adopt in dealing with a DECLINING INDUSTRY. Where the BARRIERS TO EXIT faced by competitors are low, it may be possible to gain a leadership position by investment combined with moves designed to force rivals to close. Although the associated investment of cash in a declining business may at first appear counter-intuitive, it may leave remaining firms in a position to manage the marked-down profitability with relatively little competition. By contrast, where exit barriers are high, rapid divestment or retreat into a defensible niche may be the optimal moves in the end game.

Entrants. New entrants are often dismissed on the grounds that high capital costs, technology, or scale in distribution ensure that 'Sid in the garage' would never succeed in breaking into the business. Entrants, however, are not necessarily small, undercapitalized firms.

Firms which are already in related businesses often make powerful potential entrants because, by virtue of their existing operations, they have often overcome many of the key BARRIERS TO ENTRY others may face. Potential import suppliers are one of the most important of these, since they have already overcome the majority of barriers associated with technology and production. Finding suitable distribution and establishing customer acceptance are the only hurdles which remain. Firms diversifying from other industries are the other key group of potential entrants (*see* DIVERSIFICATION). These companies often already have the distribution and customer franchise in place and may benefit from ECONOMIES OF SCOPE, which help to make them cost competitive.

It is probably even more difficult to devise strategies to deal with entrants than with existing rivals. Less is generally known about their assumptions and goals. They commonly adopt MAVERICK strategies reflecting their unique COST STRUCTURES, skills, ORGANIZATION STRUCTURES, decision processes, and resource bases, as well as their experience of different competitive norms. By redefining the 'rules of the game' they often catch incumbents off-guard and uncertain how to respond. Entrants adopting a maverick strategy may also benefit from the BARRIERS TO MOBILITY incumbents face in making the necessary shifts in strategy required for effective RETALIATION. The same plants, distribution networks, and brands which offered barriers to entry into the old game become millstones in adapting to the new competitive rules entrants have set.

Of course, potential entrants can even impact competition in an industry without actually entering it. The mere threat of their entry can be one of the FIVE FORCES which influence competitors' decisions as they attempt to deter new players from joining the game.

Environments matrix. The strategic environments matrix was conceived by the BOSTON CONSULTING GROUP, as they put it, to 'distinguish races that are worth entering'. It provides a framework for thinking about the attractiveness of a particular industry's competitive environment.

Attractiveness is distilled into two axes: one is a measure of the size of potential COMPETITIVE ADVANTAGE, the other is the number of viable sources of such advantage. The first measure reflects the idea that when competitors are fighting it out with very equal capabilities and resources even the best firms will only be marginally ahead of the pack. With the average industry price level reflecting the mid-range of competitor performance, there will be little chance of sustaining a substantial premium or achieving cost levels consistently very much lower than rivals. The second measure reflects the idea that in some industries – for example, a commodity product with a mature technology – there may be only a limited number of ways in which to compete. By contrast, those products with complex characteristics or distribution and service requirements will offer a large number of different potential sources of advantage. (See figure 12.)

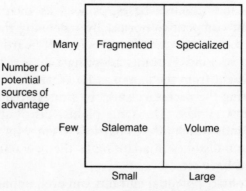

Figure 12   The Environments Matrix

Ranked along these dimensions, the world divides into four generic environments: volume, stalemate, specialization, and fragmentation businesses.

In volume businesses there are few novel ways to compete. However, they are such that firms with the right scale and execution capabilities may achieve overwhelming superiority in the one or two key areas, such as cost or BRANDING. These lands are those of the giants: Exxon, IBM or Boeing.

Stalemate businesses also have few potential sources of advantage. In these, however, the skills and resources required to gain leadership are widely available and often give only ephemeral advantage. In an industry where plant scale is one of the few ways to get ahead and market shares are volatile, for example, plenty of potential competitors might have the ability to raise the cash necessary for a large plant, but its advantage might disappear as soon as someone built a larger one. In stalemate businesses even when you do invest and open up a lead, you haven't conclusively 'won'. Success is a delusion often destroyed by a competitor's next move. These businesses are classic CASH TRAPS.

In specialization businesses, by contrast, customer needs are very varied, opening the way to product DIFFERENTIATION so as to lead in specific market segments, making use of proprietary features, unique service approaches, exclusive distribution arrangements, or particular corporate skills. There is scope for defining and exploiting distinctive COMPETENCES. Like all differentiation, however, it is not sufficient that there be many potential sources of uniqueness. These must be capable of translation into a price premium or a cost advantage in serving a particular segment. In specialization environments these advantages are both significant and difficult to imitate, allowing firms who exploit their uniqueness to sustain profitability substantially above average.

It is their failure by this last criterion which distinguishes fragmentation businesses, in which the specialization advantage is transitory or applicable to only a very small segment of the market insufficient to support significant long-run profitability. A prime example has been speciality retailing and some consumer services. Fashion boutiques or hairdres-

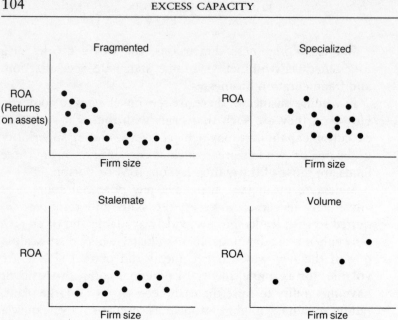

Figure 13   Profitability Patterns Differ by Industry Environment

sers have many potential sources of uniqueness, but these have historically been difficult to transfer to broader geographic markets so as to offer real profit potential for the larger corporate sector. FRANCHISING is often an attempt to convert these fragmentation environments into businesses where volume or specialization advantages can be exploited, leading to much more significant profit reward. (See figure 13.)

Excess capacity. The amount of excess capacity and its impact on the cost structure is critical to pricing and sales decisions and investment appraisal, and in predicting competitor reactions. It represents the extra volume a firm could supply without new investment in expanding the capacity of a particular activity.

Originally it was used to refer to the potential for increasing plant output without adding equipment. This would include the larger output available from existing facilities by adding extra shifts, reducing waste, increasing machine speeds, and so on. Perhaps even more interestingly, however, strategy has more recently emphasized the existence of exploitable excess capacity in 'invisible assets' such as brands, technology, or management skills. This latter type of excess capacity is more difficult to measure, but is nonetheless real. A strong brand may be underutilized when applied to a narrow product line (*see* BRANDING). There may be excess capacity in the purchasing, distribution, or maintenance functions or in an available process technology which is used in only one part of the world or on only one product application.

Companies have increasingly looked for ways to exploit these types of excess capacity by licensing, offering maintenance, distribution, and other services to third parties or by DIVERSIFICATION into new products, services, or geographic regions which can draw on the same assets.

Experience curve. The first Boeing 747 ever assembled was a costly business. By the 150th, the real unit costs of assembling the aeroplane were considerably less. The theory is simple: as workers learn their tasks and improve productivity the direct labour hours necessary to complete the product fall. As output of a particular product or model cumulates, therefore, unit cost tends to decline.

This relationship between manufacturing cost and cumulative output, dubbed the 'learning curve' has been observed in many businesses to varying degrees. In other businesses, total unit costs decline as all parts of the organization, from purchasing right through to sales and distribution and accounting gain experience of conducting their tasks with a particular product. This second relationship is commonly referred to as the 'experience curve'. Most of the thousands of studies seeking to measure these effects have found that unit costs often decline from between 10 and 30 per cent each time a business reaches a doubling in its accumulated output. (See figure 14.)

One of the earliest documented examples was that of Henry Ford's model 'T'. Between 1910 and 1927 unit costs

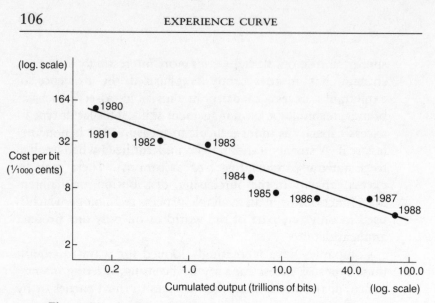

Figure 14 An Experience Curve in Semiconductors

fell by 75 per cent as Ford continued to double the cumulative output of this single model over and over again. Strategists might have told him that, as he kept accumulating experience faster than competitors, his COST ADVANTAGE relative to the rivals would be continually enhanced, allowing him to cut prices, pick up more volume, and repeat the cycle – cumulating more profit at every round. Helped by a policy of using only black paint (which dried more quickly than other colours, speeding up assembly), Ford seemed to have invented the perpetual money machine. The crippling closure of his main plant in 1927, with a loss of $200 million, however, is a lesson in the dangers of slavish application of a COST LEADERSHIP strategy based on the experience curve.

A key problem is that the experience curve has limits. In the first place, it is difficult to go on and on doubling cumulative output of a single product or design; ultimately even highly price-elastic buyers (*see* ELASTICITY) suffer from MARKET SATURATION. Secondly, those costs which fall with experience eventually become an insignificant part of the total as they decline. Ultimately, the base costs of raw materials or purchased components dominate and the curve flattens out. Thirdly, as the DISECONOMIES (OF SCALE) of running a huge plant set in, it is necessary to build others. There is no guarantee that the benefits of accumulated experience will be transferable. A new plant with 'green' employees may be starting on a virtually new curve with high initial costs. Fourthly, aggressive expansion of capacity and output to produce faster than the competition might amount to the company's betting on a technology which proves to be a loser when the market settles down. Finally, the single-minded pursuit of accumulated volume and reduced costs may, like Henry Ford, quickly result in a company losing touch with the market.

Despite all these problems there is considerable evidence that experience-curve benefits do exist and, exploited proper-ly early in the life cycle of a growing, price-sensitive market, they can offer the chance to get a valuable jump on the competition.

Externality. Business activity does not occur in a vacuum or in sealed-off, watertight containers. Its incidental effects or by-products spill over in the form of costs or benefits to those for whom the activity is not specifically undertaken. These spillovers – or externalities – occur whenever the production or consumption decision made by one individual affects the production or consumption of another, without this effect being mediated by market prices.

Such externalities are either beneficial or detrimental. Pollution is a classic example of the latter. Discharging waste by-products into a river, thereby polluting it, creates a cost for the users of the river – for example, consumers such as anglers or swimmers, or indeed other producers such as a paper manufacturer for whom a good water supply is essential. More positively, painting one's house may, to the extent that it enhances the look of the whole street, provide consumption benefits (that is, positive externalities) to one's neighbours. The difficulties posed by the notion of externali-ties are clear. What price should be put on these spillovers, beneficial or otherwise, and what role should the state play in penalizing firms (for example, by imposing fines for pollution) or individuals (perhaps by imposing road tolls on car drivers whose activity causes both pollution and congestion)?

As environmental concern deepens so the strategic implications of externalities become more serious. Companies are increasingly having to cover the *full* costs associated with their activities. For instance, the cement producer is faced with the costs of quarrying and cement production as well as the costs of making good damage to the landscape. Such costs may constitute a significant obstacle to the firm wishing to cease activity on a site, since the financial costs of closing down and making good may well outweigh the financial benefits – at least in the short term (*see* BARRIER TO EXIT).

But an equally important question for strategy is this: how can we benefit from the positive externalities generated by others and how can we avoid generating benefits of which our competitors can make use? Training is a good example. Firms which, by virtue of their track record in recruiting and training good staff become identified as ideal career starting-points or, in effect, 'schools' for the industry, continually confront the problem of how to retain the benefits of their training investment, rather than have this investment 'walk out the door', as expensively trained staff defect – or 'spill over' – to other companies. One strategic response to this particular problem might be, say, *not* to recruit new graduates but focus instead on tempting well-trained people with a few years experience away from competitors who have made the initial investment. Increasingly, strategy will have to concern itself with the issues raised by externalities and full account will have to be taken of the more general detrimental or beneficial consequences of pursuing a particular line of activity.

F

Fighting brand. On occasions a company may introduce a new
brand, not to fill a profitable gap in the market, but because
of that brand's effects on future RIVALRY between competitors. Such a Fighting Brand may be launched into a competitor's most profitable market segment as a threat to disrupt his
earnings if his own aggressive stance in other parts of the
market continues (*see* CROSS PARRY). It may be introduced in
an attempt to forestall entry or diversification as part of a
product-line strategy to achieve MARKET SATURATION. Alternatively, the introduction of a modest fighting brand could
serve to 'stake a claim' to a particular emerging segment as a
prelude to a full-scale move.

Whatever the rationale, a fighting brand is distinguished by
its primary purpose, that is, to send a signal to competitors or
potential entrants, rather than to satisfy unique customer
needs (*see* SIGNALLING).

First mover. The timing of competitive moves or initiatives plays
an important part in determining their impact and effectiveness. Moving first, thereby stealing a march on the competition, has many superficial attractions. Being first to the
market with a new product creates scope for defining the
'rules' of the competitive game, for instance in terms of
distribution channels or discount structures. More especially,
first movers can set industry standards. Establishing a strong
reputation and rapport with buyers protects these relationships from subsequent competitive entrance into the
market by building SWITCHING COSTS. Similarly, early entry
enables relationships with buyers, distributors, retailers, and
agents to be built ahead of the competition. And being first
enables the company to reap initial benefits associated with
learning.

All of which adds up to an ostensibly compelling case for
moving sooner rather than later: for taking advantage of

early entry to reduce costs, build a protected competitive position for the business and reap the high levels of profit that pre-emptive moves sometimes generate. However, beware of these superficial attractions, many of which turn out to be ephemeral. From the point of view of the follower, what has the first mover really accomplished? It has developed the product, incurred the development costs, and overcome all the initial difficulties associated with the new product's development. It has established the product's market credibility, educated the customer, created demand, obtained regulatory approval (for example, on standards) and established channels of distribution and sources of raw materials or component supply. Accomplishing all of this will have taken time and have required investment. For the follower, not only can the timetable be telescoped but many of the costs – for example, those associated with research and development, with proving the technology – will not have to be borne, or at least not to the same extent. Thus, followers may be able to enter a newly created market at a much lower cost with reduced risk, while being able to employ the latest equipment and technology.

What is at issue, therefore, is not so much the reality of first-mover advantages as their sustainability. Short-lived, unsustainable, expensively accumulated advantage is clearly of little value. Starting second, or indeed later, can enhance the chances of finishing first. Good timing is an integral element of any successful strategy and any significant strategic move should be based on a thorough understanding of the costs and benefits of acting now rather than later.

Fit (strategic fit). A specific relationship between two or more businesses can generate a COMPETITIVE ADVANTAGE when they are linked in the same corporate portfolio (*see* PORTFOLIO MANAGEMENT).

By being part of a corporate portfolio most businesses incur some costs compared with stand-alone competitors. Typically these include loss of flexibility, capital rationing, or compromise on shared facilities or services. In order to have a net advantage as part of a portfolio, therefore, it is critical that some substantial benefits flow from the fit. Three dimensions of fit are relevant: financial, functional, and formula.

As the name implies, 'financial fit' refers to benefits which might come from managing the financial resources of two businesses jointly. This may reflect offsetting seasonal-funds requirements. For businesses requiring long competitive or investment horizons, or where the strategy requires that weaker competitors exit, it is often argued that there are advantages to having a CASH COW in the same group, rather than relying on external funding.

'Functional fit' refers to the idea of gaining lower costs or better quality by sharing technical support, marketing, distribution systems, or manufacturing plant across different businesses. Finally, 'formula fit' reflects the advantages there may be in businesses with similar strategies being part of the same group. Thus a corporate group may develop special skills in achieving COST LEADERSHIP in different industries or in an area like consumer marketing, with its overall MISSION STATEMENT and CORPORATE CULTURE assisting an individual business to succeed with a particular strategic formula.

The concept of 'strategic fit' has often been important in corporate decisions regarding DIVERSIFICATION, ACQUISITION, and DIVESTMENT of component businesses. Grand Metropolitan PLC, for example, divested its reasonably profitable contract catering services business Compass on the grounds of lack of fit, with its primary emphasis on globally branded consumer products and services. On the other hand some companies believe 'fit' is relatively unimportant. They are interested in any potential acquisition which they believe to be undervalued or sitting on unexploited opportunities. The resulting CONGLOMERATES, however, have often proven a management nightmare, making them ripe for takeover and asset stripping.

Five forces. Companies often see the main pressure on profitability in their markets being generated by their direct competitors. In many cases, however, competition between rival firms is a symptom of a problematic market structure rather than the root cause of pressure on profits.

The five-forces framework, introduced by Professor Michael Porter, argues that the underlying causes of profit squeeze in a market are fivefold: BUYER POWER, SUPPLIER POWER, the threat of new ENTRANTS, the threat of SUBSTITUTION, and the nature of RIVALRY. (See figure 15.)

Early work on the five forces emphasized their identification, concluding with a ranking of the inherent attractiveness of one market relative to others. This can be useful in determining which businesses within a portfolio merit further development. However, recent empirical work has pointed to the fact that a firm's positioning within its market is a much more important determinant of its profitability than the inherent attractiveness of the market in which it is operating. This realization focuses the attention on strategy as a means of altering the forces to which the firm is subject. Therefore, strategies must be designed to reduce buyer power or build entry barriers rather than simply analysing the power relationship and threats. Our discussion of the individual forces,

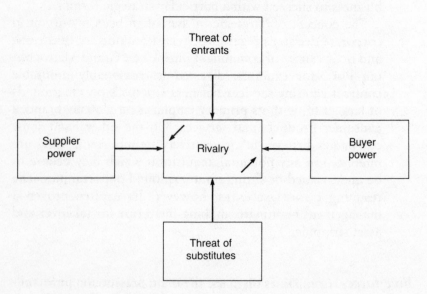

Figure 15   The Five-forces framework

under the separate subject headings, emphasizes strategy in this latter role.

Focal points. In an OLIGOPOLY individual firms generally recognize that their own actions can have a significant impact on the attractiveness of a market and the behaviour of competitors. A good example is the recognition that chasing a larger market share by price-cutting can lead to a cycle of retaliation that destroys the profitability for all.

Once firms in an industry recognize their direct interdependence the benefits of following certain 'norms of competition' designed to blunt destructive wars become clear. In rare instances a full-blown cartel emerges. More usually, firms simply keep a close eye on their competitors' day-to-day actions, and adjust their strategies to avoid upsetting too many apple-carts.

Because information about competitors' moves is often diverse and unreliable, a focal point for monitoring competition in the market often emerges. This may be the price of a key raw material or component. A substantial change in this cost may signal an 'understood' time for competitors to re-position the prices of their final product. Similarly, changes in price or product policy by an industry leader may act as the focal point around which other competitors adjust their positions. In industries facing import competition, for example, the landed price of imports plus any tariff may act as the natural focal point for domestic competitors' price-setting.

Focal points normally emerge as an industry matures and competitors accumulate experience of each other. MAVERICKS in the form of new entrants or changes in the top management of an existing competitor can therefore create disruption and uncertainty way beyond its intrinsic size or importance.

Focus strategy. The economics of an industry or the limitations of a company's resources may make it difficult to pursue either COST LEADERSHIP or DIFFERENTIATION across the full range of customer segments or a broad product line. This is often the case where the demands made on the product or the definition of 'quality' differ markedly between segments. Such a situation may also arise because it is not viable to maintain two different distribution channels in parallel (such as exclusive dealers and mass merchandisers) or because the image of one part of the product line (maybe, cheap and nasty) is inconsistent with another (precise and durable). In this environment the most successful strategy is usually to focus on a specific niche in the market and aim at COMPETITIVE ADVANTAGE through cost leadership or differentiation compared with others serving that limited target.

In a world demanding increased variety to satisfy ever more diverse needs, some broad-line producers have found their positions undermined by competitors pursuing a focus strategy which has allowed them to off-load costs by eliminating features or support not required by particular groups of users. Other focused competitors have achieved improved differentiation of their product by understanding the needs of a specific niche better than mass-market suppliers. Successful focus strategy has also been based on splitting up bundled products (*see* BUNDLING), or exploiting CROSS-SUBSIDIZATION which leads to some customers being overcharged by broad-line competitors compared with the real cost of serving them.

A focus strategy, however, carries with it certain risks. It increases reliance on a particular product variety, buyer type, distribution channel, or geographic segment which may subsequently become unattractive or even disappear as the market evolves. It may prevent cost reduction through ECONOMIES OF SCALE or SCOPE which arise if much of the fixed cost is shared across customer segments or products within the line. Finally, the size of the target market available to a focused competitor may inherently limit the size and growth prospects of the company.

Followers. One of the key strategic decisions facing a firm is whether or not it should aim for leadership in, say, the technology of its industry, or content itself with following the example set by the industry leaders. Many firms become followers by default. Good strategy requires that a follower makes a conscious, explicit decision as to which route it wishes to follow. Will it be the first to innovate or not? (*See* FIRST MOVER.) In making this decision the firm will have to weigh up the costs and benefits of being first rather than second – or third. Not being first often carries considerable benefits: for example, followers can learn from the experience of leaders to achieve lower unit costs, to tailor products more precisely to the needs of the market (needs which the leader may have originally defined), and avoid many of the R&D costs associated with innovation.

But this lower-risk, potentially low-cost strategy means that the benefits of being first down the EXPERIENCE CURVE, or of being able to establish a strong market position with a new and unique product, will have to be foregone. In choosing which route to follow the two key questions are these: will the technological lead attained by being first to the market prove sustainable or will competitors be able to erode it? Do the advantages accruing to the first mover outweigh the disadvantages?

Fragmented industry. Any industry in which there is no clear market leader, or no single dominant competitor with a large market share, is likely to be fragmented. Fragmented industries are populated by a large number of small- to medium-sized firms, often privately owned by people with highly individualized motives or aspirations and a willingness to accept the modest returns typically associated with fragmentation. Restaurants and travel agencies are good illustrations of the phenomenon.

The salient characteristics of fragmented industries are: diverse consumer needs, relatively low BARRIERS TO ENTRY, and little scope for reaping economies of scale and thereby securing a COST ADVANTAGE. Although some 'newer' industries may start by being fragmented, while new entrants acquire the requisite skills and become established, as the industry develops and consolidates this may give way to a more 'mature' pattern in which a handful of dominant competitors emerge. Alternatively, technological change may fragment – perhaps temporarily – a previously concentrated industry.

In photoprocessing, for example, the development of robust, relatively inexpensive and simple-to-use film processing and printing equipment spawned a plethora of new, small 'instant' (one- to two-hour) photoprocessing outlets with on-site facilities. Technological change eliminated the need for – and the scale advantages associated with – large centralized photoprocessing laboratories. In so doing, the rules of the competitive game changed, with increasing importance being attached to convenience, site location, opening hours and speed of response. Confronted by low barriers to entry, modest scale or volume constraints, and no dominant competitor, new entrepreneurial firms entered this developing and immature market, fragmenting it. Gradually, however, larger, well-established players reasserted control by buying up the independent operations and small chains, thereby reimposing a degree of concentration from which they could benefit – for example, by raising prices.

In this instance the competitive threat posed by fragmentation was met by a determined drive towards concentration on the part of the incumbents. Much the same pattern has been repeated in the UK brewing industry where the burgeoning demands of consumers for a wide choice of 'real ale' encouraged the proliferation of small, independent breweries (operating at relatively low volumes). Many of these have now become part of larger, national brewing companies within which the retention of their original 'name' is the sole vestige of their independence.

Developing a strategy to cope with fragmentation requires careful analysis of its causes (is it inevitable?), the relative position and strengths/weaknesses of competitors, and the alternative routes to overcoming fragmentation – profitably. Apart from forcing consolidation and concentration other competitive responses might include: specialization – by customer, product, geographical region or order types;

increasing the VALUE ADDED – by providing services not available elsewhere; and DECENTRALIZATION of the business – by setting up a number of relatively small, autonomous organizations tightly geared to the needs of the local market.

Franchising. What do the following have in common? Belgian chocolates, private investigation, roof thatching, bridal attire, vinyl restoration, tropical fish tanks and personalized colour consultancy. This title gives the answer away; all of these diverse activities are conducted on a franchise basis. Of what does this consist?

A few elements are critical. A franchise operation is a contractual relationship between a franchisor and a franchisee in which the former offers, or is obliged, to maintain a continuing interest in the latter's business. That business being operated by a franchisee will make use of a name, format and procedure developed, owned or controlled by the franchisor. In return for the licence to operate the business, usually within restricted geographical limits, the franchisee will usually be required to invest his own capital as a 'front-end fee' and subsequently to remit royalties (calculated as a percentage of sales) or a management-services fee to the franchisor. (In the UK as much as £350,000 is required to obtain a Wimpy counter-service franchise.) In return the franchisor provides support, in the form of knowhow and training, as well as services in the form of supply purchasing. Franchises may operate between a manufacturer and a retailer (as with car or truck dealerships), a manufacturer and a wholesaler (as in Coke or Pepsi distribution), a wholesaler and a retailer (such as the Spar grocery chain in the UK), or, most commonly, between the owner of a trademark or trade name and a retailer – of which there are innumerable examples in the fast-food, instant-printing and car-hire industries.

Franchising, despite its relatively recent upsurge, has a long and distinguished lineage. Its origins have been variously traced back to King John of England who offered franchises to certain of his subjects to collect taxes, of which they were entitled to keep 40 per cent for their services or, more recently, to the practices of eighteenth-century British brewers who created the system of 'tied houses' under which public houses were only allowed to sell the beer of one particular brewer.

Today, franchising is big business accounting for five per cent of UK retail sales, 33 per cent of US retail sales and more than 40 per cent of retail sales in Canada. In the UK there are approximately 80,000 franchised retail outlets and just under 500,000 in the US. Royalty payments from franchisees range from two or three per cent to as much as 45 per cent. Typically, such operations have a much lower failure rate (about 15 per cent of new franchises fail) than the average new business.

Superficially, franchising represents the best of all worlds. The franchisee gets the chance to run his own business, with a much reduced probability of failure, while the franchisor acquires a means of accelerating the growth and development of his business. Therein lies the strategic significance of franchising. It facilitates the exploitation of economies of scale, for instance in purchasing, site acquisition or distribution, that would otherwise be beyond its reach. Franchising gives smaller firms, with limited resources, the muscle usually enjoyed by larger firms. But that muscle is won on the backs of the franchisee. Hence the continuing debate as to whether franchising constitutes 'a mutually beneficial form of capitalism' or 'a form of modern-day slavery'.

Functional strategy. The building blocks of any business consist of groups of individuals who perform specific activities or functions. Those performing essentially similar activities are usually grouped together under headings such as 'finance', 'marketing', 'R&D', 'manufacturing', 'personnel' and so forth. Each such grouping represents a functional area or department (*see* FUNCTIONAL STRUCTURE). Evolving effective strategies for each such functional area is an integral part of the strategy process.

The involvement of specific functions typically occurs in two dimensions. First, functional managers do – or at least should – play a central role in developing the overall strategy for the business or the business unit. The functions for which they are individually responsible, the resources, capabilities and distinctive skills of each function, constitute both constraints upon strategy and the scaffolding around which this strategy has to be built. Recognizing the constraints or the opportunities afforded by distinctive areas of functional competence (for example, in new product design) is an essential element in strategy development.

Secondly, the effectiveness of the overall strategy will be determined in a large part by the extent to which that strategy is translated into a set of much more specific strategies for each function. Such functional strategies, often in the form of detailed action-plans, should spell out precisely how each function fits into the overall strategy, the specific contribution that is required of it and, derived from this, what the strategy calls for in terms of developing new functional skills or acquiring additional resources for a particular function.

For strategy to be translated into action, it has to become embedded in the way in which each functional area understands and performs the activities for which it is responsible. In developing strategy particular attention should therefore be given to two questions. First, does the proposed strategy take full account of our functional strengths and weaknesses? Secondly, what specific changes does the strategy require in each functional area? The answers to both questions will provide a springboard for developing precise, achievable functional strategies.

Functional structure. One of the earliest – and simplest – forms of organization is one in which common or similar activities are grouped together to make functional areas or departments: for example, marketing, finance, production and personnel. The firm is thus divided along functional lines with the responsibility for the performance of each function resting with the departmental head; for example, the finance director. (See figure 16.)

This structure – sometimes termed the 'U [unitary] form' – is most common in smaller firms with a narrow product range. It has many merits: the simplicity and brevity of its lines of communication; its clarity of job definition and accountability; the capacity of the chief executive to keep in

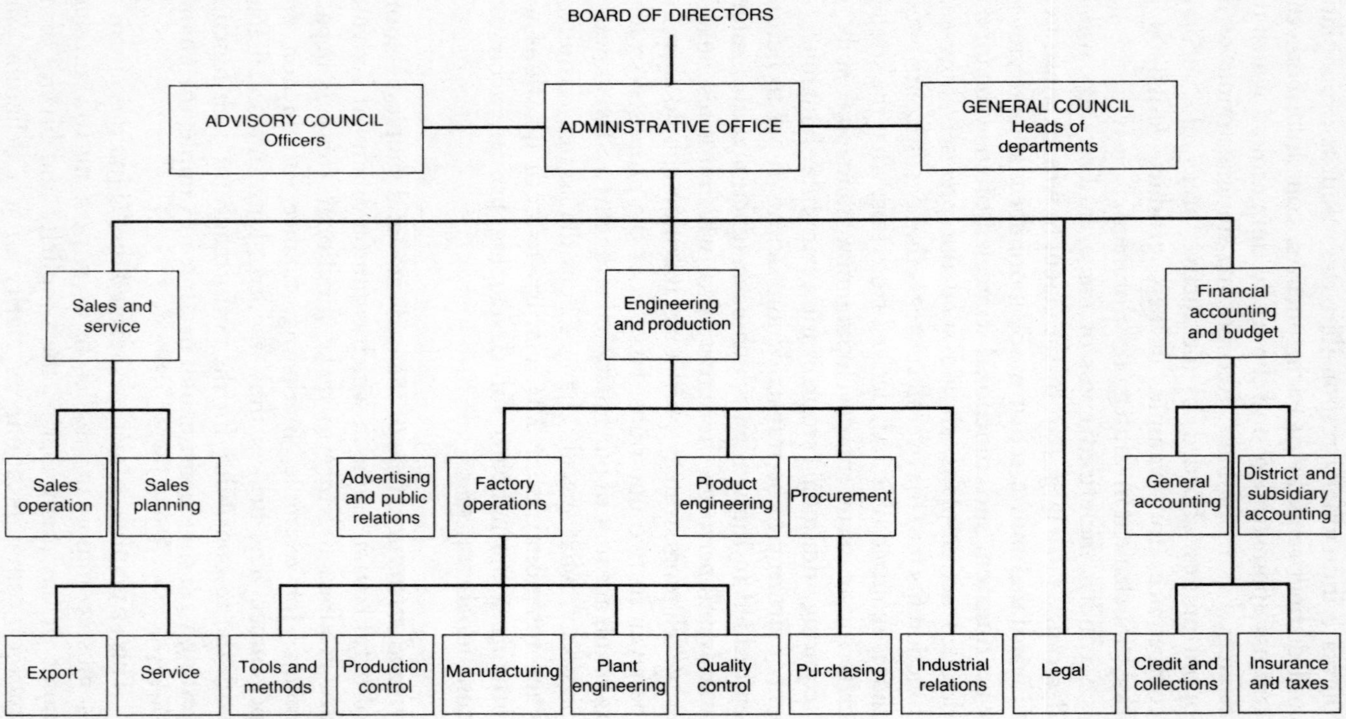

Figure 16 A Functional Structure

contact with all aspects of the business. But as firms grow, and as their range of activities becomes more diverse, the structure's limitations become more apparent. Centralized decision-making can create bottlenecks, and the referral of all decisions upwards may lead to the abdication rather than the assumption of responsibility. With size come problems of interdepartmental rivalry and a preoccupation with the interests of the department (for example, in terms of gaining adequate resources) rather than that of the firm as a whole.

Evolving a structure that is appropriate to the firm's stage of development and compatible with its strategy is one of the central tasks of management. With functionally organized firms the essential question to bear in mind is this: have we outgrown our original structure or, alternatively, is there a danger that our structure is constraining our strategy?

Excessive functional specialization and the development of tight functional boundaries accompanied by poor cross-functional co-ordination may constitute such a constraint. One solution is the creation of cross-functional teams charged with responsibility for pursuing a particular project, often a new product development activity. For example, Caterpillar, the major manufacturer of earth-moving equipment, successfully introduced integrated, cross-functional teams with the specific intention of reducing new product lead times and breaking down the entrenched functional divisions around which the firm had become organized, and through which its responsiveness, notably to the threat posed by its Japanese challenger, Komatsu, was severely blunted. Therefore, the danger with any structure is that over time it is likely to ossify. The strategic challenge is to recognize this and act upon it before it is too late.

G

Game theory. Much strategy has to do with accurately predicting or anticipating the reactions of competitors to any move the firm might make. For example, if a firm wishes to estimate the likely effect on sales of a price cut, it must take into account the likelihood that competitors will match the new price or ignore it and for how long. As in chess, a strategy's chances of success are enhanced by correct anticipation of the opponent's moves. Game theory is an attempt to formalize these types of problems where the outcome for one party depends on the actions of another.

The competitive game is described in terms of 'players' – typically single firms or organizations. The rules of the game specify how the firm's scarce resources may be used, and the pay-offs or benefits accruing to the players from particular combinations of moves. In a ZERO-SUM GAME, these pay-offs add to zero among the pool of players: what one party gains the other loses. In the case of co-operative games, the benefits may sum to more than zero; when both firms increase their profits through collusion or alliance, for example. In negative-sum games, the actions of each party undermine the positions of both itself and the opponents, as in a price war.

Although game theory provides a suggestive framework for analysis, its results have often proved disappointing. This is because the restrictive assumptions on the players' behaviour required to get a deterministic solution often reduce its effectiveness in analysing real situations. A common assumption is embodied in the so-called 'minimax' principle: that competitors will act to minimize their maximum loss.

Despite failing to reach the high hopes of its early proponents, game theory has proved useful as a way of adding a competitive dimension to problems like capacity addition. Rather than simply looking at NET PRESENT VALUE on an insular basis, for example, game theory focuses attention on the interdependency of such decisions with competitors' own plans.

Gap analysis. Identifying the extent to which the pursuit of current strategies will or will not deliver results that meet the company's long-term requirements or aims can be a major spur to action. Determining the shortfall or gap can highlight the need to re-formulate strategy. Typically, gap analysis is applied to profitability targets, as figure 17 illustrates.

Start by drawing the top line, the profit target, which represents the company's long-range (three- to five-year) target. Then draw in the profit-forecast line. That is the forecast of future profitability achieved on the basis of the existing strategies. This line may be arrived at by combining the profit targets set for individual divisions or by extrapolating the past three years' results forward for another three

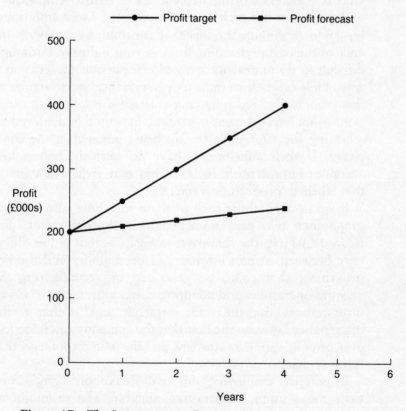

Figure 17 The Improvement Gap

years. In other words, assume that the recent pattern of growth in sales and profitability remains relatively unchanged. In arriving at the profit forecast it is obviously important to make the assumptions upon which it is based quite explicit. In this highly simplified example the gap between the profit forecast and the target is immediately obvious. If there is no gap and the forecast profit happily coincides with the profitability target, then don't rest content. Assuming the forecast is accurate, the coincidence may reflect the fact that the profit target has been set too low and does not represent a genuinely stretching or sufficiently ambitious target.

This simple gap identification can be usefully refined in two ways. First, draw in the line for industry performance. That is your best estimate of the likely levels of return being earned in the industry in which your firm operates. More ambitiously, try to reproduce the line that encapsulates the performance of the best performing firms in your industry. Although difficult to do in practice it should be possible to arrive at a reasonable estimate of industry performance and to represent this graphically. Secondly, ask yourself the following question: 'what improvement in profitability could be achieved by adjusting the strategy currently being pursued in the company?' If such adjustments have not already been taken account of in the profit forecast they may yield a new line – that labelled 'profit improvement'.

If we now combine each of these four lines into a single graph then two gaps immediately become apparent. (See figure 18.) First, the 'improvement gap' – that is the difference between current estimates of profitability and the improvement that could be generated by reconfiguring the existing operations and adapting current strategies to maximize returns. Secondly, the 'strategic gap' – that is the discrepancy between the best that the company can hope for, even after adapting its strategy, and the long-term target that it has set itself.

In practice, employing gap analysis is more complicated than these simple illustrations suggest. The technique is particularly valuable as a means of revealing the consequ-

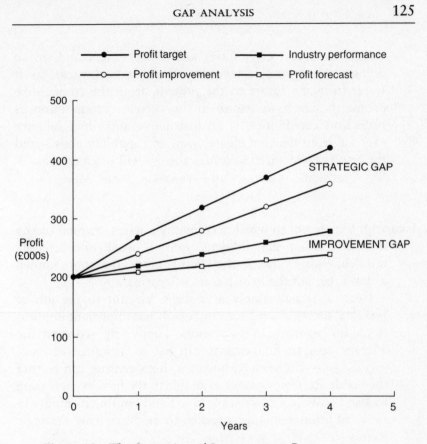

Figure 18 The Strategic and Improvement Gaps

ences of doing nothing, that is, of continuing to pursue the current strategy without alteration. Beyond this, gap analysis can be usefully applied to questions other than those relating to profitability; for example, to identifying shortfalls in productivity, unit sales volume or, more qualitatively and subjectively, discrepancies between target levels of quality or service and achieved levels.

Beyond this, the gap analysis principle has a more general, strategic value. In developing strategy a useful question to ask is this: 'in the 1990s what will the successful competitor in our industry look like?' More specifically, 'what skills, resources, capabilities and competences will be required to compete successfully in the future?' Against this profile of the ideal typical competitor the firm can then measure its current skills, resources, capabilities and competences and, in so doing, identify major lacunae. Working backwards, as it were, from the future to the present, from the competitive profile to which we aspire to the current configuration of skills and capabilities, is an instructive and often salutary exercise from which a clearer view of capability gaps – and the resources required to *bridge* them – will often emerge.

See SUPPLY-SIDE STRATEGY and STRATEGIC STAIRCASE.

Gearing. The extent to which a company's assets are financed by debt rather than shareholders' equity is usually measured by the debt/equity ratio. In the US it is more commonly known as leverage, but the British term is 'gearing'.

Gearing is not simply a concept relevant to the job of financial directors and accountants. It has important implications for strategy in two ways. Firstly, by reducing the average cost of financing it can act as a source of COST ADVANTAGE. Conversely, however, high gearing can restrict the viable strategic options available to the firm by increasing its fixed costs (*see* COST STRUCTURE) and limiting its ability to raise additional finance quickly to resource new strategic moves (*see* CAPITAL STRUCTURE).

Generic competitive strategies. The idea of dividing strategies into three 'generic' types – COST LEADERSHIP, DIFFERENTIA- TION and FOCUS STRATEGY – has become popular in much of the strategy literature. It has sometimes been suggested that companies should choose one of these as their approach to competing in the market, relying on either low costs, a unique product or specialized service to a particular market segment. Firms who failed to choose one of these were sometimes described as being 'stuck in the middle', unable to out- perform rivals in any one of these dimensions.

The problem with generic strategies is that they imply that a firm must choose only one way to compete. Strategy is then in danger of being seen as the quest for the 'big move' which achieves this single advantage, such as a massive-scale, centralized plant. More sophisticated strategy, however, recognizes that sustainable COMPETITIVE ADVANTAGE comes from building many individual advantages which cumulate across activities and strengthen over time. Such advantage is generally much more difficult for competitors to copy than the single big move. It is unlikely that every activity in the company will make its contribution to overall advantage through the same generic strategy. In some activities, the purchase of standardized components for example, it will make sense to strive for cost leadership. But in other activities, such as sales or service, it may be advantageous to accept higher costs than competitors in order to differentiate the offering in a way which is valuable to customers, thereby supporting a price premium.

Global industry. A firm's competitive position in one national market may be significantly affected by its competitive position in other national markets. This may be the case for a mixture of three reasons. First, certain basic characteristics of the technology and the buyers could result in ECONOMIES OF SCALE or ECONOMIES OF SCOPE which reach right across the world. Good examples would be airframes and aero-engines, where the required investment to produce new versions is massive, the buyers have similar needs and service networks must match the global nature of the customers' own operations.

Second, MULTI-POINT COMPETITION may occur on a global basis as competitors CROSS SUBSIDIZE their strategy in one market with cash flow from another, or respond to competitive moves in one national market by actions in another.

Third, the ability to trade in raw materials, people, components or finished goods *internally* within multinationals may render the market global, even though there are few external linkages between the markets. There is a very small international market in alumina and aluminium compared with most metals, for example, yet through domination by a few global players it is in fact a very global industry.

Global strategy. A MULTINATIONAL ENTERPRISE must respond to
and exploit the essential features of the market which make
the industry global, be they based on scale economies,
competitive interaction, or internal shifts of resources, components or finished goods within its international network.
Different commentators have advanced strategies which
emphasize each of these aspects ranging from global product
standardization and BRANDING, through emphasis on the
international distribution of a broad product portfolio, to
flexible, multiple-sourcing networks designed to take advantage of changing factor costs and market imperfections.

Global strategies attempt to find the right balance between
the benefits of international integration and national differentiation to meet local market peculiarities. This trade-off
is likely to produce different degrees of global interaction and
co-ordination across the VALUE CHAIN of a company with
some activities and functions centralized or highly interlinked
and others highly dispersed and independent. Thus many
companies have integrated their product policy and basic
marketing approach under a worldwide product manager
while leaving the advertising and salesforce structure to each
domestic organization within broad corporate guidelines.
These decisions need to take into account not only the costs
and benefits of co-ordination and centralization, but also the
shared external relationships between competitors, customers, distributors, suppliers and governments who themselves
have multinational linkages.

Decisions about co-ordination are closely related to a
global company's 'make versus buy' choices. Some global
companies subcontract or franchise the highly locally dependent parts of their business to third parties. Thus McDonald's
shifts the store-management tasks to local franchisees, while
Coca-Cola uses local licensees to undertake the management
of bottling operations in most of its international markets.

A third important concern of global strategy is the management of international risks by considering them jointly. At a
specific level, this may be reflected in systems to 'nett-out'
foreign-exchange exposure and cash positions across the
world on a continuous 24-hour basis. On a more macroeco-

nomic level it includes managing the exposure to political instability, changes in tariffs or quotas, or relative labour or raw-material costs.

Finally, global strategy seeks to identify learning and adaptation in one part of the international organization and to benefit by applying them across the global operation. The diversity of national environments to which a multinational is exposed allows it to develop a broader set of capabilities than many domestic firms. Skills and adaptations developed in one area may open the way for rich EMERGENT STRATEGY through which new products, customer segments, or processes which lead to a worldwide RE-POSITIONING of the firm are developed from the germ of problem-solving in a national context.

Goals. Goals and OBJECTIVES – the two terms are used loosely and often interchangeably. How should we distinguish between the two? The simplest way is in terms of the time scale to which they relate. A goal states what is to be achieved in the medium to long term; for example, a firm's goal might be to have the largest market share in five years' time. Objectives, on the other hand, refer to what the firm has to achieve *en route* to accomplishing its stated goal; for example, the objective for the current year might be to increase market share by five per cent, thereby moving the firm up from fourth to third position in the industry. The goal encapsulates the overall aim of the business and the level of performance that it is aiming to achieve. Its objectives are the staging posts along the way and therefore represent the dimensions of performance against which success and performance can be measured.

Why are goals important? Research indicates that individuals are essentially goal-oriented and find it motivating to be told exactly where the firm is going, why the journey is worth making and how they can contribute to its successful outcome. The combination of clearly defined goals and frequent, appropriately presented feedback on performance has been found to have a dramatically beneficial impact upon an individual's performance.

But the difficulties with setting goals are twofold. First, too often managers assume, usually incorrectly, that the goals of the firm are obvious and self-evident to all who work in it. Shared understanding of the goals by top management does not mean that the rest of the organization automatically knows what those goals are or is committed to them. Secondly, organizations typically have a number of different goals, within which there may be a hierarchy. For example, there may be a value goal that encapsulates the principles or values towards which the organization is striving, an organizational goal that describes the intended nature and structure of the company, and a strategic goal that defines the overall position within the market towards which every activity in the firm is – or should be – directed.

In formulating goals it is therefore important to consider three questions: 'are they clear, consistent and unambiguous?'; 'have they been communicated properly?'; and 'can we secure commitment to them?' In addition, any formulation of a strategic goal should incorporate a crystal-clear understanding of the goals being pursued by competitors and the ways in which these inevitably impinge upon the goals that the firm has set for itself.

See SUPPLY-SIDE STRATEGY and STRATEGIC STAIRCASE.

Good competitors. The idea that a competitor can be good for you is counter-intuitive to many businessmen. Competitors can, however, have positive spillovers onto your business and its profitability. They may help to maintain the profitability of your industry by keeping aggressive new ENTRANTS out of the market by rapid RETALIATION against any entry attempt, or by the fact they have excess capacity which makes it more difficult for entrants to find under-served customers.

Similarly, good competitors may promote technological advance in an industry from which others may benefit through low-cost imitation. They may help to develop generic demand for a product by educating customers. Good competitors may nurture suppliers to the industry, thus helping to increase the quantity or quality of raw materials, components or specialist services to all. They may help to improve the industry's image with the government or the public. Inefficient competitors, meanwhile, may be good in the sense that they provide a COST UMBRELLA which protects the profits of more productive firms.

Even where a competitor forces your company to take some unpleasant medicine it may be good in the longer run. Having tough competition in the home market has been found to help make firms more productive, innovative and responsive to customers, leading to increased competitiveness in world markets. Many have argued, for example, that the cut-throat competition which characterizes many Japanese domestic markets makes their firms very 'lean and mean' competitors overseas.

Goodwill. Expressed as the amount by which the value of a business as a 'going concern' exceeds the resale value of its tangible assets, goodwill may be the capitalized value of a company's ability to earn higher profits than a newly formed company with the same assets.

The existence of goodwill reflects the fact that companies accumulate competitive advantages which are not embodied in tangible assets. These include brand loyalty, buyer SWITCHING COSTS, barriers which prevent new firms imitating their strategy, systems, knowhow, shared CORPORATE CULTURE which aids in achievement of a strategy, and so on. Indeed, the fact that a firm has a successful strategy to deal with its market which is embedded within its decision-making processes can be an important source of goodwill.

The important contribution of this goodwill, and the 'invisible assets' it represents, to success in a market is a major reason why companies choose to make ACQUISITIONS of firms at a price premium rather than simply buying the equivalent tangible assets from suppliers.

Growth–share matrix. The BOSTON CONSULTING GROUP developed a framework to aid companies in evaluating their strategy towards individual businesses in their corporate portfolio and to guide the appropriate movement of cash between them.

The matrix, shown in figure 19, divides businesses into four classes depending on their relative market share and their growth prospects. Reflecting the dominant thinking at the time it was developed, a STRATEGIC BUSINESS UNIT's market share relative to its largest competitor was used as the indicator of profitability and hence of cash generation from operations. While this might be questioned in the current environment of the increased emphasis on DIFFERENTIATION and SPECIALIZATION as sources of profitability, it has proven a resilient indicator in many industries. SBUs with large market shares relative to competitors (greater than one on the horizontal axis) were assumed to be strong cash generators. The vertical axis, meanwhile, divided businesses into 'fast growing', which required substantial cash injections for investment in fixed assets, branding, and working capital, and 'slow growing', where investment requirements would be comparatively low.

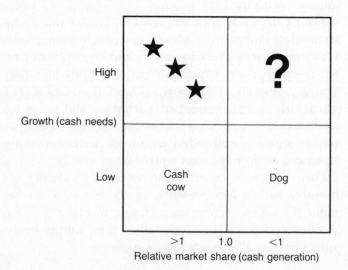

Figure 19   The Growth–share Matrix

Thus CASH COWS would be generating cash much faster than they would be using it, resulting in a cash surplus. QUESTION MARKS, on the other hand, would be using cash much faster than they were currently producing it. In these rapidly growing, EMERGENT INDUSTRIES, the 'question' was whether the business would ever develop a sufficiently strong market position to pay back the cash plus a surplus. STARS were the businesses everyone dreamed about, enjoying both market dominance and strong growth, with cash roughly in balance. 'Dogs', by contrast, had weak market positions, generated little cash and offered few prospects for growth.

The policy prescriptions following from this analysis entreated management to transfer the cash surplus from their cash cows to investment in the question marks and stars, so as to keep the portfolio in a state of renewal. As their markets matured and growth slowed down, these businesses would ultimately become cash cows to feed the future-growth SBUs. Dogs, the analysis argued, should be disposed of or closed.

While it is widely applied and in many cases can be a useful tool, the growth—share matrix has a number of problems. The first is that classifying a company as a cash cow or dog may undermine the motivation of management and employees, unnecessarily hastening the decline of a business. Secondly, it can lead to an unduly 'passive' approach to the future of a business, consigning it to low investment or even DIVESTMENT as a result of 'inevitable' market maturity. Yet, many markets which had been written off as mature in the 1960s and 1970s, such as consumer electronics, rebounded during the 1980s following the aggressive introduction of new products like the VCR and compact disc. Believing them to be cash cows, some competitors undermined their ability to keep up with the changing market and were ultimately forced out.

See CASH COW, QUESTION MARK, STAR.
See also INDUSTRY ATTRACTIVENESS.

H

Harvesting. At the end of the growing season, when crops have reached maturity, farmers reap the benefits of their previous investment by harvesting and converting the crops into cash. Knowing when to harvest and managing the process productively requires planning, skill and judgement. So too with businesses that are to be harvested for cash.

In commercial terms the objective of harvesting is to maximize short-term earnings and cash flow – both from operations and from the liberated working capital. The means of accomplishing this end include reducing or eliminating new investment; cutting operating costs – like sales representation; exploiting any residual strengths the business may have – for example, by increasing prices; ceasing to serve small customers; reducing the product range; and scaling down the range of distribution channels.

Typically, harvesting occurs when some combination of the following conditions prevails:

● the business is operating in a saturated or declining market with little future growth potential (harvesting is rarely carried out in high-growth markets);
● the profit or cash-generating potential of the business is poor;
● its relative market share is modest and can only be increased at a prohibitive cost;
● the business no longer makes a significant contribution to a firm's total sales, profitability, reputation or overall position in the market;
● more attractive investment opportunities – usually in higher-growth markets – are deemed to exist elsewhere and the exploitation of these requires that cash is freed up from current activities.

Harvesting may also be used to give a fillip to short-term profitability, thereby raising the perceived value of a firm, immediately prior to its disposal.

Successful execution of a harvesting strategy is difficult and whatever combination of means is used problems can occur in a number of areas. For example:

- where the price ELASTICITY of demand is high, raising prices may precipitate a collapse in demand, an erosion of relative market share and a net loss of income;
- sustaining staff morale and managerial commitment becomes increasingly difficult if a business is suddenly scaled down, perhaps as a prelude to its eventual disposal or closure;
- sensing withdrawal and a weakened competitive position, competitors may move to speed up a business's decline, for example by undercutting its own prices, thereby accelerating the loss of market share and volume of the higher-priced 'harvest' goods;
- achieving a gradual, controlled cost reduction is not always possible; for instance where high levels of maintenance are required for continuing operations;
- specifying precisely where the cost savings will be made and how these will translate into improved working-capital ratios is an essential but rarely an easy task.

Risks are therefore inherent in harvesting. Paramount among these risks is a danger that, in choosing to harvest a business, management may be too hasty in designating a market as mature or unattractive and therefore affording little apparent growth potential. Prematurely writing off markets or businesses – as RCA did, for example, in deciding to withdraw from the ostensibly mature television market at precisely the same time as Japanese competitors were investing heavily in the videotape market – can lead to decisions that are both irreversible and incorrect. At this point the analogy with farming breaks down: whereas the farmer replants for next year's harvest, the corporation rarely, if ever, gets the same opportunity. Once the business has been harvested that's effectively it – although competitors may have a field day!

Hedging. Price fluctuations, and rising prices in particular, create uncertainty, and constitute risks for any business. In response, firms, and individuals, can take action to reduce or 'hedge' this risk. For example, during periods of rapid inflation, buying a house – or other equities which are expected to increase in line with inflation – constitutes hedging. The risk of rising prices is offset by the purchase of an asset – in this case the house – the value of which is expected to increase at least as fast as inflation. Exactly the same principle applies in financial (particularly foreign exchange) and commodity markets. To illustrate, take the case of a printer who, anticipating an increase in paper prices, enters into a firm, fixed-price contract now for the delivery of the required amount of paper in six months time. Such a contract transfers the risk associated with the price increase from the purchaser (the printer) to the seller (the paper merchant). Hedging is therefore about transferring the risk of price fluctuations from one person or group to another.

Herfindahl index.   *See* CONCENTRATION RATIO.

Holding company. A firm may comprise a number of highly autonomous business units owned, wholly or partially, by a single, parent board. Such a portfolio of companies, which may well trade under their own names, is typically made up of businesses operating in diverse areas, offering little scope for developing interrelationships or exploiting interfirm SYNERGIES throughout the group. In many respects this type of organization resembles a multidivisional structure (*see* DIVISIONALIZATION), but the essential difference is the degree of autonomy, particularly in terms of strategic direction, enjoyed by the individual business units. (See figure 20.)

Under these conditions the role of the central holding company, which is typically small and sparing in its overhead, is to allocate capital, exercise control (particularly financial control), shuffle the portfolio (via acquisition and disposal) and, in some instances, to provide central services

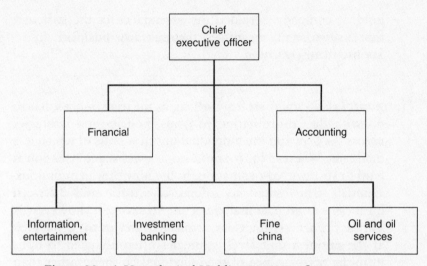

Figure 20 A Hypothetical Holding-company Structure

(for example, legal services). The availability of cheaper finance, the tight management of central overhead, and the capacity that this structural form has to offset profits earned in one part of the portfolio against losses incurred elsewhere, are all claimed as advantages. On the other hand, the lack of synergy between constituent companies, the risk of divestment facing these companies – and the adverse knock-on effect of this on management morale – and the modest role of the centre in providing skills or expertise are obvious weaknesses.

The strategic autonomy entrusted to individual companies, on the grounds that they will perform better if left alone to determine their own direction, results in a marked absence of overall strategic direction or cohesion for the group as a whole. The increasing importance of strategic co-ordination has signalled the demise of the holding-company structure. For example, in the UK during the 1960s 43 per cent of major manufacturing companies and 47 per cent of major service companies were of the holding-company type. By 1970 the figures had declined to 21 and 27 per cent respectively. A pattern repeated in many other European countries, as well as in the US. But the decade that marked the demise of the holding company heralded the ascendance of the structure that it superficially resembles: the multidivisional form. *See* DIVISIONALIZATION.

Horizontal strategy. A strategy which, as the term implies, has to do with the co-ordination of goals, policies and strategies *across* the firm and the individual business units of which it is made up. Whereas in HOLDING COMPANIES scant attention is paid to strategic co-ordination, in the now prevalent multidivisional firms such co-ordination across and between businesses is an essential element. Achieving it, however, is not easy. Formulating clear, explicit strategies to be pursued at the business unit level, strategies often designed to optimize the performance of the individual business rather than that of the corporation as a whole, is much more straightforward than identifying ways in which these individual businesses can work together within an overall strategic framework. Consequently, horizontal strategy runs the risk of being left implicit, somewhat vague and ill-defined.

In remedying this deficiency the best starting point is to identify, as precisely as possible, the linkages and interrelationships that exist between individual businesses. We might ask, for example, whether activities currently duplicated (such as distribution) might be more effectively shared throughout the business, thereby generating cost savings – in this instance the savings derived from ECONOMIES OF SCALE. Alternatively, individual firms, operating in relative isolation from each other, run the risk of continually reinventing the wheel and not sharing knowhow, expertise or experience that may exist elsewhere in the group. Pooling such expertise may yield enormous intangible value. Finally, identifying and understanding how one's competitors exploit linkages between business units is a rich source of insight into the scope that may exist for repeating this in one's own business. But beware: not all linkages are necessarily best exploited. There are many areas in which a degree of duplication may be a small price to pay for the benefits of continued autonomy.

The objective of horizontal strategy is to identify those

areas in which businesses can usefully co-operate and reap the benefits of strategic co-ordination. But the development of horizontal strategy is, by its very nature, an essentially top-down process since a degree of detachment is necessary if interrelationships are to be identified in a non-partisan way. The strategy, therefore, has as much to do with what happens within businesses as between them and, in both instances, it needs to be made explicit.

Human resource management (HRM). When asked why he interviewed every new recruit the head of Sony, Akio Morita, is reported to have replied, 'the future prosperity of Sony rests in the hands of the last person we recruited.' A more succinct assessment of the importance of a company's greatest asset, its people, would be hard to find. Human resource management, or HRM as it is usually known, is about all the decisions and actions taken by management that affect the relationship between the organization and its employees, its human resources.

Traditionally, this dimension of management was regarded as the domain of a particular functional department, personnel, which was primarily responsible for devising effective policies for recruiting, training, rewarding, retaining and, where necessary, discharging employees. Much of the work done by the personnel department was reactive (as when dealing with personal crises or responding to labour demands) rather than pro-active, in the sense of actively shaping the relationship between an organization and its employees. But this narrow definition of the scope of HRM is no longer valid.

HRM is now widely seen to be a central part of the general management function; human resources are now recognized as a critical asset constituting the firm's 'intellectual' or 'social' capital. A number of pressures have combined to make the management of this asset a crucial area: for example, demographic changes and the impending labour shortages that will affect every firm; intensified competition, particularly for staff; changing values and the ascendance of concepts such as consensus, mutual commitment (between staff and management) and participation; increasing organizational size and complexity; finally, developments in information technology that facilitate much better tracking of staff and their careers.

These developments have profound implications for strategy. They involve the recognition that a firm's human resources are a critical constraint in determining the strategy it should pursue. Just as it needs a strategic response to its external environment (that of competitors, markets and customers), so too it needs an internal strategy in respect of its staff; achieving a good FIT between these two dimensions is a prerequisite of success. The effectiveness of human resource management hinges upon its becoming an integral part of daily activity. Making strategy happen fundamentally involves shaping the deep-seated, often unconscious, beliefs that people have about their jobs, their place in the organization, and their contribution to its success (see CORPORATE CULTURE). Strategic redirection can only take place if such changes take place at the individual level. Hence the telling observation of Cor van der Klugt, formerly president of Philips, who described the challenge of restructuring the company in terms of a 'change in religion'. HRM is therefore the responsibility of every manager – a responsibility perfectly encapsulated by Akio Morita.

I

Incrementalism. 'I knew the new model wouldn't be profitable on a stand-alone basis, but it contributes to our overhead recovery.' 'We try to avoid getting into the commodity end of the business but the additional volume there costs us very little, it's just a way of filling up the plant.' These statements are examples of incremental decision-making.

Economists often remind us that profit is maximized by continuing down a path for as long as the extra benefit (marginal revenue) is greater than the extra marginal cost. Many businessmen apply this rule in practice, extending product lines on the grounds that they can share the existing distribution system at little extra cost, or chasing extra volume for as long as it covers variable costs. All this might be true, yet it is not the whole story.

First of all, those economists sometimes forget to mention that the maximum profit available from an inherently poor strategy may be a whopping loss. A firm can still go bankrupt maximizing profit if its total revenues don't cover total costs. Suppose you start with an unprofitable business. Each incremental decision may add a little more revenue than cost, so you make the extra investment required – introducing an extra model, for example. So it goes on; a few extra customers, a little extra capacity, R&D to keep up with competitors improving their product, a bit of extra stock – each decision viewed on its own looks sensible. Then you look back over your shoulder; the business is bigger, but still making below-acceptable returns. More cash has gone in with little chance of enough ever coming out (*see* CASH TRAP). This is the first danger of incrementalism: every step on the way makes some progress although the destination is still unattractive when you get there. So strategy needs to consider critically the final result as well: is there sustainable COMPETITIVE ADVANTAGE at the end of the road?

The second pitfall is that while the extra revenues are obvious, it is harder to identify all of the extra costs. Many of these may take the form of adverse effects on the existing business: reducing the responsiveness of the plant in producing the core products on time, for instance, or overloading the salesforce with information, diluting the firm's marketing image, distracting management from the core business, and introducing other COSTS OF COMPLEXITY. Incrementalism often fails to take account of these additional costs.

Since much strategy deals with the uncertain, a degree of flexibility and step-by-step decision-making is often necessary. Strategies almost always evolve over time, new issues arise and details are finalized along the way. These are facts of life. What distinguishes incrementalism, however, is a failure to reassess critically the overall profitability of both today's results and tomorrow's goal at every step of the way.

Industry attractiveness. A more elaborate means exists of analysing and assessing the potential of an industry than the two-dimensional GROWTH–SHARE MATRIX developed by the BOSTON CONSULTING GROUP. The BCG matrix provides for the distribution of businesses within a portfolio on the basis of the attractiveness of an industry, as measured by its rate of growth, and the internal strength of the firm in respect of that industry, as measured by its market share. The key premise of the framework is that rates of market growth determine long-term industry profitability. But this somewhat narrow, two-dimensional focus prompted the search for a broader framework; a framework that would take account of other critical factors.

One such framework is that developed by MCKINSEY & CO., in conjuction with General Electric: the industry attractiveness–business strength matrix. This is a multi-dimensional matrix in which equal attention is paid to both internal and external factors. Key external factors (over which the firm exercises relatively little or no control) that determine industry attractiveness include market size, market growth, barriers to entry, government regulations, and social, environmental, legal and political issues. Critical internal factors are typically market share, product line, customer service, R&D,

distribution, company image, managerial competence and financial resources. Having identified the critical factors businesses may then be positioned in terms of (a) their strength – that is, the extent to which they possess the factors critical to success in the industry; and (b) the overall attractiveness of the industry itself. One way of assessing each of these factors, and the firm's position in relation to it, is by weighting and prioritizing them. Having assessed and ranked such factors the firm can then be positioned in the attractiveness–strength matrix. (See figure 21.)

The difficulties of using this matrix are at once obvious. In place of the simple – or as some have argued, simplistic – growth–share matrix we now have a complex multidimensional matrix in which the criteria must be defined in an unambiguous manner and, importantly, limited to a manageable number. Weighting each criterion, though necessary, is clearly complicated and may lend the exercise a spurious objectivity. Using the factors consistently, and

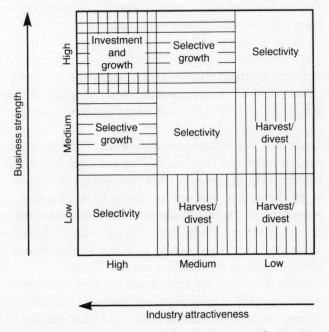

Figure 21 The Industry Attractiveness–Business Share Matrix

achieving consensus among managers as to both the meaning
and relative significance of each, is inevitably difficult.

Putting into operation the concept of industry attractiveness is therefore a problematic process, whichever matrix or
analytical framework is adopted. But beyond this there is an
inherent weakness in the concept itself, namely its incorporation of an essentially *passive* view of strategy. This view treats
industry attractiveness as a 'given', as something that is
determined entirely by external forces (like market growth
rate) over which an organization has little or no control. Such
a deterministic view leaves little scope for the firm itself to
influence or mould the potential or attractiveness of an
industry. The remit of strategy is thereby limited to determining the optimal position of a firm within a predetermined
industry context. But this truncated view is unnecessarily
limited. Ostensibly 'unattractive' industries, which may have
been vacated by disillusioned competitors, often provide rich
opportunities for those firms which, taking a more active
view of the role of strategy, recognize that far from being a
fact of life, industry 'attractiveness' is something over which
they can exert a decisive influence.

Industry definition. Defining the scope of an industry is an
essential but difficult first step in developing strategy. Essential, since strategy must be based upon a clear answer to the
questions, 'in what industry do we compete?', and derived
from this, 'what business are we in?' Difficult, because there
are no hard and fast rules or unambiguous criteria to guide
the drawing of the industry's boundaries. A narrow approach
is to define an industry in terms of a group of firms that
supply products or services that are close substitutes for each
other. In other words, the industry is defined on the basis of
the range of products from which a typical consumer would
choose to meet a particular need.

Take the need to type a letter. The typewriter industry
could be defined in terms of the range of typewriter manufacturers, who collectively constitute the industry. But this
example highlights the dangers and risks inherent in a narrow

definition of the industry. For in this case the industry which meets the need for typed letters, could equally well be defined in terms of all those suppliers of personal computers, word-processors and so forth. A typewriter manufacturer who restricted the scope of his definition to other *typewriter* suppliers would, at a single stroke, eliminate all potential competition from PC/word-processor suppliers – competitors who have, as it happens, virtually eradicated the traditional typewriter industry.

Now this example is extreme but it serves to make a number of key points. First, do not assume that just because you define an industry in a certain way, others (like potential competitors) will do the same. The scope of your firm's activity is not necessarily the same thing as the scope of the industry's activity. Be careful therefore not to mistake a segment of the market for the industry as a whole. Secondly, do not assume that industry boundaries are immutable. They change frequently and often very rapidly, thereby invalidating prevailing distinctions and definitions. Thirdly, correctly defining the scope of an industry is not the same thing as correctly defining what should be the COMPETITIVE SCOPE of the firm. An integral part of strategy development is specifying precisely what limits the firm should set to the range of its activities and, having done this, how it should compete within its chosen areas.

Essentially, these three notes of caution come down to the same thing. The greatest threat to industry definition is myopia. The myopia that prevents a firm from noticing potential new rivals in its market, the ways of which market/industry boundaries are changing and the emergence of new products that could render existing products redundant and thereby wipe out the demand for them. Of course, drawing industry boundaries is a matter of debate and often the source of much controversy. Strategy need not concern itself with the niceties of this debate, but it must remain centrally concerned with this question, 'what business are we in?' Once you lose sight of this question the risk is that the business might disappear, before you've had time to realize what is happening.

Industry life cycle. One approach to the analysis of an industry focuses on the stages through which it develops; stages which, taken together, represent a complete cycle, paralleling the stages through which the life of each person progresses. Using the criterion of sales growth, industries are said to proceed through four stages: embryonic (product introduction), growth, MATURE, and aging or DECLINING.

In the first two stages, sales steadily increase, then reach a plateau as the industry matures prior to decline. Other financial factors, such as profitability and cash flow, are also supposed to track industry evolution, as figure 22 illustrates.

As depicted here, cash flows for example are largely negative during the embryonic and early growth stages, becoming positive as maturity sets in and continuing to be positive (although declining) as the mature stage evolves into the final period of aging. Once the principle of an industry life cycle is accepted then the following question arises: 'how do we locate business within this cycle?' One answer is provided by A. D. Little, an early exponent of the life-cycle concept, who identified the following positioning criteria: the role of market growth and market potential; breadth of product

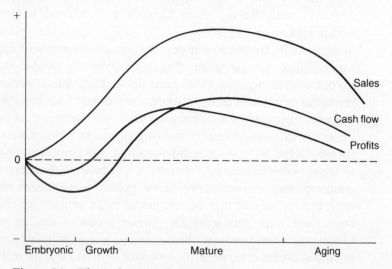

Figure 22 The Industry Life Cycle

line; number of competitors and their relative market shares; entry barriers; the state of technological development. The life-cycle approach therefore provides a framework within which industries can be analysed and businesses allocated to particular phases or stages of the life cycle. But how useful is such a conceptual framework? Does it really do justice to the real world? Critics would answer 'no' and, in support of their answer, would typically provide the following reasons:

- Life-cycle stages vary widely in length between industries. Generalization is therefore dangerous and it is rarely easy to identify exactly what stage in the cycle a specific industry has reached.
- The gentle, regular 'S' shape of figure 22 does not hold true for all industries. Indeed, stages can be telescoped, for example, in the aging stage, or truncated through obsolesence.
- The shape of the curve is not entirely outside the firm's control. For example, the rate of new product introduction may well alter it.
- It is impossible to draw general strategic inferences applicable to all industries on the basis of the stage in the life cycle a particular industry has reached. Strategies appropriate to, say, the mature stage of one industry may be wholly inappropriate to the same stage of another.

As with most good frameworks the life-cycle approach is useful in providing a well-organized, disciplined and fairly rigorous methodology for analysing industries and the position of incumbent firms within it. But if you make use of such a framework bear in mind its limitations and don't look upon it as a source of strategic prescriptions. It isn't.

Input costs. What would be the true cost of producing cement at a plant sited in central London? Apart from the obvious impact of congestion, the opportunity cost of the alternative use of premium land would be enormous. Yet the accounts of the company might well show the high profitability of the operation since the implicit rental of the site would not be counted among its input costs. Likewise, we might ask what

COSTS OF COMPLEXITY are imposed on manufacturing by expanding the product line, or what is the cost of the scarce management resource devoted to an ALLIANCE? Again, most accounting systems would not count these among the cost of inputs to either venture.

Successful strategy, by contrast, needs to account for input costs broadly; not only short-term, but also long-term costs; not only tangible, but also intangible inputs like management time or the opportunity cost of land. Moreover, the full input costs must include the cost of transacting business to acquire them, not only the price paid.

Casting the net even wider, strategy decisions might need to make allowance for the loss of flexibility associated with particular input decisions which could impose future strategic disadvantage on the firm. Understanding the true cost of a product by looking at a broad definition of the inputs expended by the firm in supplying it is therefore an important role of strategic analysis.

Integration. Combining quite distinct activities – for example manufacturing, marketing, distribution and sales – within a single firm. Integration takes place in two dimensions: vertical and horizontal (*see* HORIZONTAL STRATEGY, VERTICAL STRATEGY).

Vertical integration refers to a firm's movement up or down the industry VALUE CHAIN. By moving up – or backwards – the firm elects to take over activities that previously occurred at an earlier stage in the process than that at which it is primarily engaged. Movement down – or forward – represents a move into those activities relating to what the firm produces rather than how it produces its goods. To illustrate: publishers typically concern themselves primarily with tasks relating to the selection, editing, marketing and distribution of titles. A move into printing or into bookselling would represent, respectively, a form of backward or forward integration. Both take place on the vertical axis.

If, having set up in bookselling, the publisher moved into the business of record retailing this would constitute horizontal integration: that is, a move into a comparable or competitive activity. The UK brewing industry is a classic example of integration in both dimensions, with many brewers owning, apart from the breweries themselves, wholesalers and retailers (pubs, for instance), as well as – on the horizontal axis – hotels and restaurants.

The extent to which vertical linkages are in the public interest has become a focus of debate in both the UK and Europe, with suggestions that they mute competition and reduce consumer choice. The UK's Monopolies and Mergers Commission has ruled against the brewers with a set of proposals for diluting or eliminating the linkages – for example, between the brewer and the pub.

The rationale for vertical integration usually takes the following form. It creates scope for achieving economies, both in terms of costs and in less tangible areas such as internal control and co-ordination. It assures supply and, to an extent, creates the scope for ensuring demand, effectively stabilizing the relationships between buyers and sellers. In strategic terms it creates a source of sustainable advantage, in that it is difficult for new entrants and non-integrated competitors to replicate.

But what of its costs? Vertical integration may mask or conceal the real level of profitability being earned by a business at each of the different stages of activity in which it is engaged; such has been the case with UK brewers who have consistently overstated the profitability of their brewing businesses whilst substantially understating the profitability of retailing. The result was a long period of relative under-investment in the pub estate. It increases a company's proportion of total fixed costs, it ties the fortunes of the whole of the business to cycles (for example in retailing) that may affect only one part of the entire business, and it creates a BARRIER TO EXIT, often in the form of an emotional, historical commitment to one part of the business on the part of its management. And precisely because it stabilizes the buyer/seller relationship, making it an essentially captive one, it creates distortions – for example, in the price at which goods are transferred within the business – that may well dull the competitive appetites of managers or lull them into a false sense of security.

Thus the decision to integrate has to balance carefully the costs and benefits of so doing, as well as to consider the feasibility of 'deintegrating'; that is, decoupling activities and businesses in the event that the deteriorating performance of one business threatens to undermine the performance of the rest of the firm. The choice between making or buying, between doing something oneself or farming it out, must include a rigorous assessment of the strategic advantages and disadvantages and not simply the economic costs and benefits. Indeed, buyers who can credibly threaten to integrate backwards may achieve just as much leverage over suppliers, with resultant financial benefits, as those who actually make the move upstream.

The key strategic question to bear in mind is this: are the requirements for success, particularly in terms of management skills and expertise, the same in the upstream and downstream ends of the business? Usually they are different – for example, manufacturing and retailing, which require radically different management skills. If they are different then how can the firm acquire the requisite skills or refine those it already has? What reason is there to suppose that success in one part of the business will translate into comparable success in another? If integration does not work out then what are the costs and consequences of the subsequent deintegration or decluttering? And, finally, does the firm really understand the business into which it proposes extending its activities, and how can it add value to these activities?

Internal growth. *See* ORGANIC GROWTH.

J

JIT. See JUST IN TIME.

Joint venture (JV). Simple forms of ALLIANCE have traditionally
been used as a method of extending the span of a company's
operations into new geographic markets or new activities
(such as raw-material processing, or distribution and service)
in the pursuit of HORIZONTAL or VERTICAL STRATEGIES. Common examples include joint ventures between multinationals
wishing to extend a proven product or technology 'formula'
and national partners who provide local knowledge and
customer, supplier and government relationships. Vertical
joint ventures were often established with the aim of assuring
suppliers of filling high fixed-cost capacity, of cementing
technological co-ordination, stabilizing intermediate-goods
prices, or reducing in-pipeline inventories. Research indicates
that these have been most frequent in businesses with substantial scale economies, global similarity in demand, and
high R&D or CAPITAL INTENSITY and business RISK.

Recently more JVs have been concerned with the joint
development of new products. As firms have faced increasing
investment stakes associated with financing such development, shortening product life cycles and fighting international standard battles, many have looked to JVs as a means of
spreading their risk exposure across competing base technologies and economizing on scarce development funds. This
had led to a growing number of JVs between companies
which are otherwise competitors in the market, and ultimately to more complex networks of alliances where broadly
comparable global competitors seek to fill in complementary
gaps in their capabilities by co-operating in some areas while
competing in others.

Many joint ventures have ended in the separation, often
acrimonious, of the parties involved. Some point to this as
evidence of their failure. It may be, however, that many JVs

actually *should* have a limited life. As the JV grows and the environment changes, the needs, strategies, contributions and balance of power between the parties change with it. The original rationale may no longer persist. Given these facts, the strategy associated with a JV needs to be continually reviewed and a smooth provision for a possible future buy-out by one party or disbandment considered when framing the initial agreement. In some cases a JV has led to its flotation as a separate company. Perhaps the best-known example is Unilever, which rapidly grew to become much larger than either the British (Lever Bros) or Dutch (J. Van den Bergh) companies who originally established it as a JV operation.

Just in time (JIT). This innovative manufacturing and inventory-control system remains, nearly 25 years after its first introduction, a source of mystery and confusion in many Western companies. In part this derives from a preoccupation with the *techniques* of just in time (and with trying to replicate these techniques) while failing to grasp that JIT is as much a philosophy as a technique. The essence of this philosophy or approach to manufacturing is a commitment to minimizing expenditure – for example, in inventory – until the last possible moment.

This approach originated in the early 1960s with work done by Taiichi Ohno at the Japanese Toyota motor company which, in response to changing demands for particular models or colours of car, to be supplied with minimum delay, developed a manufacturing approach with two distinctive features. First, it created a system whereby each production centre calls off parts, usually in a standard container, as and when it requires them – between five and ten deliveries per day is not unusual. Secondly, it developed a whole series of small factory units (300 staff or fewer), each delivering to one another in successive production stages and, eventually, to the final assembly plant. Inventory movement and parts production is triggered by completing a card known as a 'Kanban' at Toyota, an 'action plate' at Nissan and 'DOPS' at Honda. It was under the name 'Kanban' that JIT (of which the Kanban system is but a part) became known in the West in the late 1970s – until then it was known not as JIT but as the 'Toyota Manufacturing System'.

Used effectively, JIT affords many benefits: minimizing costs, in the form of both wastage/scrap and inventory; reducing bottlenecks; facilitating rapid response to engineering changes; and minimizing downtime and set-up time. For example, Toyota has estimated the set-up time for a typical hood-and-fender stamping operation at an automobile plant as follows: USA, six hours; Sweden and West Germany, four hours; Toyota, 12 minutes. JIT also facilitates highly flexible manufacturing processes that are well adjusted to coping with variety, with rapidly changing consumer needs and the demand for quick response; it marries a high degree of responsiveness with the capacity to produce in relatively small run-lengths.

But beyond these tangible and largely quantifiable benefits JIT creates value in other, less direct ways. The most significant of these is the maintenance of good production discipline. This operates at the level of both suppliers and assembly-line workers. Knowing that surplus parts have been eliminated from the assembly line, suppliers take particular care to ensure that those parts that are supplied meet the required quality specifications. Similarly, the absence of excess stocks and the sense of security that these gave encourages workers on the line to make every effort to eliminate mistakes and keep the line going.

Supplier co-operation and support is clearly critical to the success of such an approach, as is a commitment throughout the organization to understanding and making it work. It is here that many attempts to replicate JIT in the West come unstuck. Simply copying the techniques is insufficient. Its successful implementation usually entails a complete reformulation of the philosophy and approach to manufacturing; a renegotiation of relationships with suppliers and, in many instances, a reduction in the number and geographic dispersal of suppliers. At the same time it is typical for companies operating JIT systems to enter into longer-term contracts with those suppliers able to guarantee quality, delivery and flexibility. Finally, JIT often entails a redefinition of manning agreements and the introduction of flexible working that may require a complete renewal of the CORPORATE CULTURE. JIT is seen as an integral part of the continuing Japanese quest for productivity improvements: 'chasing the last grain of rice in the bowl'.

The process has been taken significantly further by Toyota at New United Motor Manufacturing Incorporated (NUMMI), a joint venture with General Motors in the US set up in 1984. Here the development and application of the JIT approach has had remarkable results. For instance, new car output from the plant, originally forecast at 200,000 units per annum, is currently running at 244,000 units, only 10,000 below the level achieved in Japan using the same equipment. But operating in the US creates a new dimension, conspicuously absent in Japan: distance. JIT originally developed in a context in which all of Toyota's suppliers operated within a 50 km radius of the main plant. In the US, suppliers are geographically dispersed and the NUMMI plant itself is thousands of miles away from head office. In place of the primitive card system, Toyota is now developing sophisticated electronic communications systems, both with Japan and its US suppliers. The objective is nothing less than moving from JIT to real time – the ability to produce cars in the shortest possible time in response to specific, real orders. *See* TIME-BASED COMPETITION.

JV. *See* JOINT VENTURE.

K

Kinked demand curve. In 1939, theorists began looking for an explanation of a phenomenon from which businessmen had long suffered: price increases leading to large loss of sales, yet price reductions picking up only modest additional volume. This was formalized in the concept of the kinked demand curve in oligopolistic markets, based on the following logic. When one competitor raises price, rivals do not follow. The 'deviant' therefore faces a highly elastic demand curve and heavy loss of sales. Should a black sheep decide to cut prices, however, his rivals would rapidly follow to stem their loss of sales. The demand curve would be inelastic in the downward direction, with little gained by cutting prices. (*See* OLIGOPOLY, ELASTICITY.)

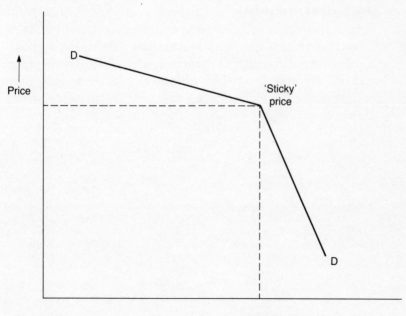

Figure 23   The Kinked Demand Curve

The result of this kinked demand curve – shallow above and steep below – would be so-called 'price stickiness'. Only when all its competitors faced similar types of cost increases could a price leader initiate a price increase, confident that all others would want to follow to restore their margins. Tacit collusion on price rises in favourable circumstances would result. (See figure 23.)

This theory was found to explain price behaviour quite well in many industries where domestic markets were closed from foreign competition. As markets became more international, however, each firm tended to face a mix of rivals operating from different home bases. As a consequence, they suffered different cost pressures at different times. RIVALRY around the 'kink' therefore intensified, with chronic price weakness as a result.

The strategic response to being caught in a kinked demand curve situation is to find a way of differentiating your product in the eyes of customers so that, despite an increase in price, they are unwilling to defect to the competition. (*See* DIFFERENTIATION.)

L

Learning. By 1983 one third of the *Fortune '500'* companies listed in 1970 had disappeared. Why? One answer, albeit partial, is that the extinct companies had failed to understand and adapt to a changing environment. They had, in effect, failed to 'learn'. The nature of institutional, that is company-level, learning as distinct from individual learning, has been neatly encapsulated by Arie De Geus (formerly Head of Planning for the Royal Dutch–Shell Group) in a classic definition. 'Institutional learning is the process whereby management teams change their shared mental models of their company, their markets and their competitors. For this reason we think of planning as learning and of corporate planning as institutional learning.' ('Planning as Learning', *HBR*, 2 (March–April 1988), p. 70.) This definition provides the clue to what learning, at the corporate level, is fundamentally about: changing mental models. But of what do these models consist?

Each individual carries in his head a mental model of the world made up of a set of core, taken-for-granted assumptions. We all assume, for example, that the sun will rise in the morning, and all our plans can be predicated, quite reasonably, upon this assumption. Deciding what we might do were the sun not to rise would doubtless throw us into a state of confusion and probably paralysis. Similarly at the corporate level, managers have mental models or representations of the world, grounded in core, taken-for-granted assumptions and associated expectations. None of these assumptions may be of quite the same fundamental order as our belief that the sun will rise in the morning, but there are some – for instance that we'll still be in business in, say three years time – that approximate to it.

To illustrate the point with another example, made popular by De Geus's work. In 1984 the price of a barrel of oil was $28. In the same year a planning group at Shell postulated a situation in which the price fell to $16 per barrel. From the planners' point of view what was of interest was how the company, which had become used to steadily rising prices, might react to this seemingly improbable development. From the point of view of many managers at Shell the likelihood of this happening seemed so remote, and the exact nature of the price fall so imprecise, as to make even thinking through the consequences appear somewhat futile. And yet by April 1987 the price per barrel stood at $10. Was Shell prepared? The answer is that to a very considerable extent it was. Why?

Undeterred by the initially sceptical reaction of colleagues, the planning department had developed a hypothetical case study sketching out the '$16 per barrel' scenario. The management was invited to enter into the spirit of this 'game', and think through and discuss its consequences. When the improbable happened the organization was reasonably well prepared; learning had taken place.

This episode highlights a number of fundamental points. First, a central task of strategy is to encourage – and if necessary to force – managers to think the unthinkable and, moreover, to analyse the implications of the unthinkable coming to pass. To us it is inconceivable that the sun will not rise tomorrow, but in business the unthinkable has a nasty habit of occurring, often faster than one ever imagined. How many of the decreased *Fortune '500'* companies had failed to imagine what might happen (to their market, their competitors or to themselves), or having raised an improbable spectre had moved swiftly to rationalize it away?

Secondly, there is nothing like a major crisis or severe external pressure on an organization to accelerate the rate at which it interprets what is happening, learns from this and adapts accordingly. The trick is to engender the same degree of urgency without there being a full-blown crisis. Thirdly, the learning process needs to start by elucidating and explicating management's mental model of the world, including as it does markets, competitors, buyers and suppliers. This implicit model or point of view on the world, and the equally implicit assumptions upon which it is based, need to be made completely explicit, brought out into the open so that its core assumptions can be challenged, discussed and, where appropriate, validated.

Fourthly, a variety of mechanisms and devices exist to facilitate this process in which well-established, hallowed rules and beliefs are suspended. Game playing, SCENARIO ANALYSIS and computer modelling techniques designed to capture and re-present mental models have all proved their worth in this regard. Finally, the learning process requires that those taking part in it evolve a new way of both thinking about and communicating their insights. Adherence to rigid procedures and routines inhibits the development of a new language in which learning can be conveyed. Rapid and unpredictable changes in the market and competitive environment place an absolute premium upon institutional learning and adaptation, without which companies risk the fate of those 165 *Fortune '500'* companies which passed away in the brief period between 1970 and 1983.

Levels of strategy. At one level strategy must analyse, respond to and help shape the forces operating in a market. At the same time, it must be put into practice, and the details of different initiatives worked out and adjusted, by individuals acting on perceptions of what their job is and when they have done it well. In addition to the classic distinction between corporate and business-unit strategy, therefore, we must distinguish between various levels of strategy within any business unit or activity. To be effective, the strategy must be consistent from the broadest level right through to its impact on the end activities of 'front line' staff and the incentives they perceive. Many strategies fail because they stop halfway. Figure 24 sets out a blueprint for ensuring the main of the levels of strategy are addressed and consistency achieved.

A successful strategy begins with a vision of the market. Many strategies run into problems right here: either the market VISION is unrealistic, a product of a 'we know best' delusion, or different people in the company are working on very different visions of what makes the market tick, what

Time horizon	Corporate roles	Levels of strategy	Business-function roles		
5–10 YRS	Shared assumptions	Vision		↑	
3–7 YRS	Shared aims	Mission/ goals			
2–5 YRS	Synchronized moves	Plan/staircase		Consistent vertical links	
1–3 YRS	Resource provision	Step-by-step initiatives			
1–2 YRS	Employee priorities	Individual objectives			
1 YR	Satisfied capital markets	Annual budgets		↓	

Figure 24   Corporate-functional Strategy Links

drives customers and who are the most important competitors. FIVE FORCES analysis, competitor BENCHMARKING and STRATEGIC GROUPS are important tools at this level. Market vision provides a map of the territory. Accuracy is critical and it is helpful if everyone is using the same map.

Based on the market vision, the next level is for the firm to develop a realistic MISSION STATEMENT of how it is to prosper in this environment in the future. Many strategies have failed because they started out at this point. By missing out the market vision, however, missions are apt to operate in the realm of dreams rather than reality.

In addition to a mission for the business unit as a whole, various functional or activity groups within the business often need their own missions. At this sub-level the mission sets out a goal for how that group is going to make a real contribution to achieving the overall mission of the business.

An important corporate role here is to ensure these individual missions form a set of shared aims.

To make a mission happen requires a plan, setting out the 'how' in a sequence or 'staircase' which identifies the milestones which will lead to one level of COMPETITIVE ADVANTAGE being built upon another (*see* SUPPLY-SIDE STRATEGY AND STRATEGIC STAIRCASE). This is important both to ensure that the strategy doesn't 'run before it can walk' and to provide the motivation to undertake difficult steps (such as cost reduction) because it opens the way for new opportunities at the next stage. Synchronization across functions is also important here, preventing, for example, the marketing function announcing to customers something which operations are not yet in a position to deliver.

The danger with an ambitious strategy is that employees are simply 'swamped' with the enormity of the task, and the organization suffers the paralysis of 'indigestion'. The next level therefore requires each great step forward to be broken down into specific initiatives: things which individuals can both relate to and believe to be actionable. At the centre this requires the support of appropriate shifts in resource allocation to make these initiatives possible.

In achieving these initiatives, individuals will have to make trade-offs. Even strategic objectives which have made it this far can expire under the pressure of employee priorities which are inconsistent with what the strategy deems important. Often these dysfunctional priorities result from incentive and measurement systems which encourage individuals to act at variance with the strategy. No amount of communicating strategic priorities will be effective if the promotion and bonus systems are making their voices heard loudly in a different direction. Making sure the strategic initiatives are reflected in individual objectives, and priority through incentives and evaluation consistent with them, is an essential level of the strategy process.

The final level of strategy is its contibution to the annual budget. Too often strategy and the budget never meet. However, since the long term is in practice no more than a series of annual budgets, both the costs and investments required to achieve the strategy, as well as the benefits coming from it, must appear in the annual budget. Where this level is absent, the strategy is prone to float free like a cloud above reality.

Despite these many levels, one aim is shared: to provide a consistent set of links between market reality and day-to-day behaviour.

Leverage. *See* GEARING.

Licensing. There may be advantages to a transaction in which a licensor assigns a licensee the right to make use of a technology, process, trade mark or patent in exchange for a payment (the latter usually takes the form of a royalty payment, calculated as a percentage of sales revenue). Typically, licences are assigned for a specified period of time and have attached to them precise conditions, for example, governing the manner in which the technology will be exploited, specifications relating to the equipment to be used or the level of output to be generated. While retaining ownership of, say, the technology the licensor assigns a degree of control over it to the licensee. But why would a firm do this rather than produce the product itself?

Numerous circumstances favour licensing, of which the following are the most important: where the firm has developed more products and associated patents than it could produce itself; where exploitation of a particular technology exceeds the financial resources available to the firm; or, particularly in the area of international business, where access to foreign markets is restricted either by import barriers or by local requirements relating to indigenous ownership and manufacturing. In such circumstances the firm is exporting an intangible – the licence – rather than the tangible product itself, thus circumventing many obstacles for the licensor. Equally, it may play a strategically significant part in the development of a licensee's business. Rather than develop its own technology (and thereby risk reinventing the wheel), a firm may be able to short-circuit the laborious and expensive process by licensing the technology which, once it has been mastered, enters the COMPETENCE set of the company and can be improved upon.

The strategic equation is therefore finely balanced. If we licence our technology do we forfeit our competitive edge to potential competitors or do we create additional sources of highly profitable income? One company that has provided a clear answer to this question is SUN Microsystems of California, the maker of a range of highly innovative desktop computers incorporating a range of potentially proprietary features. 'Potentially', because SUN – which has grown from nothing to a company with annual sales of two billion dollars in seven years – has deliberately chosen to open the door to its technology by issuing a series of licences (notably for its powerful microprocessor) to a range of current and future competitors such as Toshiba and Fujitsu.

But what benefits does SUN reap from a policy that ostensibly at least looks like a case of corporate hara-kiri? SUN identifies a number of advantages. For example: licensing disperses the technology more widely, thereby increasing customer familiarity with a particular technology and, it is believed, improving receptivity on the part of the users; innovations made by licensees can be taken advantage of by SUN; without the safety-net of proprietary technology, which may engender complacency, the company is forced to search continually for new ways of retaining its competitive edge, via service, reliability, quality and so forth. Licensing, while it brings new competitors into play, may actually lead to an overall increase in the size of the market and, finally, it yields a highly profitable income stream that can be invested elsewhere.

But others who take a more sceptical view of this matter point to the experience of IBM whose initial personal computers, based as they were on non-proprietary technology, spawned a plethora of cheap clones which effectively eroded IBM's position in the market. Licensing therefore poses a real strategic dilemma, the resolution of which entails a careful balancing of the costs and the potential competitive benefits that might accrue to the licensor.

Logistics. All activities to do with the movement and storage of goods or raw materials come under the logistics rubric; that is, the process of getting the right goods or services in the right quantity, to the right place, at the time required and, if possible, at the lowest possible cost. Principal among these activities are those associated with transportation, stock or inventory control and order processing. Three activities which typically account for a high proportion of the total cost of logistics.

But the remit of logistics also encompasses a range of support activities such as warehousing, materials handling, packaging and product scheduling. Historically, logistics or, as it used to be termed, 'distribution', was a Cinderella in many industries. Compared with areas such as marketing or finance, distribution often received inadequate management attention or resources. But in the last decade logistics has come of age. This development has been driven: by dramatic improvements in information technology; by a new determination by purchasers of all sorts to optimize and in many cases to minimize their stockholdings; and by a recognition of the critical part played by appropriately configured and adequately supplied distribution channels in achieving and sustaining market penetration.

For so long the preserve of the military, for whom co-ordination of supplies has always been of paramount importance and from whom the term itself is borrowed, logistics now occupies a pivotal strategic position in many industries. With this has come an improvement in the calibre of people working in the area, a high degree of professionalism and expertise and, of course, a burgeoning number of professional associations to which 'logisticians' (as they are called in the US) can belong.

See also JUST IN TIME.

Loose bricks. It is sometimes useful to think of a competitor's existing sales in the market as a castle wall made up of interlocking product/segment combinations. Some firms mount their attack with a battering ram at the first broad stretch of wall they see. Often they dissipate their resources and mangement time with too broad an assault. Many of the most successful drives for increased market share or profitability, by contrast, have begun with very focused attacks on the loose bricks which exist in every competitor's wall. These may be the customer segments which the salesforce has tended to ignore, pockets of dissatisfaction with performance, the products which are relatively overpriced so as to CROSS-SUBSIDIZE low profits elsewhere, or the parts of the line or customer base where SWITCHING COSTS are lowest.

Having identified the loose brick the aggressive competitor sharply focuses his attention and resources on offering, in that segment or product category, better value or service at a lower cost. History is littered with examples. The market for television sets in the US and Europe is a classic instance. In the 1960s the Japanese recognized the private-label segment as a loose brick because of lower retailer switching costs. With a volume base established they recognized the lack of interest of US producers in small-screen, portable and black and white sets. The incumbents felt that small and portable sets were a low-margin business and the black and white technology obsolete. This gave the Japanese a keyhole into the branded business (*see* BRANDING). In Europe the loose brick was the supply of picture tubes, entry into which provided the Japanese with intimate knowledge of the markets, supported capacity expansion, and allowed the building of volume and cost advantage in a key component. With these new resources they were then well placed to expand the initial window hole.

This illustrates another key problem with loose bricks: it doesn't take the removal of many before an interlocking wall starts to crumble. The loss of extra volume which at first appeared marginal turns into a substantial cost disadvantage, the advertising and branding channels become more crowded, loyalties come under pressure as the market begins to churn. Then one wakes up to find the wall is now no more than a decorative border.

M

Management buy-out (MBO). When a management team
within a company or division buy that business and become
owner-managers, they will usually be required to find something like five or ten per cent of the necessary investment
from their personal assets, in return for which they receive a
substantial shareholding in the new company, in many cases
a majority stake. The remainder of the investment will be
supported by high GEARING and possibly some modest equity
investment from employees or a venture-capital firm. The
financial structure of an MBO has important consequences
for its behaviour in the market and hence both for its own
strategy and that of its competitors.

The viability and increasing popularity of MBOs also exert
an important influence of the PORTFOLIO MANAGEMENT of
large corporate groups, offering a powerful new route for
divestment. It is also suggestive of the inadequacies of much
corporate-level strategy to harness the potential of their
senior middle management and individual STRATEGIC BUSI-
NESS UNITS.

Faced with the need to meet higher interest payments, the
management of an MBO is under strong pressure to eliminate
all unnecessary costs and 'buffers' in the form of excess
working capital and 'safety stocks'. They can be expected
quickly to eliminate CROSS-SUBSIDIZATION which supports
uneconomic products and customers. Seeking COST ADVAN-
TAGE and greater focus are therefore probable strategic
responses which the competitors of an MBO need to understand. A shift to a much more entrepreneurial approach,
taking more reasonable (and sometimes unreasonable!) risks,
because of the direct relationship between success and reward, is another common change in strategy following an
MBO.

MBOs are often an attractive route through which a
corporate group can divest itself of businesses which it might
be difficult to sell on an open market. Putting up a business

for 'auction' may substantially reduce its value as management and staff become demotivated and uncertain of their future. The best employees often depart and customers become wary of dealing with the business in case it closes or falls into the hands of a competitor. These problems are aggravated the longer a business remains 'on the market' before it is sold. The MBO route eases many of these problems: staff motivation is often improved, the company's performance is maintained in the expectation that the business will shortly be theirs, and the transaction can be concluded more quickly with less market disruption.

Any corporate group faced with many offers for MBOs, however, needs to ask some searching questions about its ability to motivate its management properly and the impact of its control and decision-making systems on the SBUs. MBOs are a clear sign of value which is currently unrealized, not because the existing management is unaware of what should be done to improve the business, but because the corporate system fails to motivate them into doing so – or even inhibits them.

Management information system (MIS). The traditional focus of MIS has been on speeding up existing business processes and hence containing costs and enhancing administrative efficiency. Its emphasis has been on internal information flows. Looking to the 1990s, however, a recent survey of European businesses ranked customer service, managerial effectiveness and competitive position as the key areas where MIS could be of most benefit. Its role is thus becoming much more outward-looking, shifting towards the flow of information between the businesses and its customers, distributors, suppliers and sub-contractors, and towards the collection of data on changing customer needs and competitor behaviour.

Cast in this broader role, an MIS can assist a business both to gain COMPETITIVE ADVANTAGE (or reduce its disadvantage) in each activity within its VALUE CHAIN and to improve co-ordination across the chain. The use of MIS to communicate with far-flung customers, for example, has allowed smaller companies to offer high-quality service without an extensive, high fixed-cost service network. A major source of advantage formerly held by the established competitors has therefore been eliminated. This use of MIS to handle variety and reduce set-up times has increased the possibilities for DIFFERENTIATION and product tailoring at an economic cost. Computerized warehouses have increased companies' ability to share distribution costs and exploit ECONOMIES OF SCOPE without being swamped by the COSTS OF COMPLEXITY. As these developments continue, the interaction between strategy and MIS will also increase; becoming a tool for changing the RULES OF THE GAME, creating additional sources of customer value, and spawning entirely new markets.

Market dominance. Dominant competitors are those who have a large MARKET SHARE both as a percentage of total sales and relative to the next largest competitor. They are often credited with advantages such as the ability to take PRICE LEADERSHIP, or to establish their own technology as the industry standard for the next generation of products. Market dominance can provide a company with strong cash flow and low costs through the benefits of ECONOMIES OF SCALE and EXPERIENCE CURVE EFFECTS.

Although many companies see market dominance as their Eldorado, recent evidence across a variety of industries suggests that businesses with very large shares of their market, over 65 and 70 per cent are often *less* profitable than firms with a lower market share. This probably reflects the fact that cost control often becomes lax, innovation languishes and DISECONOMIES OF SCALE are accepted in the absence of strong competitive pressure. Even at high prices, therefore, dominant firms often fritter away their potential profits through excessive costs. Second-ranking companies, meanwhile, can often enjoy high profitability by combining their lower cost base with the high price umbrella set by the dominant firm.

While BARRIERS TO MOBILITY often protect the dominant firm from ME-TOO STRATEGIES, experience has shown that they are often extremely exposed to MAVERICK competitors in a changing market. Mavericks are often successful in challenging market dominance by redefining the basic RULES OF THE GAME, rather than attacking head-on. Faced with a completely different approach to the market and encumbered by a history of beliefs and unquestioned assumptions institutionalized in the organization structure and decision-making processes dominant firms often find it very difficult to respond (*see* CORPORATE CULTURE).

The lesson is that market dominance does offer potential advantages, though not a royal right. The advantages underpinning it must be continually improved and replenished and adjusted to the changing market in order to retain the lead.

Market penetration. Generally refers to the percentage of a company's target customer population who are now buyers of its product or service. It differs from MARKET SHARE in that the relevant definition of potential sales includes all those who could reasonably be expected to be purchasers, rather than only those currently buying. Thus a company may have high market share in a new product, but low market penetration, since only a fraction of the potential customers may have sampled, or even heard of, the product. Bank accounts have very high penetration, around 90 per cent of the earning population in the UK. By contrast, shares and unit trusts have market penetration of only five or ten per cent of savers.

Strategies for penetrating markets include policies designed to expand availability through broader distribution, increase awareness through advertising, or generate demand through sampling or 'starter incentives'.

Market saturation. Strategists perceive that there are certain goods of which customers want to build up a 'stock' for their use; once reached, they will only purchase what is necessary to maintain the stock, or replace it once it wears out (*see* REPLACEMENT DEMAND).

Market saturation is often discussed in the context of durables like refrigerators; over a long period of time each household obtains one of their desired size until most of the buyers are simply replacing what they have. At this saturation point demand is reduced to some basic level based on the effective life of the durable. But saturation can also occur over much shorter cycles. Each year, for example, the market builds up towards a saturation of summer clothing. Each week the demand for Sunday newspapers probably becomes saturated, but fortunately for publishers the valuable life of a newspaper is short!

Market saturation is often depicted in the form of the familiar 'S' curve (see figure 25). Demand builds up slowly when a new product or variant is introduced and 'experimenters' try it. The 'mainstream' consumer then becomes convinced, sales quickly reach high levels and the stock rapidly increases towards saturation. Apart from a few 'laggards',

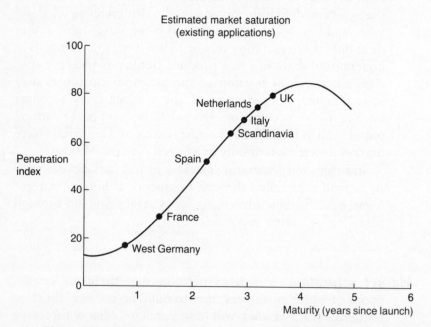

Figure 25   The Market-saturation Curve for the European Stretch-film Industry

the market then settles down to ongoing replacement demand plus a long-term market-growth factor.

Saturation raises some critical issues for strategy. An important strategic decision concerns how much to expand capacity. If a company gears up to meet the unusually high sales level associated with reaching saturation, it faces EXCESS CAPACITY when demand levels off. Not to do so, however, risks being left with a small installed base and a relatively little-known brand with which to capture replacement demand and base-market growth in a market which is highly competitive.

Some suppliers choose to position their product as a high-quality, limited-volume brand during the initial market expansion, banking on customers 'trading up' to a better product when saturation is reached. Others seek to expand volume rapidly, relying on lower costs through ECONOMIES OF SCALE and EXPERIENCE CURVE effects to give them a COST ADVANTAGE in the saturated market.

An important strategic role of TECHNOLOGICAL CHANGE and improvement in markets which face long-term saturation is to enable the launch of successive products which make obsolete the existing stock in the hands of consumers. On a shorter time-scale, fashion is used as a powerful weapon against the threat of saturation. Companies as diverse as ETA – with 'Swatch' watches – and stockbroking firms have sought to encourage their customers to 'turn' their stock more rapidly in an attempt to mute the impact of market saturation.

Market share. A common, 'rule of thumb' strategy argues that by striving for a large and growing market share profitability will take care of itself. A very substantial amount of empirical evidence does, in fact, support the view that market share and return on investment (ROI) do move together. In one of the most comprehensive recent studies Buzzell and Gale re-explored the market share–profitability relationship using data from 2,611 business units across a wide variety of industries. They concluded that for every ten per cent in-

crease in market share, return on sales increased by an
average of 1.4 per cent, adding 3.4 per cent to ROI. This
improvement in ROI was, however, down on the five per cent
increase estimated from a parallel study a decade earlier (by
one of the same authors), suggesting a decline in the value of
market share.

There are a variety of reasons why market share may
enhance profitability. Traditional arguments have centred on
ECONOMIES OF SCALE in manufacturing, distribution, marketing and advertising, and on the ability of firms with a large
share to reduce BUYER and SUPPLIER POWER. Economists,
meanwhile, have argued that when an industry is inhabited
by a few firms with large market shares, they recognize the
futility of price wars and hence 'tacitly collude' to maintain
higher prices. It has also been pointed out that firms with
large market share, especially where they achieve MARKET
DOMINANCE, find it easier to attract the best management in a
'virtuous cycle'. They may also be more able to justify the
employment of specialists which firms with smaller shares
cannot afford.

But a number of these arguments have come under strong
questioning. In the first place, it is likely that the best firms
will have the highest market share simply because they are
better at meeting the needs of customers. Market share is
therefore a result of success, efficiency, skill and quality,
rather than a cause of above-average performance. Secondly,
larger organizations have increasingly suffered DISECONOMIES
OF SCALE and added COSTS OF COMPLEXITY which have offset
the benefits of a larger market share. Thirdly, much of the
best management now prefers to work in smaller, entrepreneurial units without the burden of procedures necessary
to co-ordinate large organizations. It is also a fact that with
the huge growth in specialist sub-contractors who can offer a
company high-quality support, from technological advice
through to cleaning services, a large market share no longer
gives unique access to specialist skills.

Looking at the relationship between market share and
profitability on an industry-by-industry basis, researchers
have found that in a number of key sectors, notably services

and semi-finished goods and components, small-share firms were just as profitable or even more profitable than those with large shares. In these industries, high profitability is achieved by strong NICHE players or leading mass-market firms. The medium-sized competitors typically have low returns. This point to the growing importance of segment share rather than broadly defined market share (*see* SEG-MENTATION), and to the rise of successful, focused companies at the expense of the 'medium-sized, all-rounder'.

Matrix structure. To cope with its rapid development after the Second World War, Philips, the Dutch-based multinational, developed a structure which accorded *joint* responsibility for the group's activities to the national organizations (which were primarily responsible for sales and marketing in each country) and the product divisions. The resulting structure, in which different divisions work in tandem with each other, is a matrix.

A defining characteristic of such a structure is that there is no single source of authority or individual accountability, since each individual has dual reporting relationships and responsibilities. Thus in Philips many individual managers, particularly those working in the national organizations (NOs) outside Holland, would report to both a manager within their respective NO and to one within a particular product division (PD).

The potential drawbacks of such an arrangement are immediately obvious. Distinct lines of authority, such as one would find in an organization structured on functional lines, are replaced by a 'network of relationships', by dual sources of authority and overlapping areas of responsibility. Ultimate profit accountability is ambiguous and difficult to pin down. In Philips's case the question is, which should be held accountable for profit and loss, the NOs or the PDs? Throughout the 1960s and 1970s the answer was 'both'.

The complexity of reporting relationships in the matrix further creates problems of co-ordination, fostering the growth of co-ordinating committees (to which all significant decisions are referred) and inevitably slowing down the decision-making process. Finally, a fundamental difficulty is that the matrix itself is inherently volatile, making it extremely difficult to keep the organization balanced or in equilibrium. Thus the 1960s and 1970s marked the ascendancy of the NOs over the PDs within Philips. Throughout the 1980s, however, Philips responded by trying to re-balance the matrix, tilting it in favour of the PDs which were given enhanced power and authority. By the end of the decade this process culminated in a completely redefined structure; one based around a limited number of PDs, each of which had exclusive, worldwide profit responsibility. The role of the NOs was subordinated to servicing and supporting the PDs. Thus the ambiguity which had pervaded the organization for so long was now removed and with it the matrix structure, in all but name.

This particular illustration should not, however, obscure the potential benefits of this type of structure. For instance, it encourages informal, lateral communication across functions within the firm. Although it may be slower, the decision-making process is often enhanced, particularly in situations where there is a conflict of interest or a danger that one sectional interest may dominate all others. Cross-functional communication broadens an individual's perspective on the firm, enabling him to see more clearly how the various parts fit together to form an integrated whole, and where, moreover, his own area fits in.

In general, matrix structures work best where there is a high degree of mutual trust, a willingness to compromise and a strong, shared sense of purpose. Hence a matrix approach is often best suited to specific, time-bound projects (for example NASA's 'Apollo' project) to new product groups, R&D teams and so forth. Although difficult to pull off, the best way of extracting the benefits afforded by the matrix is to manage in effect with an implicit matrix; that is, to adopt a matrix style of management within, say, a functionally organized structure. Informing staff that they are now working in a matrix structure often creates confusion and uncertainty. But applying a matrix approach covertly often serves

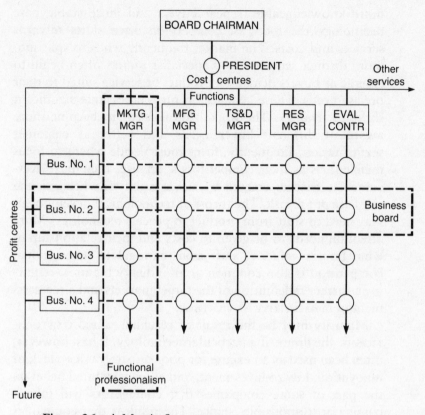

Figure 26 A Matrix Structure

to enhance understanding of the firm as a whole, to strengthen motivation and commitment. (See figure 26.)

Mature industry. This third stage of the INDUSTRY LIFE CYCLE is characterized by a combination of slowing growth in demand and the rate of technological change, a prevalence of repeat rather than first-time buyers, and a more stable group of competitors who have experience of each other's market stance and competitive reaction.

In this mature environment company growth must increasingly come from wresting market share from competitors rather than from the expansion of market demand. With more knowledgeable, repeat buyers and more stable base technology the focus of competition often shifts towards services and costs. The market frequently tends to split into more distinct segments and specialist NICHES often begin to emerge as buyers demand a product or service suited to their precise needs. These changes, in turn, necessitate significant shifts in strategy. The organization needs to become more aware of different buyer needs and better at customer segmentation. Frequently, firms must decide where to focus their efforts as their competitors specialize; they must overcome the friction created by MIXED MOTIVES when existing sales are put at risk. The thrust of technological development may need to shift from product to process technology. More attention needs to be given to costs and their relationship to what buyers value. A shift from national to international competition is also common as an industry matures, requiring a further redefinition of the target markets and a reassessment of COMPETITIVE ADVANTAGE.

Maturity may be the result of reaching MARKET SATURATION or the limits of a particular technology. It has, however, often been used as an excuse for poor SEGMENTATION, lack of innovation, low re-investment, and an unwarranted belief on the part of some companies that competitors will take a passive or 'responsible' stance. The result is that companies often 'write off' a market as mature and lacking in potential long before this is justified. By HARVESTING their position and starving the business of investment, they often make decline a self-fulfilling prophesy.

Some strategists argue that there is no such thing as a mature market except in the minds of companies within it. The ability of many Japanese competitors to revitalize 'mature' markets, like consumer electronics, photocopiers or photographic equipment, with step changes in technology or cost, and introduce reverse-engineered 'personal' versions which open up entirely new market segments, lends weight to this view. One of the greatest advantages an aggressive competitor may have in a mature market, therefore, is the myopia of incumbents, combined with a common delusion among competitors that the market is set to decline and hence is not worth investing resources, time, or top management attention in.

Maverick. A competitor who redefines the RULES OF THE GAME associated with a business, may adopt a strategy which defies the conventional wisdom of the majority of market suppliers.

New ENTRANTS, looking at the industry afresh or diversifying from different market environments with different skill bases, often adopt maverick strategies because their past experience leads them to approaches which have been ruled out by existing players. Mavericks often switch the distribution channel, as Amstrad did when it launched its PCs through discount electrical chains rather than specialist computer stores. Canon emphasized direct sales of photocopiers which had traditionally been sold on leases. They commonly reconfigure the production process and stockholding points; Benetton, for example, made up its clothing before colour-dyeing it, completely reversing industry norms. Discount brokers proved that broking execution could be sold without associated advice.

Changing market needs frequently open up opportunities for mavericks. 'Traditional' competitors, in turn, find it very difficult to respond because to do so threatens existing market relationships with distributors and suppliers and calls for substantial shifts in the skill base, ORGANIZATION STRUCTURE and CORPORATE CULTURE. Although some of the most potent competitors, mavericks are often wrongly ignored as 'not being in our business' until after it is too late.

MBO. *See* MANAGEMENT BUY-OUT.

McKinsey & Co. Often described as the 'IBM' or 'Blue chip' of the strategy-consulting world, McKinsey has been at the forefront of the development of some of the key tools used in strategy, and in matching strategy and ORGANIZATION STRUCTURE.

Throughout its history, McKinsey has assisted clients to move their organization structure from simple functional forms (U forms), through multidivisional (M form) structures towards the modern 'network' organizations designed to meet the new market demands for flexibility, speed of response and global linkages. It was also important in popularizing the approach of analysing a business in terms of the characteristics of the market sector on one hand, and the competitive position of the unit or product on the other. The VALUE CHAIN concept and the 7-S FRAMEWORK also have their roots in the work of McKinsey.

See also INDUSTRY ATTRACTIVENESS.

Me-too strategy. Approaches to the market which are carbon copies of another competitor's rely entirely on better execution as their potential source of COMPETITIVE ADVANTAGE. It is most unlikely that a strategy of abandoning other opportunities to steal a march on the competition by doing things differently – and better – will be optimal. By singling out a set of customers with slightly different needs it is usually possible to DIFFERENTIATE the product or service the better to satisfy them or to gain a COST ADVANTAGE from a FOCUS STRATEGY. By exploiting the peculiar history, skills and resources of your enterprise to achieve differentiation or lower costs, new sources of advantage are opened up.

Despite this compelling reasoning, many firms end up following me-too strategies either in the belief that risks will be reduced by copying others or because they become mesmerized by 'industry norms' and conventional wisdom about the way the business 'should be' conducted. Yet a me-too strategy means meeting the competitor head-on. In pitting strengths in this way it is likely that the potential profit will be eliminated for both. Indeed, MAVERICK competitors are often some of the most successful because by avoiding head-on confrontations and redefining the RULES OF THE GAME they force the competition to battle on unfamiliar territory and to face the friction of changing long-held beliefs and engrained procedures.

M-form organization. *See* DIVISIONALIZATION.

Minimax principle. *See* GAME THEORY.

Mintzberg, Henry. Once described as 'the scourge of strategic orthodoxy', Mintzberg, currently Professor of Management at McGill University, is the author of numerous books and articles on issues relating to ORGANIZATION STRUCTURE, strategy and the links between the two. His ideas are most neatly synthesized in the article 'Crafting strategy' (*Harvard Business Review*, 1988).

The strategic orthodoxy against which Mintzberg inveighs is the notion that strategy is best understood as a deliberate process in which carefully defined objectives and moves that are designed to achieve these objectives can be specified in advance of action and embodied in a strategic plan. Within this view of strategy the manager's task is to implement this plan. Thus the process of formulation is quite distinct from the temporally separate stage of implementation. This conception, Mintzberg believes, ignores the reality of managerial life. In practice, strategy – far from being specified and articulated clearly in advance – typically *emerges* from past action. The job of mangement is to be sensitive to emerging patterns in past behaviour and to shape these patterns into coherent strategies.

The process most closely resembles the work of a potter who, in shaping a piece of clay, is receptive to emerging – and often accidental – forms that combine together with an original image to produce the finished object. In place of the formulation/implementation dichotomy Mintzberg substitutes a seamless web within which strategy is crafted by a process of continual movement, back and forth, between formulation and implementation; between recognizing patterns in past behaviour and actively shaping and making these patterns more explicit.

An important corollary of this view is that just as strategy is not deliberate, so too the idea that organizations can be reshaped or restructured to fit a chosen strategy is unrealistic. To argue that structure follows strategy is, in Mintzberg's view, to ignore the inertia of organizations and their resistance to change. Structures, like strategies, evolve over time. The strategic task of managers is to shape this evolutionary process (*see also* EMERGENT STRATEGY).

MIS.   *See* MANAGEMENT INFORMATION SYSTEM.

Mission statement. 'What business are we in?' That is the question to which any mission statement should provide a clear, concise answer. But good mission statements go beyond this simple though fundamental question to consider other issues equally germane to the organization. For example, they include: purpose – that is, the expression of the guiding purpose or *raison d'être* of an organization – understanding why the organization exists, and what its overriding aim is, is a prerequisite of securing commitment to that purpose or aim; strategy – that is an explanation, necessarily brief, of how the organization will accomplish its chosen purpose and realize its ambitions; values – good mission statements encapsulate the core beliefs or guiding principles that should underpin everything the organization and its members do. These values may relate to employees, customers or the community within which the firm is operating as well as to more general management philosophy and style. Examples would include respect for the individual; dedication to customer service; learning and co-operation. Implicit in such statements of value are expectations relating to the standards – of both performance and behaviour – that should be achieved and against which individuals will be judged.

Defined in these broad terms the value of a mission statement becomes clearer. Knowing not only what business they are in but why they are in this business, what their aim is, how they will accomplish it, and which core values underpin what they do helps individuals make sense of what they do on a day-to-day basis. It imbues action with a sense of meaningful purpose without which work has little point or rationale above the instrumental requirement to earn a certain amount of money. Instilling, throughout an organization, a shared sense of mission therefore provides individuals with a basis on which they can readily make the choices and trade-offs that crop up each day. Sharing a sense of purpose engenders loyalty, commitment and a degree of co-operation and mutual trust which organizations with little or no clarity of mission conspicuously lack.

But this is not to say that simply producing a mission statement will accomplish all of this overnight. Clearly it won't. Indeed, the process of developing the mission, of communicating it, of endlessly repeating its message and imbuing an organization with an almost intuitive understanding of that mission, is a process that takes years, rather than months. Writing the mission is relatively easy. Communicating it is invariably more difficult and time-consuming.

In embarking upon this process it is worth bearing in mind three broad principles. First, whatever the process of consultation that precedes the formulation of the mission statement and out of which it is built up, senior management will be closely identified with the result. It is essential, therefore, that complete consensus on key issues prevails at senior management level, and moreover, that this consensus is embodied in everything that senior management does in both communicating and promoting the mission. Senior management needs to give overt and public support to the mission and it has to ensure that the message is communicated in a disciplined and *consistent* manner.

Secondly, the mission itself must be kept grounded firmly in reality. Quixotic statements that express a wish, that represent a radical departure from the present, or that entail an enormous leap are doomed to fail. Rather than inspiring and encouraging people, such expressions of hopeless ambition simply serve to create frustration, disillusionment and a sense of helplessness. In such circumstances the mission literally makes no difference; it has no impact on what people do every day and the process is thereby discredited. Always take care, therefore, to subject any mission statement to the 'reality' test.

Thirdly, the statement of mission or values needs to have a clear voice or identity; sanitized, neutral statements usually betray their origins – the committee. This is not to say that developing the mission should not be the work of a group, but what is required is that, once the work has been done, one individual is given the responsibility and authority for writing the mission: that one voice is, as it were, imprinted on it.

Once produced there is always a danger that the mission statement will be seen as something sacrosanct, not to be changed. But casting a mission in concrete is a mistake. Change will be required so as to ensure that the mission does not become outmoded, anachronistic or overtaken by events. In some instances the first attempt may be simply wrong or misguided; change will be essential. A company's mission therefore should be seen as a living thing; as something that guides the organization, providing it with a point of reference, but which requires adaptation and renewal in the light of experience. In pursuing a chosen path, the organization will learn much about the viability of the aim and the obstacles to accomplishing it. The challenge is to feed that learning back into the mission statement, reinforcing it in some areas and adjusting it in others.

Mixed motives. As markets evolve, new segments emerge which often require different channels of distribution, product technology or brand image from those appropriate to the more mature parts of the market. A classic example was the shift of volume watch sales away from jewellers towards mass-merchandisers and drug-store outlets, supported by television brand advertising, in the post-war US market. In chainsaws a 'casual user' segment that demanded a light-weight, low-cost product from discount stores emerged in what had been until the mid-1970s almost exclusively a durability-conscious, professional market. More recently, a growing 'voice plus data' segment has been demanding changes in the installed base of private branch exchanges (PBXs).

These types of market evolution pose dilemmas for established firms: how to exploit the new opportunities without gravely undermining their positions in mature segments of the same market. The Swiss watchmakers did not wish to disenchant their formidable network of jewellers who provided both sales and service. Some chainsaw manufacturers feared diluting their quality-brand image if they produced lightweight, private-label products. The large telecommunications companies resisted the introduction of integrated voice-and-data PBXs which would have rendered much of their installed base obsolete.

These kinds of dilemmas are often termed the problems of 'mixed motives' – the desire to exploit a new segment conflicting with the motive of protecting an existing one. Firms with mixed motives often find themselves stuck in the middle and fare poorly in the face of a focused, single-minded competitor. Their strategies inevitably involve compromises which impede success. Indeed the mixed-motives problem is probably the most important reason why established firms often fail to react aggressively to thwart expansion by a new ENTRANT or smaller existing competitor – even though the ultimate loss of market share and profitability can be catastrophic.

Multinational enterprise (MNE). In the narrow sense MNEs have been with us a long time: some of the earliest emerged in the 1890s with companies like Swift which had established a meat-packing empire right across the globe. Kellogg's and Kraft had expanded their production and marketing networks as far as Australia by 1919.

The term was originally coined simply to refer to the growing number of companies who had established manufacturing, distribution and marketing operations in many national markets to serve local demand across the world, rather than simply exporting or trading goods between them. The early MNEs took their plant technology and marketing formula and basically transplanted it into a domestic economy. There was little co-ordination between the national units, in many cases because of poor communications infrastructure and little need to take account of transnational relationships. Thus the home-country strategy was essentially duplicated to form what is now described as a 'multi-domestic' group. The term MNE, meanwhile, has come to connote a company which comprises an interrelated network of national units with a substantial degree of co-ordination between them. The aim is to pursue, to varying degrees, a GLOBAL STRATEGY which takes into account the interactions between the national markets, possibilities for intra-company trading of components or finished goods, and the presence of MULTI-POINT COMPETITION with other MNEs.

Multi-point competition. Companies that span a diversified product range or numerous geographic markets often meet the same competitor in more than one area. This so-called 'multi-point competition' potentially opens up a panoply of competitive interactions where the response to strategic moves in one market may show up as a counter-move by the competitor in another, indirectly related, marketplace.

The airline industry is a classic case of multi-point competition. British Airways and British Midland, for example, meet each other in a number of markets including the London to Edinburgh and London to Dublin routes. In responding to a competitive move by British Midland in the Edinburgh market, for example, it may pay British Airways to plan its counter-move on the London–Dublin route where British Midland has a weaker position and more limited capacity to react. On the other hand, making this CROSS PARRY would risk retaliation by a third competitor like, for example, Aer Lingus.

In the tyre industry Goodyear reacted to the build-up of Michelin's US market share by attacking it in Europe rather than by direct action in the American market. As the US leader, Goodyear had a great deal to lose by cutting prices in the US while Michelin's strong European cash flows could continue to finance an extended US price war. Instead Goodyear attempted to discipline Michelin by building its share in Michelin's key European market where any price cut would cost Michelin dearly.

Although ultimately a matter of judgement, analysis of multi-point competition suggests that counter-attacking in a second market is likely to be a more favourable option than direct defence; the lower a responder's existing MARKET SHARE in that market, the lower the BARRIERS TO ENTRY around it, and the more significant the source of CASH FLOW it represents to the opponent.

N

Net present value (NPV). An important quantitative tool in investment appraisal, NPV is a summary measure of the value of the future cash flows expected to arise from an investment over its life, net of the cash injections necessary to establish and maintain the activity. These cash flows are 'discounted' to reflect the fact that cash now is worth more than cash in the future because of its interest-earning capacity.

Estimates of the future cash flow of a project embody the associated strategy and as such, depend on market and competitor reaction to it. One of the great dangers of net present value estimates in practice is that, wrongly interpreted, they may give the illusion of accuracy to what is a very uncertain market response. Moreover, if narrowly applied, the NPV estimate can fail to reflect the contribution of an investment to the sustainability of a company's position or the future options which might be opened up by entry into a new market or development of a new competence within the firm. NPV calculations should therefore be seen as a complement to, rather than a substitute for, strategic debate.

Niche. A company may choose to concentrate its activities on a small market segment which is separated from the mainstream by special buyer needs or a unique COST STRUCTURE. The existence of niches opens the way for FOCUS STRATEGIES where a business obtains COMPETITIVE ADVANTAGE by concentrating specifically on a small part of the market.

Focusing on a niche has a number of possible advantages. RIVALRY may be less severe because the mainstream competitors ignore the niche, regard it as too 'unimportant', or wish to avoid the additional COSTS OF COMPLEXITY in serving it. By focusing on a specific set of customers the firm's mission is clear and easy to communicate. It can offload all costs which are not necessary to serve its niche. Finally, by concentrating on a limited set of buyers a competitor is likely to develop special skills, knowledge and brand preference which act as BARRIERS TO MOBILITY, offering protection against the advance of rivals who discover the niche.

NPV.   *See* NET PRESENT VALUE.

O

Objective. Companies must provide a yardstick, or dimension of performance, against which progress in achieving a stated goal or level of performance can be measured. Objectives deal in shorter terms (typically one year) than GOALS (typically five years or more). But they are of longer duration than targets, which usually relate to quarter- or half-yearly periods. Objectives tend to be more specific, therefore, than goals but less specific than targets. Objectives translate overall corporate goals into more narrowly defined and therefore more accessible ends. But from the point of view of developing effective strategies it is more important to pay attention to the quality of the objectives than to the distinction between goals, objectives and targets. What therefore constitutes 'good' objectives? There are five criteria that they should all meet; objectives should be:

1 precise – vague and loosely formulated objectives will not provide a reliable guide to action;
2 measurable – quantifiable objectives are more easily measured than qualitative ones, but both types need to be measured using indices that people find both intelligible and acceptable;
3 feasible – pursuing quixotic objectives may be fun but ultimately ends in disappointment. Feasability or achievability is therefore essential and should be measured;
4 consistent – typically an organization will pursue more than one objective, although pursuing too many at once dilutes effort; care must be taken therefore to ensure that the complete set of objectives, which should rarely exceed more than five at any one time, is internally consistent and contains no pairs of objectives that are mutually exclusive. Reconciling conflicts between objectives is the job of management – not that of the staff who are expected to achieve them;
5 suitable – good objectives spring from a thorough under-

standing of how your industry operates and which factors are critical to achieving competitive success. Objectives that are precise, measurable, consistent and feasible will be of no value if they do not provide the appropriate keys to competitive success.

But beyond these criteria by far the most important thing is to ensure that commitment to the objectives is shared throughout the firm. This entails communicating the objectives, explaining clearly why they make sense and how their realization will enhance both corporate success and the individual fruits of that success. Ideally, the process of defining and communicating objectives should therefore challenge staff to achieve levels of performance which they had hitherto considered to be beyond reach.

Obsolescence. An activity that is no longer practised, a process that ceases to be employed or a product that is discarded are all said to be obsolete; what has rendered them so is the process of change. Traditionally understood, this process resulted in the steady and gradual erosion of a product's utility until it eventually fell into disuse. Biologists, for example, see obsolescence as the gradual disappearance or atrophy of an organ as it ceases to be used. But the metaphors of biology need revision in the context of strategy. Rapid rates of change, particularly TECHNOLOGICAL CHANGE, have dramatically accelerated rates of obsolescence. Many investment decisions in plant and equipment that could be justified in terms of five to ten years' life-expectancy – or more – now have to earn an adequate return far more quickly. Shortening PRODUCT LIFE CYCLES, and the more rapid move from one version or generation of a product to another, places buyers in the situation in which their purchases (for example, computers) rapidly become obsolete. For some buyers the costs of obsolescence take the form of continuing investment in new versions of a product so as to maintain their competitive positions. Where buyers can derive all the benefit they require from the first version of a product the costs of obsolescence will be correspondingly lower. Thus analysing rates of change and their impact upon the life-expectancy of a product or service, constitutes an important part of strategy. Consideration must be given to the extent to which a firm is vulnerable to a new product or process that will eliminate the need for its own product, thereby rendering it obsolete. Unlike much biological change, strategic and technological change now occur with ever increasing speed. Strategy must therefore take full account of both the manner and speed of the process of obsolescence and avoid committing to heavy fixed costs or inflexible assets which, although attuned to a particular product or technology, are exposed to obsolescence.

Oligopoly. An industry in which a few firms, around four to eight, account for the bulk of total sales in the market is commonly known as an 'oligopoly', a term borrowed from economics. But this definition loses a great deal of the managerial usefulness of such a concept. The key point is that an oligopoly is a market where the decisions of individual firms reflect their mutual interdependence: that the profitability of a large new plant will depend on whether another firm is bringing a similar plant on-stream at the same time, a clear indicator of a likely price-war as both scramble to fill their new capacity; that the impact on an increase in advertising will depend on whether one or two key competitors are also planning a blitz of the TV screens; that the impact of a price cut depends on whether one or two direct competitors choose to match it or hold their prices down. In a market with hundreds of small competitors, by contrast, the impact on the whole market of decisions by one firm is generally so insignificant that others do not need to take it into account in formulating their own strategy unless it is part of a bandwagon where all firms are moving in a particular direction.

The best-known cases are those where whole national or even international markets exhibit oligopolistic behaviour, such as detergents, disposable nappies or earth-moving equipment. Oligopolies can exist on a much smaller scale: the set of four petrol stations in a town or the three airlines serving the same pair of cities may act as a 'local oligopoly'.

Acting within an oligopoly can mean that strategic flexibility is reduced. In particular, price is often a blunt and ineffective competitive weapon in an oligopolistic environment where action and reaction can lead to a KINKED DEMAND CURVE. As a result, non-price forms of competition such as advertising or frequent launch of new products tend to be more common.

Successful strategy in an oligopoly depends critically on anticipating competitors' actions and reactions and adjusting one's own strategy to take these into account. Here COMPETITOR ANALYSIS, an appreciation of the 'gaming' aspects of a market such as the PRISONER'S DILEMMA, and the ability to influence competitors' behaviour successfully by signalling an intent to respond or retaliate come to the fore. There is a premium on finding strategies which go around the competitors rather than attacking them head-on and on devising strategic initiatives to which they will find it difficult to respond because of their own BARRIERS TO MOBILITY.

Operating leverage. The ratio of fixed costs to total costs. High operating LEVERAGE is an important constraint on making short- to medium-term changes to strategy. A high ratio of fixed costs to total costs means that a company's profits are highly sensitive to capacity utilization. Thus markets supplied by firms with high operating leverage are prone to price cutting and high RIVALRY during cyclical downturns. Increased operating leverage is often one of the indirect costs incurred in the quest for ECONOMIES OF SCALE and DIFFERENTIATION, reflecting heavy capital investment in plant or the form of high fixed-cost marketing expenditures and distribution networks. Recognition of the dangers of high operating leverage for strategic flexibility in an uncertain environment can focus attention on finding sources of advantage which are less dependent on high fixed costs and hence more flexible as conditions change. Likewise, the desirability of reducing operating leverage increases the attractiveness of subcontracting.

Operations strategy. The strategist must specify how a firm's overall strategy will be accomplished at the level of an operational function; for example, production. That is, given a firm's chosen strategy what specific changes are required at the operational level so as to ensure that the overall strategy is effective? Traditionally, 'operations' has been seen as little more than a 'productivity machine' (that is, how can we squeeze more productivity out of our existing physical and human resources?), or as a route to improving financial performance (how can we cut operating costs while increasing revenue?). But what this approach ignores is the scope that exists to use operations, and the way in which operations are conducted, as a competitive weapon. To see in their workings potential sources of COMPETITIVE ADVANTAGE rather than simply a set of assets to be 'sweated', or worked harder. Operations are therefore, to paraphrase an observation made by Professor Wickham Skinner in the early 1970s, either a competitive weapon or a millstone; the latter because operations have traditionally figured little in the strategic equation, with the result that managers responsible for operations have been left to make decisions or devise operations policies that may be inconsistent with the core assumptions upon which a firm's strategy is based.

But to ignore operations is to forfeit an opportunity to use this area of the business as a base on which to build real competitive advantage. Moreover, operations decisions typically have enduring consequences for the firm which cannot be easily undone; for example, decisions relating to the choice of plant and equipment, the location of manufacturing facilities, the configuration of these facilities, technology, inventory management, automation, delivery capability and control systems. Structural issues, far from being peripheral to strategy, lie at its heart since the choices that are made here, and the way in which these choices do – or do not – reinforce each other, will exert a profound influence upon the firm's success in achieving its chosen goals.

Thus the intersection of operations strategy and strategies devised in other functional areas, like marketing, requires careful analysis so as to ensure that decisions made in one area are not incompatible with those made in another. In developing strategy it is important therefore to ask: 'is there a key operating task on which our competitive success depends or can we identify one operations element within the business on which we can build a sustainable competitive advantage? – for example, quality, delivery time, new product development, cost reduction or parts elimination.' Operations should, in other words, be seen as a potential competitive and strategic resource rather than as a clutch of often neglected secondary activities; to take the latter view is to risk converting operations from a source of advantage into a millstone.

Organic growth. In pursuing growth, whether it is measured in terms of sales, profitability or market share, firms face a number of alternative routes: ACQUISITIONS, JOINT VENTURES or ALLIANCES, DIVERSIFICATION or INTEGRATION. Much strategy revolves around appraising the merits – or otherwise – of these very different routes to growth. But there is another increasingly fashionable route: that of organic or internal growth. That is, growth that springs directly out of, and is supported by, the firm's current activities. For example, the design company that achieves a 20 per cent annual increase in sales, for three years running, by means of steadily expanding its client base, or by taking on more and preferably larger repeat assignments from its existing clients, has achieved organic, internally generated growth.

But sustaining high – say 20 per cent or more – rates of profitable organic growth is notoriously difficult to achieve, for a variety of reasons, including resource limitations like physical plant, space, staff and, particularly for smaller companies, management time. Growth requires investment, usually at the expense of profitability – at least in the shorter term; a conspicuous feature of organic growth in small- to medium-sized companies is a dramatic increase in size, as measured by turnover, accompanied by an equally dramatic decrease in profitability. A third key problem is that of time: whereas an acquisition can have a strikingly quick effect upon a company, organic growth is, by its very nature, a much slower process.

The principal appeal of internal, organic growth is that it is relatively controllable; it builds upon the firm's existing skills and can be achieved without loss of competitive focus. Moreover, as a route to growth it harmonizes with an organization's existing CORPORATE CULTURE, building upon it rather than threatening it in the way that other routes to growth (such as acquisitions) frequently do. In other words, the cultural 'costs' are fewer, at least until such time as the organization reaches the size at which it has, in a sense, outgrown its original, founding culture. Growth, even where it is achieved organically, places immense strains upon an organization as the traditional beliefs and assumptions that held the business together in the early years start to come under pressure. For example, as new staff join to match the demands of growth so the organization's core beliefs may no longer be either self-evident or necessarily valid, in the way that they were at the outset.

In pursuing a strategy of organic growth it is essential to be clear about (a) the precise ways in which such growth will be achieved (will it, for example, come at the expense of your competitors, and if so, how will you accomplish this?); (b) the increasing difficulty of sustaining adequate rates of growth as the firm grows; and (c) as in all strategy, what exactly are we trying to achieve, maximum revenue growth or profitability — often two very different things?

Organization structure. The internal design of an organization comprises a number of elements such as:

- the definition and allocation of specific tasks – 'who does what?'
- the grouping of similar tasks into functional departments – for example, marketing;
- the creation of systems that facilitate the co-ordination of activities between and within departments;

- the allocation of responsibility within a department – for example, along hierarchical lines; and
- the distribution of formal authority across the organization.

Having defined a structure in these terms one question immediately arises: what determines this structure? The classic answer, provided by Alfred Chandler of Harvard Business School, is that strategy determines structure, and moreover, achieving a good FIT between strategy and structure is crucial in determining a firm's success.

Let's deal with the first half of Chandler's thesis. A firm's growth strategy shapes its structure and, as the firm expands, for example by way of geographical dispersal, so its structure will change. But, as Chandler noted, structural change takes place more slowly than strategic change and, therefore, changes to an organization's structure lag behind changes of strategic direction.

Since its publication in *Strategy and structure; Chapters in the history of the industrial enterprise* (MIT Press, 1962), Chandler's thesis has been subjected to extensive empirical testing, principally in terms of the question: do diversification strategies result in the multidivisional structure? The answer is broadly 'yes': the diversification surges of the 1960s and 1970s, in the US and in Europe, have been accompanied by an increased incidence of firms organized on a multidivisional basis. But there is an additional factor of key significance: competition. That is, under conditions of intense competition, strategy – in the form of diversification – does shape structure; but where competition is weak, as for example under conditions of monopoly, then strategic re-direction is less likely to be accompanied by structural reorganization. The conclusion to be drawn therefore is this: structure follows strategy where structure makes a competitive difference. Moreover, it is quite clear that in competitive circumstances those firms that achieve an early and effective fit or match between their strategy and structure do gain a competitive advantage – at least temporarily, until such time as competitors follow suit and catch up.

Under some conditions, therefore, structural change has

been shown to accompany strategic change and structure itself is clearly an important variable in determining a firm's overall performance. However, it is but one of a number of variables influencing performance. Other key issues are: the prevailing conditions of the market in which the firm operates – for example, is the market growing and does it enable the firm to make full use of its basic strengths?; the systems by which the firm is managed; the processes that exist for resolving conflict; and, not least, the appropriateness of the firm's culture to its strategy.

From the strategic point of view there is therefore an essential point to bear in mind. Do not assume that if, having formulated and agreed your strategy, you reorganize and adapt the organization's structure, the work of strategy is complete. It has only just begun. All too often firms make the mistake of thinking that success lies in changing the way in which the business is organized; moving people around, changing reporting relationships, redefining responsibilities. Five reorganizations later, little may have been accomplished, and that usually at the expense of considerable wear and tear.

Finally, a word of caution: structure has been defined in terms of the observable, internal design of the organization. As such, structure has been presented as something that is formal, explicit, governed by clear rules, relatively malleable, fundamentally stable; a system embodying clear rights and obligations, rules and procedures. But every organization has another structure; one that is informal and, to a large extent, invisible. This structure has to do with the currently accepted practices and ways of doing things or of getting things done; temporary alliances and networks; debts and obligations; tacit norms and expectations that govern behaviour. More succinctly, the formal structure describes how things *should* work; the informal structure reflects how things actually work in practice.

When embarking upon your next reorganization take care, therefore, to ensure two things: that the structural change is not completely at odds with the way in which the informal structure works; and that structural change is not, along with strategy, the only item on your implementation agenda.

P

Payback. One method for evaluating and choosing between investment opportunities is based on the time taken for the initial capital outlay to be recovered. The payback method addresses the question 'how long will it be before the proposed project pays for itself?' To obtain the answer, the future annual cash flows expected from the project are added together until they equal the original investment. The method is simple, easy to use and intelligible to non-specialists. Indeed, after a period in which its use declined, the payback method is currently enjoying something of a renaissance, being frequently used in conjuction with other appraisal techniques, such as discounted cash flow.

However, it has a number of serious drawbacks. First, it accords equal weight to each cash flow – irrespective of the year in which it occurs – and it completely ignores all cash flows occurring after the payback period; but the speed of payment and total project profitability are not necessarily the same thing. Second, the choice of cut-off period – deciding that project A must pay for itself in, say, five years – is often an arbitrary process, and the use of standard payback targets within a firm fails to take account of the distinctive nature of different investment proposals. But perhaps most damagingly, the simple version of this method ignores the fact that the value of money changes over time, and that income, in the form of cash flow, received today is more valuable than that occurring in say two years' time. Recognizing this, some companies calculate payback after they have discounted projected cash flows. But again, the cut-off period may be a matter of guesswork and, importantly, cash flows after the period are still ignored. The best solution to the problem is to use the NET PRESENT VALUE method of evaluating all investment proposals.

PIMS. Profit impact of marketing strategies. This is an important database designed to link the performance of different businesses with measures of their underlying strategies (such as MARKET SHARE, advertising and R&D expenditure, quality, breadth of product line, and vertical INTEGRATION) and the characteristics of their markets (such as total size, CONCENTRATION RATIO, and growth).

One of the most important distinguishing features of PIMS is the fact that the data is held at the level of a STRATEGIC BUSINESS UNIT (a division, product line or profit centre), rather than at the company level. Many interesting results have come from analysis of PIMS, including estimates of the value of shares in different competitive environments and the impact of CAPITAL INTENSITY and vertical integration on long-run profitability.

Portfolio management. The DIVERSIFICATION of a company across a portfolio of different businesses raises important questions for the management about the interrelationships between them. Early strategic frameworks dealing with this portfolio-management task emphasized the re-allocation of cash between the businesses. Models like the GROWTH–SHARE MATRIX viewed the portfolio as a means of achieving cash balance between profitable but low-growth businesses generating more cash than they required (CASH COWS) and businesses experiencing the heavy cash demands of their growth phase who could benefit from being part of a cash-rich corporate group.

The increasing sophistication of external capital markets, however, questions the role of the portfolio as an internal money market. Would not the individual businesses be better off without the weight of corporate overhead, exchanging cash with shareholders and financial institutions in the form of dividends, share re-purchases, new issues and borrowings? With an efficient capital market the CORPORATE VALUE-ADDED as a bank seems insufficient to justify its existence.

In response many companies have re-evaluated their portfolios, divesting themselves of those businesses not closely related to their core activities (*see* DIVESTMENT). The emphasis of portfolio management has shifted towards exploiting the benefits of transferring skills between the businesses, or organizing so as to reap ECONOMIES OF SCOPE by sharing distribution channels, salesforces, basic R&D or manufacturing facilities. Those with unrelated portfolios have generally moved to create 'common control systems and management processes in pursuit of corporate value-added. For example, they have instituted tight financial disciplines and cost-rationalization mechanisms driven from a small centre which manages 'through the numbers' to increase the performance of a portfolio of mature businesses.

The view of individual businesses as channels through which to exploit the distinctive COMPETENCES of the firm, rather than sources and uses of cash, now dominates port-folio management. Thus the Dutch electronics giant Philips, for example, has sought to restructure its portfolio so that each business draws on its basic strength in electronic-component technologies, deploying this in professional systems, consumer electronics, lighting and medical systems. Honda has built a portfolio around its strengths in small petrol engines with a portfolio of businesses including motor-bikes, snow blowers, generators, lawnmowers, and small construction and landscaping equipment. Consistency, either in terms of related business activities or common management and financial-control processes, is now the byword of portfolio management.

Price leadership. A firm that takes the initiative in making price changes which others then follow is pursuing a price-leadership strategy. The conditions under which such strategies are pursued fall into three main categories. In markets where there is a single large firm whose actions will materially affect market prices, the firm is effectively acting as a monopolist. Under these conditions the price set by the dominant firm is taken, by the competitive fringe, to represent the market price. The second category, sometimes referred to as barometric price leadership, occurs when the identity of the price leader changes frequently. The competitors' response to a price initiative will typically be less rapid and will be determined not so much by the identity of the price leader as by an assessment of the extent to which the price initiative reflects a real change in the market or in costs. Thirdly, where there are relatively few firms enjoying similar market shares, operating with comparable costs and producing slightly differentiated products, the initiative of a price leader is more likely to be accepted, this acceptance representing a form of covert 'collusion'.

The efficacy of a price-leadership strategy in improving a firm's market position and profitability depends in large part upon the speed with which competitors follow suit. Judging correctly the length of the lag between raising prices and the others matching this is critical. Until such time as the gap is closed other firms may gain at the price leader's expense as consumers switch into the less expensive product. This gain will be eliminated if the firm that took the price initiative is forced to revert to the original price. Thus firms will often choose to be followers rather than leaders in setting prices. In strategic terms the success of a price-leadership strategy depends crucially upon firms having a shared, mutual understanding – and acceptance – of the rules of the competitive game and the conditions under which the industry is operating.

Prisoner's dilemma. A concept drawn from GAME THEORY presents the following dilemma. Two prisoners, arrested after a bank robbery, are kept in isolation from each other and interrogated. Obtaining a conviction requires at least one confession. If neither prisoner confesses, both will go free. If both confess, both will receive the statutory ten-year gaol sentence. Each prisoner is advised that if he alone confesses he alone will go free and the other will receive a heavier – twenty-year – sentence. Since the prisoners cannot communicate they cannot agree upon the best strategy; that is, that neither should confess and both can go free.

Left alone each is faced with a dilemma: to confess – and get the ten-year sentence, or go free if the other does not confess; or not to confess – and go free if the other does not confess or, if he *is* betrayed by his fellow prisoner, to get the heavier, twenty-year sentence. Since they can neither communicate nor rely upon the loyalty of the other not to confess, the most likely outcome is that they will both choose the second strategy, to confess, so that they each receive a ten-year sentence.

In strategic terms firms that are mutually dependent, and therefore strongly affected by each other's actions, face much the same dilemma. For example: should a firm pursue a high-price strategy that will, if followed by competing firms, enhance the profitability of all players; or should it cut prices and thereby risk sparking off a damaging price war? The firm is like the prisoner. If all firms co-operate, each can make reasonable profits; if one breaks ranks – and others do not retaliate – it will reap the benefits in the form of higher profits; but if, as is likely, competitors do retaliate then everyone is likely to be worse off. But unlike the two prisoners, firms can communicate, signal their intentions and, over a period, develop informed expectations about the likely behaviour of others.

Profit centre. An identifiable, discrete unit or part of a firm may be made responsible for its own costs, revenues and therefore profit. Managers of such units are said to have profit and loss (P&L) responsibility, being free – in principle – to make key decisions relating to price, product positioning, output and so on; the underlying premise being that such managers have control over both costs and revenue. But therein lies the difficulty. Policies within the firm, for example those relating to the price at which goods or services are traded internally or to the criteria determining the allocation of fixed, central costs, may leave a profit-centre manager with less than complete control over key elements that go to make up his unit's profit or loss.

Genuine profit centres increase visibility within an organization; they provide an effective control device and serve as a way of focusing managerial effort. But in situations in which the performance of a profit centre is compromised by

the policies or performance of other units within the organization, then the use of this device may serve as a recipe for
internal conflict and dispute, rather than as a spur to
improved performance and profitability. In some instances,
the manipulation of a profit centre's performance is deliberate. For example, profit centres are widely used in multinational corporations for which they provide an opportunity,
using TRANSFER PRICES, to depress the profitability of those
subsidiaries operating in high corporate-tax environments.
But very often, quasi-profit centres emerge by default rather
than by design, leaving managers notionally responsible for
profit without full control of revenues or, more usually, costs.

Purchasing strategy. All activities associated with the acquisition
of resources, materials, equipment and other items required
by a firm in order to carry out its business and meet its
long-term supply needs come under the rubric of purchasing
or procurement. Narrowly defined, purchasing relates solely
to the selection of suppliers, and the placing and chasing of
orders. But this conception obscures the strategic significance
of purchasing – a significance that has historically been
ignored.

A firm's total purchases will have a major impact upon its
overall cost position and it is important, therefore, to see
purchasing as a strategic resource, rather than as a neutral,
strictly functional exercise. Failure to do this may result in
unexpected and costly anomalies occurring. To illustrate:
what was Chrysler's largest single purchase from a single
supplier? Not steel, not automotive parts, but Blue Cross
health insurance: a 'product' bought by a relatively lowly
personnel manager. Upon discovery of this Chrysler instituted a new purchasing policy in respect of health insurance,
thereby cutting the bill dramatically. This episode, which is
not apocryphal, neatly illustrates the ease with which significant purchasing decisions can fall from view.

In devising an effective purchasing strategy the following
elements are critical: evaluation and selection of suppliers in
terms of quality, price, reliability and delivery time; length of

supply contract; centralized versus decentralized buying; relations with suppliers – are they managed in a competitive or a co-operative manner? More specifically, purchasing strategies should address the question of how best to reduce the total costs of all purchased inputs; for example, by using many suppliers, thereby fostering competition, while still remaining an important customer to any one supplier; by varying the volume of purchases from a single supplier; by helping the supplier to cut his own costs, for example by introducing improved order-handling processes; and according status to the purchasing function commensurate with its strategic importance within a company. The usual framework for systematically thinking through these issues is the VALUE CHAIN which throws into sharp relief the strategic significance of purchasing or procurement. Purchasing plays a part in almost every activity in which the firm engages, it has a decisive impact upon an organization's overall cost position and therefore requires effective strategic management.

Q

Quality circle (QC). Mention quality circles and people immediately think of Japan, the country in which they originated and initially flourished. Yet the origin of quality circles owes as much to the US as to Japan. Essentially, QCs evolved out of three related developments. First, the introductuion – spearheaded by the American quality-control expert, Dr W. E. Demming – of statistical quality control (SQC) techniques into Japanese industry. From its inception at the Bell Laboratories in the 1930s, SQC was developed as a rigorous, scientific method of analysing both the quality and productivity that could be expected from a given production process and, on the basis of this estimate, building measurement systems to monitor discrepancies between actual and target (for example, zero-defect) performance levels.

The second thrust was provided by another American, Dr T. M. Juran, who, during a visit to Japan in 1954, argued strongly for the assumption of responsibility for quality by the entire workforce, rather than pigeon-holing quality control in a separate department. The final link in the chain was provided by Dr K. Ishikawa who promoted the idea of book-reading circles in which Japanese managers read about and discussed quality control related literature. As these groups became more concerned with doing, with solving problems rather than simply reading about them, so QCs emerged. It was not until the early 1970s that the concept was transplanted back into the US under the auspices of a team from the Lockheed Missiles and Space Company of California that visited Japan in 1973 to investigate the concept. They found it appealing, and launched a programme within Lockheed.

Typically, QCs now comprise an average of eight to ten voluntary members who meet regularly, often weekly, during company time to identify, analyse and resolve a range of work-related problems, of which quality control *per se* is but one. Other topics falling within the remit of QCs often include issues relating to staff communications, staff morale, personal development needs, training, and quality of working life more generally. Most commonly, QC meetings are chaired by a group leader (often – but not necessarily – a first-line supervisor) whose role is principally one of co-ordination rather than control. Many groups, particularly during the initial stages, work with facilitators, whose task it is to provide training, guidance and encouragement while the group members learn how to work with each other, to identify problems and allocate responsibility for their further analysis and investigation.

The apparent simplicity of QCs is, however, deceptive. To be successful, they require careful planning and management. More specifically, the chances of success will be improved in circumstances where:

- management realizes the legitimate role that workers have to play in decision-making, particularly as it relates to issues and problems within their own work area;
- management itself receives prior training in both the techniques of QCs and the principles underlying them;
- groups themselves receive continuous training and guidance, often from a facilitator;
- inter-group co-ordination is carefully handled, in some instances by a designated company co-ordinator;
- expectations are not unduly raised and the initial pace of progress, which is often painfully slow, is not forced;
- suggestions emanating from QCs are either acted upon quickly, or useful feedback is provided indicating precisely why a suggestion cannot be taken up;
- the groups are used as a way of developing individuals, rather than simply as problem-solving, task-orientated groups.

Finally, it must be remembered that the origin of QCs is in statistical control and the principles it embodies of producing accurate and reliable feedback. Where groups receive vague or ambiguous feedback, their effectiveness will be blunted. Indeed, as Peter Drucker has noted: 'most US QCs of the last 20 years have failed despite great enthusiasm, especially on the part of workers. The reason? They were established without SQC, that is, rigorous and reliable feedback' (*HBR*, 3 (May–June 1990), p. 96).

Question mark. Businesses occupying the upper right quadrant of the BOSTON CONSULTING GROUP'S GROWTH–SHARE MATRIX are typically found in high-growth markets. Such businesses are characterized by relatively low market share and poor cash generation, combined with high cash needs to finance growth. In strategic terms there are three ways of dealing with question-mark businesses: invest, often heavily, in an effort to convert the question mark into a STAR and, eventually, a CASH COW; manage the business in such a way that it generates the maximum possible cash before becoming a 'dog'; and thirdly, divest it. In ACQUISITION terms question marks may make good targets, provided the resources and commitment exist to make them stars.

R

Regression analysis. Regression has been widely used in an attempt to estimate inputs to strategy such as the price ELASTICITY of demand for a product or the slope of an EXPERIENCE CURVE. It amounts to estimating the 'line of best fit' between a scatter of observations. Mathematically, it finds a line which minimizes the sum of squared deviations between the actual observations on for example, costs, prices or volumes, and what would be predicted by the line.

Many analysts feel more comfortable drawing a scatter diagram and plotting the line of best fit by eye, rather than using regression. While scoring high on simplicity, this plotting technique can lead to identifying spurious relationships and consequently making incorrect decisions. Take, for example, a set of data on unit costs which suggests an experience curve as operatives learn by repetition. Running a regression on the same data, but taking into account data on changes in technology which are also occurring, may show that it was really technological improvement which was improving costs and that experience and learning were relatively unimportant. This is because multiple regression can estimate the impact of more than one factor simultaneously. This amounts to drawing lines of best fit in many dimensions, so that it can estimate the effect of price changes in sales, for example, taking into account the fact that advertising is having an effect at the same time.

Regression is therefore a powerful tool for trying to separate the impact of different causes and for testing the sensitivity of sales, profit or costs to specific business decisions in the messy real world which cannot be plotted on a simple graph. It also quantifies the size of the impact (for example, costs fall by 15 per cent when scale doubles) as well as how good the fit is (R^2), and how reliable is the result about a specific relationship ('t' statistic). Despite all of these advantages, however, the regression results must pass the ultimate tests of 'reasonableness' and 'common sense' which are frequently forgotten in the enthusiasm for 'hard numbers'. Equally, it is important to bear in mind that if you put garbage in you will only get neatly processed garbage out.

Replacement demand. Typically, rapid growth in an industry begins to tail off once the market has been penetrated fully, and very little scope remains for increasing the customer base by adding more first-time buyers (*see* MARKET SATURATION). From this point, the subsequent growth rate is determined by the appetite of repeat buyers to replace their original purchase with a new one. In the case of many consumer durables, such as washing machines or vacuum cleaners, once saturation is reached, demand may decline more rapidly than the growth in replacement demand.

Replacement demand can be stimulated by the rapid introduction of new models offering novel features; by technological or design developments that render obsolete earlier purchases; or through reductions in the cost of new versions of the product relative to its predecessors. For example, buying a new car may have as much to do with the availability of new models as with the costs of continuing to run the current but aging one. In Japan, the process of stimulating replacement demand has been taken a significant step further. Toyota's Japanese customers can now choose the individual specifications for their new car (out of thousands of possibilities), and have that car delivered within a week. What could be a more powerful stimulus to replacement demand than giving the customer the option of specifying his own car, whenever he likes?

Re-positioning. Firms may need to shift their position with respect to the FIVE FORCES: buyer and supplier power, the threats of entrants and substitutes, and competitors. In practice, companies are re-positioning themselves continuously by minor adjustments relative to these forces. Over time, these incremental moves may cumulate into a major re-positioning through the process of EMERGENT STRATEGY.

In other cases, businesses may undertake a planned re-positioning in response to significant changes in their market environment. This may involve a shift in the market segments (*see* SEGMENTATION) on which they FOCUS, their CHANNEL STRATEGY (for example, from the private-label to the branded sector), their COST STRUCTURE, MARKET SHARE targets, or quality levels.

The concept of positioning has long played an important role in strategy as a way of defining the relationship between a firm and its market. Some have suggested, however, that an excessive concern can blind a firm to the fact that even the best positioning in a market does not guarantee eternal success. Even very favourably positioned companies need to devote attention to maintaining flexibility – avoiding rigid structures and dogma which will act as a yoke, creating BARRIERS TO MOBILITY when the market changes. This requires the firm to be continually improving its core COMPETENCES – basic capabilities in technology, marketing, or distribution on which tomorrow's positioning can draw.

Responsibility accounting. A large and increasing proportion of the costs incurred by a business, including the extra costs associated with differentiating particular products or services, are ending up as 'overhead' in the accounting system. This overhead is then often allocated on a rather arbitrary basis like direct labour hours. Such trends mean that the relationship between activities and costs is becoming opaque in many companies, and that managers responsible for the profit line are lumbered with a rising proportion of costs for which they do not have direct responsibility. Yet fundamental to strategy is the ability to add those costs which will be more than compensated for by higher customer value through DIFFERENTIATION, and to eliminate costs which add little or nothing to buyer satisfaction to gain COST ADVANTAGE. A clear link between costs and activities, and direct management responsibility for the costs of each activity is therefore crucial.

Responsibility accounting is a tenet of system design which

seeks to trace all costs back to the activity and associated decision-maker who were responsible for incurring them. Such systems are often complex. In the case of the cost penalty in processing a rush order, for example, they would need to allocate this cost back to the sales department that initiated it. Only with this information can proper strategic decisions on pricing and service be made to ensure that the extra VALUE CAPTURE available through differentiated service takes place.

See COST CENTRE.

Retaliation. An inward-looking approach to mission and strategy – 'what we want to do' – often pays scant attention to the likely retaliation by competitors. Yet if we add our target of ten per cent growth to last year's budget to get next year's, in a market that is growing only three per cent, the implication is that the competitors are ceding MARKET SHARE if we succeed. Can they be expected to do so without some reaction, such as price erosion in the market, or higher advertising, or a direct attack on our key customers?

The nature of the retaliation we might expect should have an important role in determining the risks and rewards of different strategic moves, as well as in anticipating that retaliation by moving early to neutralize it. Retaliation depends on whether the competitor notices the impact of your moves, much more likely in a concentrated market (*see* CONCENTRATION RATIO). It is also a function of the competitors' ability and willingness to take action. What constraints do their ORGANIZATION STRUCTURE and CORPORATE CULTURE place on moving quickly to respond. Improved prediction of likely retaliation is a major benefit of COMPETITOR ANALYSIS.

In environments of MULTI-POINT COMPETITION the issue of retaliation is complicated. A move in one market may result in retaliation in another where the penalties are more severe. Thus companies seeking to expand internationally can face costly retaliation against them in their home market by a foreign competitor (sometimes known as a CROSS PARRY).

Retaliation is also a critical aspect of dealing with the

threat of ENTRANTS. Companies are often slow to fight back against new entrants which are perceived as small and unimportant. But once a new competitor develops a solid foothold, even if small, preventing its further expansion may prove difficult. Even more importantly, the success of one entrant often signals to others that entry is possible, risking a wave of new competitors, or attracting the interest of larger firms seeking diversification.

Return. There are a variety of different ways of quantifying returns: return on sales (ROS), return on net assets (RONA), return on capital employed (ROCE), return on investment or equity (ROI or ROE), and CASH FLOW. Each has its own role as a tool of strategic analysis.

ROS is useful in measuring the amount of value created by the business for each pound received from sales. Much strategy revolves around attempts to increase the value created (by DIFFERENTIATION), to set a price premium to reflect the worth of the product (VALUE CAPTURE), or to gain COST ADVANTAGE while maintaining value in the customers' eyes, and hence improve the ROS. Return on sales, however, is not an end in itself. Many businesses have run into trouble through fruitless forays into differentiation which cost money, but generated little value for the customer. Ignoring the market, their attempts to drive up ROS actually reduced it.

Strategists also make extensive use of the return on net assets (RONA, or its counterpart ROCE) as a basic measure of the profit the assets are generating, be it from high ROS or high asset utilization. By ignoring the impact of GEARING (which shows up in ROI), it provides a guide as to the relative operating performance of competitors. All of these measures, however, are open to accounting distortions created by different reporting conventions. Cash flow and its cousin NET PRESENT VALUE thus play an important role in deciding whether the cash put behind a strategy will ever again see the light of day, not to mention with a premium.

Risk analysis. The weighing up of alternative strategies is more an art than a science. Nonetheless, there are a number of techniques which can be marshalled to structure the task and – it is hoped – improve the result. SENSITIVITY ANALYSIS tests the robustness of a strategy to changes in the underlying assumptions about the market, speed of execution by the business, RETALIATION from competitors and so on. Strategies will be more responsive to changes in assumptions the more they involve high OPERATING LEVERAGE and high GEARING. SCENARIO PLANNING can be useful in deciding under what environmental assumptions to test the strategy.

More generally, it is important in assessing strategic risk to develop a clear understanding of how transportable the strategy is into a different market environment. Since the success of strategies depends importantly on the FIT with their market segments (*see* SEGMENTATION), successful NICHE strategies often fail when projected into the mainstream. Strategic approaches embodied in the organizational structure, culture, and decision-making processes, which work well in one market may be a route to failure when carried into a diversification, acquisition or other changing competitive situation. What is a low-risk strategy in one context, therefore, may be highly risky in another.

Rivalry. Though it is often blamed as the cause of low profitability in a business, rivalry is only one of the FIVE FORCES which can exert profit squeeze, and in many respects it is a symptom of BUYER and SUPPLIER POWER, and the threats of ENTRANTS and SUBSTITUTION which impact upon it.

The intensity of rivalry also reflects the number, balance and objectives of competitors relative to demand and its rate of growth. The higher the *concentration* of industry sales among a few players, the more likely it is that they will recognize the ruinous nature of intense competition on the profitability of the whole group. On the other hand, slow growth or declining demand, high fixed costs, lack of DIFFERENTIATION, and low SWITCHING COSTS (buyers suffering little penalty for being fickle) will all tend to encourage rivalry. Similarly, rivalry tends to be higher when competitors have diverse goals and face different pressures from their other operations (a particular problem when competing in markets with many foreign players or in those with firms who have diversified from other industries).

Industries where capacity has to be added in large lumps (relative to the size of the market) also tend to suffer higher rivalry. When new capacity is added the competitor will rapidly strive for volume to fill it. If a large shift in existing market share is required to do so, the market will be severely disrupted each time a new facility comes on stream. Frequent capacity addition or renewal, therefore, can lead to almost chronic price warfare.

Some strategies assume, either implicitly or explicitly, that long-run market share will be gained by forcing smaller competitors to exit. The idea of coming to 'dominate a FRAGMENTED INDUSTRY' is often advanced. If one or more competitors pursuing this goal have underestimated the BARRIERS TO EXIT competitors face, the industry is likely to end up with excess capacity for an extended period with consequent high rivalry as competitors struggle to improve their *capacity utilization*. This is aggravated if the business in question is considered by many players to be the core of their portfolio, hence a WALLED CITY which they will defend 'at all costs'.

Businesses that have built a COMPETITIVE ADVANTAGE will always be better off in dealing with rivalry than marginal players. The impact of rivalry can also be reduced by improved market segmentation, differentiation, and building switching costs around buyers as well as minimizing the size of capacity increments, thus reducing the risk of costly RETALIATION.

See also MARKET SHARE.

Rules of the game. In chess the pieces have different values and you win by launching a targeted attack on your competitor's position; chess is a game of profitability and positioning. In the game of 'go', all pieces are of equal value and the game is won by surrounding your opponent's pieces before eliminating them; go is a game of market share and staying power.

Much strategy has been cast in the mould of optimizing competitive position within a set of market rules (*see* COMPETITIVE STRATEGY). Those rules, however, have often been set by the interaction of the market with incumbent players. Not surprisingly they are skewed in the existing leaders' favour. The most powerful form of strategy is therefore to change the rules of the game.

Many Japanese competitors started playing their game, go, instead of chess. The incumbents cried 'foul'; the results are well known. When the small private branch exchange (PBX) supplier Intecom entered the market it faced the prospect of matching the nationwide network of local service agents which its rivals had established in vigorous competition to offer the best support. By installing duplicate back-up components and self-diagnostic systems in its PBXs, however, it changed the rules, making its rivals' networks redundant. When Canon entered the photocopier business it was also at a disadvantage through lack of a network to provide immediate service to all of its customers. It would be a long time before it could hope to match Xerox on service speed. It responded by offering three alternative service contracts with a discount for accepting delayed priority. It was then able to even out the peaks in service demand and improve personnel utilization. It had thus switched the basis of competition to cost, where Xerox was weak (*see* COST LEADERSHIP).

The lesson from each of these examples is that ME-TOO STRATEGY, playing by rules established by others, would surely have failed. The breakthroughs came from rewriting the rules of the game.

S

Satisficing. 'Individuals will seek a course of action that is "good enough" – or satisfactory – as distinct from one that represents the "best" move.' This conception of how we make decisions is radically different from the classical economists' view which represented individual decision-making in terms of the application of a set of preferences to a given set of alternatives and outcomes; a process intended to maximize or optimize the outcome – that is, to choose that alternative which is 'best'. But do individuals – or indeed firms – operate like this? Herbert Simon, the American scholar of organizations who introduced the notion of satisficing, answered resoundingly 'no'.

In Simon's view individuals start with an 'aspiration' level – that is, a level of expectation that they regard as satisfactory or acceptable, but not necessarily optimal. A limited number of alternatives are then considered, in sequence, and the first to meet the desired level is accepted; for example, the first alternative that yields a satisfactory financial return, or an acceptable degree of risk. The premise underlying this model is that an individual's capacity to process information and consider alternatives is strictly limited, or bounded by 'cognitive limits', a fact ignored by the classical model. The attraction of Simon's view, therefore, is that it provides a more realistic description of managerial behaviour; one that recognizes the efficacy of choosing a course of action, the outcome of which would be acceptable or satisfactory without necessarily being the 'best'.

But this raises a series of intriguing questions for strategy. For example, good COMPETITOR ANALYSIS should give consideration to the possibility that, in terms of the desired level of profitability, a particular competitor is a satisficer rather than a maximizer. Returns currently being earned in an industry may reflect levels that, possibly for historical reasons, have come to be seen as adequate or satisfactory whereas the real returns that could be earned are somewhat higher. Assessing the extent to which competitors are satisficers provides, therefore, an insight into their behaviour and, more pertinently, into likely shifts (including retaliatory actions) in that behaviour should you decide to pursue a particular course of action.

But in developing strategy we need to turn the spotlight on ourselves, as well as others, and ask: 'are our managers pursuing sub-optimal goals that they deem to be satisfactory?' 'Is the underlying level of return that we *could* earn greater than that currently regarded as adequate?' 'Is there a "best" move that we could make that our satisficing competitors will not imitate or match?' More fundamentally we need to ask whether or not there is a commitment throughout the organization to 'doing things right' (that is, in a manner considered satisfactory), as distinct from 'doing the right things.' Much strategy has to do with identifying the 'right things' and the obstacles – both internal and external – to doing them. Paramount among these obstacles may be a degree of organizational complacency that perpetuates sustained under-performance based on continually setting satisfactory rather than genuinely stretching goals.

The notion of satisficing may actually reflect how decisions are often made, but that is not to say that it justifies or excuses not pursuing 'better' courses of action and aiming at a much more challenging target.

SBU.   *See* STRATEGIC BUSINESS UNIT.

Scenario analysis. Credit for the term 'scenario' is claimed by Herman Kahn, the famous futurist, whose stylized narrative portrayals of the hypothetical future of the world first appeared in the 1950s. More recently, Royal Dutch–Shell has done much to promote the use of scenarios in the strategic context, to which credit is given for enabling the company to anticipate successfully the world oil crises of both 1973–4 and 1989. Does this mean that Royal Dutch–Shell simply forecast accurately what would happen? The answer is 'no'; a scenario is not simply a forecast (*see* LEARNING).

Underpinning many forecasting techniques is an assumption, often tacit, that the world of tomorrow will be much like that of today; that tomorrow's world is susceptible to an essentially quantitative statement encapsulating its essential features. But forecasting, as we know, is fraught with difficulty and rarely proves accurate. Why? Research indicates that the problem lies not in the methodology used (indeed, errors attributable to methodological flaws in forecasting are trivial), but rather in the core assumptions upon which the forecast is based. If the assumptions are invalid then there is, of course, no chance that the forecast itself will be correct. It is precisely this difficulty that scenarios are designed to address.

The essential features of scenarios – or scenario planning – are these:

- Scenario analysis presents alternative and novel ways of seeing the world; ways that break out of the straitjacket of everyday, habitual perception.
- This is accomplished by providing a series of qualitative, as distinct from quantitative, descriptions or narratives displaying alternative ways in which the present might evolve into the future.
- The future is projected in plural not singular terms. That is, more than one possible future is represented; there are often three, each of which could plausibly occur. Whereas a forecast is essentially a prediction of what *will* happen, scenario analysis is a way of conceiving and representing alternative *possible* outcomes.
- Central to this analysis is uncertainty. The task of scenario analysis is to acknowledge the reality of uncertainty, to understand its significance, and to integrate uncertainty into alternative representations of the future. Representations that bring together an array of diverse information relating to economic, technological, industrial, social and political change.

Thus the essence of a scenario is that it portrays *different* worlds, *different* futures, and not, as in forecasting, projected outcomes in the same world. The intention is not to produce one 'right' scenario but rather a set of possibilities which between them shed light on what is happening in, say, a particular industry and how the major forces in this industry interact.

The approach lends itself therefore to longer-term planning horizons. Five-year periods are quite typical, although Royal Dutch–Shell worked with 15-year time spans. Situations in which it is possible to identify a limited number of key factors that will between them decisively effect the future are more amenable to this approach than those in which there is a multiplicity of comparably significant factors which render the analysis unwieldy. Similarly, the number of scenarios themselves must be kept in check, with three being the optimal number. Restriction to two scenarios tends to lead to one being labelled 'optimistic/good' and the other 'pessimistic/bad', with the difference between them typically being split. More than three scenarios become difficult to manage, although care should be taken to ensure that a projection of three alternative scenarios does not automatically engender a bias in favour of the 'safe' middle option (*see* SATISFICING).

Two tests for scenario analysis have been suggested by Pierre Wack, formerly of the group-planning department in Royal Dutch–Shell. First, what do they leave out? Managers should not be able to say that a scenario was fatally flawed because it omitted a key event that subsequently occurred. Secondly, does the scenario analysis lead to action? Does it encourage managers to do something different, rather than repeat the same formula that has worked well in the past? Ideally, scenario analysis will encourage managers to see the world in a new way, to see the future as being something more than an extension or continuation of the present and as such it should be a spur to action that breaks the mould of past practice.

Search good. Within a single shopping area the prices of essential foodstuffs are likely to vary slightly between different supermarkets. It is nevertheless unlikely that the typical consumer will invest much time in comparing prices in all the supermarkets before making his purchases. Food, which is bought frequently, is not subject to very wide price variations (at least among competing supermarkets). It is not, therefore, a search good – there is insufficient incentive for the consumer to initiate a search for the lowest price every time he buys the product.

But other goods, particularly those that are purchased infrequently, may well provide the consumer with an incentive to search, notwithstanding the time, effort and sometimes actual cost that this will entail. The benefits of search, in the form of identifying a low-cost supplier, are likely to be greatest, therefore, where the consumer has relatively little 'experience' of purchasing the good and where expenditure on it represents a relatively significant outlay. Furniture or bathroom fittings are search goods in the consumer arena, as are major equipment purchases for industrial buyers. To some extent the costs of searching will be determined by the number of firms offering the product in question – the greater the range of supply the wider the search – or the way in which the product is advertised and prices announced. In principle, more search and more information should increase competition and reduce price differentials between competing suppliers.

Segmentation. In strategic terms, market segmentation is the most obvious example of the process of disaggregating or dividing an entity into a number of smaller, discrete entities or units. But the process has equal relevance and value in the context of firms, competitors or industries. Take the firm. Firms operating across a number of different markets, with a diverse array of products, raise the question 'how do we disaggregate this total span of activity into a smaller set of, as it were, "natural" businesses?' One answer is to use not a set of criteria gounded within the firm – for example the functional commonality of activities such as marketing – but rather those rooted outside the organization – for instance, competitors, customers, prices or substitutes. In other words, we may group together that set of products that face similar competitors, that are aimed at the same group of customers and which serve as substitutes for each other. Employing such criteria provides clues as to how best the firm might be organized or structured – for example into product-based divisions.

The reference to customers brings us back to one other key dimension of segmentation: the market. Common to all attempts at market segmentation is the assumption that the demand for products is differentiated and that we can therefore identify groups of customers who exhibit similar characteristics or types of purchasing behaviour. But again, the question that arises is, 'on what basis should the segmentation division be made; what criteria should be employed?' A question around which debate continues to rage, the only certainty being that no single variable will capture all the attributes or differences between buyers that will serve to distinguish one segment from another. A number of variables have been – and continue to be – used. For example, demography – that is, age, sex, household size, income, educational background and so on; geography – county, region, urban versus rural; psychographic or lifestyle criteria which play an increasingly important part in many consumer, as distinct from commercial or industrial, markets, such as those for clothing, cosmetics, magazines and TV channels.

The upshot of such an analysis, at both the market and the industry levels, will be the elucidation of segment differences in terms of their relative size, rates of growth, change in consumer populations, vulnerability to new entrants or the erosion of demand resulting from product substitution. The analysis will illuminate, too, questions such as to the robustness of the boundaries of the segments, that is, the degree to which changes in technology may render obsolete the needs of a particular buyer group; the competitive dynamics, both in terms of the basis on which competition occurs (is it on price, distribution channels or product range, for instance?), and, importantly, the intensity of the competitive battle.

In the final analysis, however, we are interested in defining different segments not because of their inherent fascination, but because they distinguish parts of the market with different profit potential. From the strategic viewpoint a new segment needs to be isolated for any combination of customers and products which differ in terms of the FIVE FORCES which drive profitability. (See figure 27.) If the buyer power or rivalry associated with a particular group differ from that of its neighbours, for example, both its profit potential and the strategy required to reap that potential will also differ. Strategy therefore needs to treat it as a separate segment and adjust accordingly.

See also BARRIER TO MOBILITY, COMPETITOR ANALYSIS, STRATEGIC GROUP.

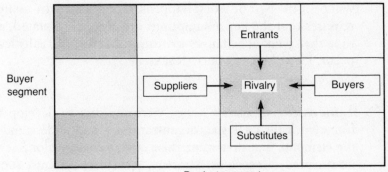

Product segment

Figure 27   Forces Generating Segment Differences

Sensitivity analysis. Every strategy, or a part thereof, is at some point translated into a budget, a business plan or a model that sets out the financial consequences of pursuing that strategy. Underpinning this budget, plan or model, is a set of assumptions, the validity of which is obviously critical in determining the accuracy of the predicted outcomes. Let's suppose, for example, that a forecast assumes that demand will increase by ten per cent per annum for the next three years, and that capacity utilization of plant and equipment will not fall below 80 per cent. These assumptions may not be correct. What we need to know, therefore, is what would happen if, say, demand grows by five per cent rather than ten per cent, or capacity utilization averages 60 per cent in the first two years of the forecast and 85 per cent in the third year. By varying the assumptions, usually one at a time, it is possible to isolate the effect on performance and profitability of any change in a key variable. The process can be repeated for each critical variable and the result consolidated into a set of forecasts reflecting 'best', 'worst' and 'most likely' cases. In developing a strategic plan or business model it is therefore essential to identify the key factors and to analyse how sensitive the model is to changes in these critical variables. The advantages of sensitivity analysis are that it provides a way of isolating major assumptions underpinning any proposed project and it shows just how good or bad the project will be if the best or worst happens. Good sensitivity analysis requires that the key assumptions are correctly isolated, and that the 'what if' changes are ones that could realistically occur. (*See also* SCENARIO ANALYSIS.)

7-S framework. MCKINSEY & CO. were the first to develop the framework for analysing organizations – and understanding the elements that determine their effectiveness – along seven interrelated dimensions: strategy, structure, systems, superordinate goals, skills, staff, style – the seven Ss. This was subsequently popularized by Tom Peters and Robert Waterman in their bestselling book *In Search of Excellence* so that the framework is now widely used and provides managers with a useful tool for thinking systematically about organizations. Proponents of the 7-S framework argue that:

• The effectiveness of an organization is determined by a multiplicity of factors and that changing an organization is not, therefore, simply a matter of changing its structure or reorganizing. Equally, organizational effectiveness is not simply a matter of defining a strategy and adapting the organization's structure to fit that strategy. Other critical elements are involved. These elements are:

   • Systems – all the formal and informal procedures that govern day-to-day activity
   • Style – how the management team spends its time, and presents itself to staff

- Skills – the distinctive capabilities or competences of an organization
- Superordinate goals (subsequently relabelled shared values in search of excellence) – the fundamental values and aims that guide an organization
- Staff – the human resources of the firm
- Structure – how the firm is organized
- Strategy – the route chosen by a firm to achieve success.

The relationship between all seven Ss is shown in figure 28.

- As figure 28 makes clear, all of the seven Ss are interconnected and interrelated. A change in any one element therefore has an effect on all the other variables, and moreover, it is impossible to make progress in one dimension (say, strategy) unless equal attention is given to the other six dimensions. But which of the seven variables is the most important? The answer is that they are all equally important. There is no hierarchy, as the circular nature of the figure deliberately indicates. The critical variable at any one time will change – it may be any one of the seven Ss.
- Clearly, it is easier – and usually quicker – to change some of the variables rather than others. For example, strategy or structure may be altered relatively quickly whereas the process changing staff or skills is much more gradual and, indeed, difficult. Given the interconnectedness of all seven Ss the pace of change is inevitably determined by the speed with which all the Ss are changed, not just one or two.
- In effecting organizational change it is essential that equal attention is given to all seven Ss. Typically the 'hard' Ss (like structure or strategy), receive a disproportionate amount of management time and attention at the expense of the 'soft' Ss – (superordinate goals or staff). Change, which is not directed at all the S's, hard and soft alike, is unlikely to succeed. Successful change is about aligning each of the Ss and ensuring the whole organization is in balance. An effective strategy has to be based upon complete consistency throughout the entire range of the firm's activity and the responsibility of management, therefore, is to focus on the interrelationships between the key elements of the organization, to

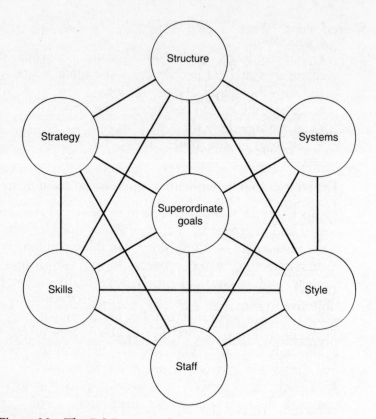

Figure 28   The 7-S Framework

understand how these elements interact and to strive for balance – or FIT – between them. In doing this it is just as important to attend to the 'soft', informal elements – such as staff or shared values – as the more formal and seemingly more malleable elements of strategy and structure.

The realization of strategy depends crucially upon how well you have aligned each of the elements of which your organization is made up. Using the 7-S framework is a way of thinking about the organization and what makes it successful.

Shared cost. When a particular function serves a range of products or a number of different businesses within a portfolio its costs may be distributed among them. Classic examples include sales representation and distribution, the costs of which are frequently shared between different product lines or businesses. The existence of shared costs implies the existence of shared experience: that is, experience gained in one sphere of activity (for example, by selling product A) can be usefully applied to another (selling product B). Exploiting that experience, via sharing, should serve to reduce costs and avoid redundant 're-invention of the wheel' within a business.

For many firms the process of allocating shared costs across the business, for example to different PROFIT CENTRES or product lines, is the focus of political infighting and conflict. Cost attribution is rarely possible on the basis of objective, transparent and non-contentious criteria. Typically, the final outcome is a negotiated one and, as with all negotiations, achieving a satisfactory outcome entails compromise.

For the strategist, the essential point is this. The basis on which shared costs are allocated should, as far as possible, accurately reflect the economic rather than the political reality of the situation. Where politics dominates, the risk is that the real costs associated with a particular activity will be masked or obscured, thereby distorting the perceived profitability of that activity. Much strategy is about making choices and trade-offs. Where cost plays a part in making such choices, as it almost always does, its allocation must be fair, rigorous and, above all, as accurate as possible.

SIC. *See* STANDARD INDUSTRIAL CLASSIFICATION.

Signalling. Any action that a competitor makes which provides an insight into his future intentions, actions, motives or strategic goals constitutes a signal. Such signals come in a variety of forms and fulfil many different functions. For example, announcing an intended price rise, publicizing a

new product prior to its launch, foreshadowing the construction of a new plant, cutting a product line, or indeed, passing
judgement on the industry in a trade journal. Potentially each
of these actions is laden with competitive significance: it
means something. But what? Herein lies the problem.

Signalling may be used for many purposes: to confuse, to
warn or threaten, to intimidate, to mislead, to pre-empt, or to
convey a message to an important audience, like the financial
community. Interpreting the status of signals is therefore
fraught with difficulty, and a particular signal taken in
isolation rarely provides a sufficient basis on which to react
or respond. A useful starting point is to ask yourself the
following question. In the past how has a competitor followed up a particular signal and what is that competitor's
track record in matching signals with action? For example,
did the threatened price increase materialize or was capacity
added to in the way that was announced? Of course, there is
no guarantee that history will repeat itself but it provides the
best starting point. The essential point about signalling and
its interpretation is that they contribute to good COMPETITOR
ANALYSIS, and although there is danger of becoming ensnared
in a web of guessing and second-guessing it is better to run
this risk than to ignore competitor signals, however incom-
plete they may be. Competitor analysis will be enriched by
judicious interpretation of any action that provides some
indication of what a competitor will do or how it might
retaliate to a move that you make (*see* RETALIATION).

Simulation. A fundamental approach to decision-making rather
than a specific technique, simulation entails the construction
of a theoretical model of a real-life business situation. By
using a variety of conceptual tools and techniques the model
may be manipulated to provide conclusions about the real
world.

Just as children explore reality through games and 'pretending', so too managers can explore new business possibilities through the formalized pretending involved in simulation
models. What these models do is predict the consequences of

different decisions; they do not necessarily indicate the
optimal choice or decision available. But once a model is
constructed it can provide managers with a better understanding of major cause-and-effect relationships and an
insight into how key variables interact – for example, price
and sales volume. Of course, the value of these insights
depends crucially on the validity of the model. In assessing
this, managers should ask the following sorts of questions.
Does the model react reasonably when it is manipulated? Do
the relationships between the variables in the simulation
correspond to those in real life? To what extent does the
model enable the user to predict *observable* events (such as
oil-price fluctuations), changes affecting the industry as a
whole (like major technological developments), and events
which will have a direct bearing upon that part of the market
in which a particular firm, and its principal competitors, are
operating?

Spin-off. Data General was set up by a small group of former
employees of Digital Equipment Corporation when, so it is
widely believed, that company proved reluctant to develop a
new product idea that the group felt had potential. The new
company continued to operate in the same sphere as Digital,
becoming thereby one of the best-known examples of a
spin-off.

   During the early phases of an industry's development, at a
time when technology is changing rapidly and opportunities
are burgeoning, the lure of a spin-off is likely to be greatest.
Frustrated by the unwillingness or inability of a firm to
pursue a new product idea, aware of the untapped potential
afforded by new opportunities, or attracted by the prospect
of operating a business in which significant equity participation is possible, ambitious employees may be tempted by the
idea of 'spinning off' their own business.

   But in some instances the spin-off process is controlled by
the parent organization itself; for example, a firm may
actively decide to spin out a separate business activity or
technology from itself, and will accomplish this by setting up

a new company in which it will almost certainly retain a minority investment and to which it might supply production or marketing resources, management advice and, importantly, credibility. For example, Liber Developments is a company which started out life as an in-house Ferranti project concerned with developing new telecommunications products. In view of the marketing risks and funding requirements Ferranti decided against funding the project internally. Other investment partners were brought in, with Ferranti retaining a 25 per cent stake in the newly established, independent company Liber. In spinning out Liber, Ferranti effectively spread the risk (by securing other investors), without forfeiting all the potential gains. Liber acquired finance, credibility and a degree of support not normally available to independent start-up companies.

SQC (Statistical quality control). *See* QUALITY CIRCLE.

Stalemate cycle. In industries where technology is undergoing continual improvement, yet heavy investment at any point will lock the company into a particular technology, stalemate cycles will typically occur.

Suppose a company builds a new plant with larger-scale and more cost-effective technology than any of its rivals. In the short term, while demand stays strong and capacity is limited, it makes high margins at prices comparable to those its competitors with less efficient capacity can offer. When another competitor subsequently decides to replace its plant, however, the technology has improved, possibly requiring an even larger scale. This competitor therefore builds an even more massive plant with lower costs in order to re-establish its competitiveness. This large increase in capacity drives down the price. A third competitor then finds he cannot make a profit. His only alternative is to re-invest. The plant he builds has yet better technology, lower costs and larger scale. When it comes on-stream prices fall yet again. Our original company's modern plant now looks sub-scale and high-cost, yet it has often not fully returned its original investment and is far from the end of its productive life. If it is written off and the company invests even more cash in a yet larger 'state of the art' plant, capacity will be increased and prices will fall yet further in an attempt to fill it.

This is the stalemate cycle. Each competitor has to bet higher and higher stakes to play each round, prices keep falling and the customer rather than the investors benefit from the cost reductions. Yet while costs and prices keep moving down together, no competitor can win. The industry becomes a CASH TRAP.

Stalemate cycles have been observed in a number of high-volume, commodity-type businesses such as acrylic fibre and paper production, zinc smelting, petroleum refining and steel making. Some strategists recommend avoidance of industries with these characteristics. Others suggest *pre-emption* to deter competitors from building capacity. Recognizing the problems of stalemate, other companies have successfully re-positioned their businesses to specialize in MARKET SEGMENTS with particular needs. They have designed smaller plants with much greater flexibility to take advantage of short-term shortages in particular products, and made provision in the original design for subsequent upgrading as the technology changes (*see* RE-POSITIONING).

Standard industrial classification (SIC) . Firms may be classified on the basis of their principal products according to this numerical scheme. In most Western countries the classification is based on a maximum of seven digits, with each successive digit refining the product sector to which the company contributes. The first digit, therefore, will distinguish the broad area of the industrial economy, agriculture and forestry for instance, extractive minerals or metal manufacturing; the second digit will distinguish sectors within that first grouping and so forth. In the British SIC, for example, category '321' is 'agricultural machinery and tractors'. This is a sub-group of division '32', 'mechanical engineering', which is itself part of the broad sector '3', 'metal goods, engineering and vehicle industries'.

This classification system has its drawbacks. Categorization based on similarities in production, rather than product substitutability (*see* SUBSTITUTION), results in a situation, for example, where plastic buckets are classified as 'plastics', metal ones as 'metalworking' and wooden ones as 'wooden products'. Faced with this limitation the strategist should conduct an industry analysis on the basis of as detailed a breakdown of the SIC as possible – typically according to a three- or four-digit classification – and be prepared to reclassify firms as appropriate. Beware also that the system may distort CONCENTRATION RATIOS by allocating the whole of a firm's output and employment to the one census class that its principal products indicate, thereby discounting minor product lines falling within other classes.

Star. An occupant of the upper left quadrant of the BOSTON CONSULTING GROUP'S GROWTH–SHARE MATRIX. Competitively strong, such businesses have relatively high shares of fast-growing markets. This means they are generally both strong generators and users of cash, but roughly in cash balance. In subsequent refinements of the original BCG matrix, stars are further defined in terms of businesses exhibiting a high degree of product or market specialization, on the basis of which they may achieve positions of dominance. Sustaining stars requires continual investment, and their growth potential and competitive advantage may be destroyed if treated too early as CASH COWS.

Statistical quality control.   *See* QUALITY CIRCLE.

Strategic business unit (SBU). Clearly it makes little sense to try to assemble a single product-market strategy for a diversified conglomerate. Nor can a regional organization serving multiple product markets with different competitors necessarily adopt a uniform strategic approach. The concept of a strategic business unit (SBU) therefore emerged for the purposes of developing a collection of active responses directed towards broadly the same market, with a common set of competitors and similar strategic problems.

SBUs were often collections of smaller units which had been run independently. In many other cases, they cut directly across organizational lines. Recognizing that in most cases it was desirable to run strategically similar businesses under the same management umbrella, many corporations subsequently restructured their organization into SBUs for operating and reporting purposes as well as strategy formulation. Within such an SBU-orientated structure, the artificial distinction between strategy formulation and implementation tends to fade away, helping to bridge the unwanted gap between strategy and operations.

Strategic choice. In the eyes of some, chief executives are men and women who can move mountains with a memo. Many of those further down in the organization envy the breadth of choice they perceive those at the top to enjoy. Like others, however, the strategic choices open to chief executives are constrained by a host of limitations.

Some of these constraints stem from the demands of the three main CONSTITUENCIES which the firm must satisfy: the capital market, the product market and the individuals who make up the organization itself. Much strategy is about positioning the firm so as to minimize the adverse impact of these constraints and extend the range of future choices available. The desire of many firms to generate most of their cash-investment needs from internal sources can be seen as a device for minimizing the direct constraints to strategic choice imposed by the capital markets. Research and development, meanwhile, is often designed to improve strategic choice against the constraints of the product market. The desire to maintain open-minded, entrepreneurial employees and an adaptable company structure is part of a drive to reduce the organizational constraints on strategic choice.

Retaining strategic choice by these types of actions may conflict with the successful execution of the specific strategy currently being followed. Flexibility and HEDGING may have costs in the form of reducing the external financial resources currently available, increasing costs compared with a single-minded strategy, and may impede the development of a strong CORPORATE CULTURE totally attuned to current strategy. An important role of the chief executive is to resolve these conflicts between retaining strategic choice and excelling within the current strategy.

Another important set of constraints on strategic choice may arise from the beliefs of the top management itself. These beliefs, which tend to evolve into a shared 'company vision', may exclude important strategic alternatives. In extreme cases there is a lack of any real strategic choice as a result of 'tunnel vision' management. This is the classic signal for new competitors, with a different view of the strategic choices, to enter by redefining the basis of competition (for example, by using a totally new distribution channel), often with devastating results.

Strategic distance. In analysing competitors it is often useful to make a distinction between those who are 'close' competitors and those who are 'distant' rivals. Take the simple example of ice-cream sellers on a beach. Comparison with the variety of flavours and prices offered by the vendor a few metres from your stand is of much more immediate concern than that offered by a vendor one mile along the beach, since few customers are willing to walk so far from their swimming place even for a better or cheaper ice-cream.

The two key dimensions of strategic distance are:

• the magnitude of the difference between your target segment's needs and buying behaviour, and the segment aimed at by the competitor; and
• the degree to which you and your competitor are following similar or differentiated strategies for serving the chosen segments.

A firm competing in the heavy branded end of a market and distributing through specialist outlets where customers receive high levels of service is strategically distant from a counterpart competing for price-sensitive customers through a low-cost, private-label product.

Much short- and medium-term strategy is concerned with dealing with the competitive interactions with the STRATEGIC GROUP of rivals who are close in terms of strategic distance. In the long term, however, the most potent threat can arise from companies who, while historically separated by a wide strategic distance, move into your market segment and use the skills accumulated through their very different experience to undermine your position by changing the RULES OF THE GAME.

Strategic distance is also an important concept in assessing the likelihood of more intense RIVALRY as a market develops. In some markets, the strategic distance between competitors grows as individual firms refine and differentiate their strategies during the maturation. Rivalry thus becomes more gentlemanly. In other industries, the market evolves so that competitors converge along one dimension of strategic distance while remaining apart on the other. This can lead to the situation where competitors with very different strategies are competing for the same segments causing RIVALRY to intensify. This often occurs when industries internationalize, leading companies with very different home-bases – and hence cost structures and macroeconomic pressures – into competition for the same set of global customers.

Strategic group. Firms in the same industry or market often employ a range of quite different strategies in approaching the business. It is not just that some firms have inferior resources; there is generally more than one route to success. We commonly find, for example, branded, full-line competitors co-existing with low-cost suppliers to the private-label channel, alongside NICHE players focusing on particular applications, types of buyers or geographic segments.

In analysing an industry it is often useful to divide competitors into strategic groups each made of up firms pursuing similar strategies (see figure 29). These commonly line up roughly with different market segments. Thinking about these in terms of different strategic groups, however, high-lights the differences in skills, scale, financial resources and so on, which are necessary to succeed in any segment. It can also raise a number of other interesting questions.

Suppose we find growth in one segment beginning to take off. Clearly this segment starts to look more attractive to those firms who traditionally focused their attention else-where. If these firms wish to start seriously pursuing this newly growing segment they must make some important strategic choices. One approach would be to shift their strategy so as to emulate more closely that of the strategic group already serving the segment; they could start supplying to private-label channels, for example. Making this kind of shift, however, often lands them with the problem of MIXED MOTIVES; what would such a move do to the brand image of their existing sales? Would it undermine the loyalty of their existing distributors? There is often something to lose.

In shifting its strategic group a firm may also face BARRIERS TO MOBILITY. Moving into a lower-price segment means more unit sales for the same revenue, hence the need for more production capacity, and perhaps, therefore, a shift towards standardization and away from customer options. Putting in new capacity often takes time, and re-orientating the goals of both management and employees towards the new strategy, obtaining new skills and so on, may prove major obstacles to such a move. Conversely, establishing the brand image, distribution or after-sales servicing network necessary for a move into a premium-price segment may provide mobility barriers of its own. Nor would it be clear how the firm would gain COMPETITIVE ADVANTAGE against those already inhabit-ing its new strategic group. Being on par is probably not enough to guarantee to profit or win market share there against those with experience of the strategy.

An alternative approach might be to apply major elements of your existing strategy to the growing segment. In this case firms from different strategic groups come head to head in competition for the same segment. National brands of beer competing with those of regional breweries is an example. Here the judgement is how successfully the behaviour of the segment can be changed so as to exploit the non-traditional strategy. Is the market becoming more susceptible to national advertising, for example?

The concept of strategic groups is also valuable in assessing the viability of different strategies in declining markets. Which strategic group will be hit hardest as sales decline? How easy will it be for them to change their strategy to dodge the decline, possibly resulting in a direct assault on our own sources of advantage? Can I build barriers to mobility to prevent emulation of my strategy, such as patents, exclusive distribution contracts, product line or geographic MARKET SATURATION?

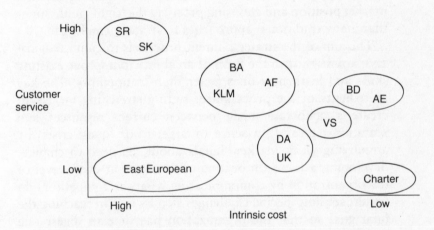

Figure 29   Strategic Groups in European Air Transport

Strategic intent. The concept introduced by G. Hamel and C. K. Prahalad in their *Harvard Business Review* article of the same name encapsulates the process by which a company embeds in the organization an obsession with winning at all levels and guides a 10- to 20-year drive for global leadership. It is often expressed in terms of a simple and very long-term objective, like Komatsu's 'Encircle Caterpillar', Canon's 'Beat Xerox', Honda's avowed aim to become 'a second Ford', Coca-Cola's drive to put Coke within 'arm's reach of every consumer in the world', or ETA's target of selling a 'Swatch' to 'one per cent of the world's population'. Each of these provides a much more powerful motivational umbrella for individual actions than, say, maximizing shareholder wealth. They can also be a consistent guiding light over a long period of time.

How does a company know what its strategic intent should be, especially if it has already achieved the status of leader in its market? Many companies adopt grandiose MISSION STATEMENTS with little hope of ever achieving them. Hamel and Prahalad would probably argue that, as long as the strategic intent is broadly consistent with long-run trends, the precise mission doesn't much matter. What really lies behind strategic intent is a view that success comes from having the right strategic process rather than from identifying the best market position and choosing precisely the 'right' goal, things that many traditional approaches to strategy emphasize.

The aim of the strategic-intent process is to gain COMPETITIVE ADVANTAGE in the form of an ability to improve existing skills and learn new ones faster than competitors. The key ingredients of the process are: setting stretching targets to create a deliberate misfit between current resources and ambitions; creating a sense of urgency or 'quasi-crisis' by amplifying weak market signals about the need to change; developing a focus on beating competitors at every level of the organization by communicating what the competitors do better; settling specific challenges step by step in reaching the final goal so that the organization has time to digest one before launching another; and establishing clear milestones combined with mechanisms to track progress and reward achievement in moving towards the long-term goal.

Strategic map. The trick of preparing maps is in knowing what to leave off. A good road-map illustrates the essential detail only; it avoids the distraction of supplying information when no real choices are available, while it highlights complex decision points like five-way intersections.

In business, individuals, dealing with confusing details, need to exclude extraneous material and adopt a few key indicators with which to measure their contribution to the success or failure of the firm. Therefore, the strategic road-map must highlight who are the key customers, what are their essential needs, how does competition in the segment work, what are the economics of the business? These maps become ingrained in an organization and condition the upcoming generation, influencing what they see as the firm's mission and the questions they do and don't ask about the business and the world.

The strategic maps which built many successful Western businesses, like automobiles, motorcycles and machine tools, incorporated the idea that customers wanted broad product lines and chose on the basis of a huge array of options; the wisdom of following this axis was never questioned. New focused competitors had a different map: price was a motorway, not a byway. This led them to believe that consumers would prefer to forego much of this individual choice in exchange for standardized features and lower prices. The result is history.

It is important, for strategy implementation, to recognize the existence and nature of these maps. Requesting preparation for a 'right turn' in strategy will fail if individuals' maps deny there is a road there. Beliefs must be redrawn first (*see* CORPORATE CULTURE).

Strategic staircase. *See* SUPPLY-SIDE STRATEGY AND STRATEGIC STAIRCASES.

Strategic trade. The exchange of businesses between two firms – with a cash transfer to make up any nett difference in value – often makes sense where two groups have peripheral businesses which are complementary to each other's core activities. It has generated recent interest as many companies have sought to become more focused in their activities. A good example is the trade which took place between Pabst and Stroh in the US brewing industry. Pabst was facing some $9m redundancy costs in closing its plant at St Paul, Minnesota, part of the area where Stroh was hampered in building itself a strong regional position by capacity constraints. Stroh gained St Paul, plus its associated distribution network, in exchange for a plant in Florida, peripheral to *its* business, but key to Pabst's expansion plans. Likewise BP and ICI exchanged businesses in speciality chemicals to improve their respective positions in particular markets.

Strategic trades may offer a number of advantages relative to outright sale. They can avoid the potential decline in a business which often occurs through demotivation when a company is put on the open market. They ensure that the business goes to a competitor interested in developing it as a complement to established activities in its existing market, rather than to a third party who may use it as a base to enter the core business of the seller. They are often very financially and tax efficient, since little cash changes hands.

Stretching. Companies prefer to go on doing what they know how to do well. When markets change, therefore, they often seek to 'stretch' rather than replace their existing strategy to encompass the new customers, shifting needs or different priorities associated with the change. Many initially specialized firms also attempt to stretch their strategy into new segments, countries or products in the pursuit of growth.

Some strategies are more elastic than others; when stretched, a strategy can break. Take, for example, a company which is successful because of a unique product, its close personal relationship with a few customers, hands-on management and low overhead. It is acquired by a larger company which attempts to grow it quickly into the mass market. Its strategy, however, is highly specific to its particular environment and the stretching fails. A branded-products company sees strong growth in private-label goods and decides to expand into this segment. The required emphasis on tight cost control and reverse engineering to succeed in the private-label segment, however, makes its existing strategy and skills unsuitable to the new environment. A charter airline extends its operation to target the business-travel market as well; the two parallel businesses sit uneasily together.

In each of these examples it is essential to understand how much of the success of a strategy is due to its fit with a particular 'micro-climate' and how much it can be stretched. It is also critical to recognize that a 'strength' compared with one set of competitors may be a weakness when taken into a new product or customer environment where different competitors are much more expert in that dimension. An exceptionally strong goldfish, the envy of its tank-mates, is still a 'minnow' in the open sea.

Sub-contract. A firm may wish to use external suppliers to provide components or services which it is either unable to provide itself or deliberately chooses not to do so. Decisions of this type typically fall under the rubric 'make versus buy'. Appropriate choices between these two alternatives often exert a profound influence upon a firm's success or failure.

The dilemma is particularly acute for small or newly established firms. Prevailing wisdom suggests that such firms should keep the business simple and sub-contract out as much as possible. Yet many firms, both large and small, are loath to forfeit a degree of control over the product that sub-contracting necessarily entails.

In making this choice a number of factors come into play:

- the relative cost of making in-house as compared with buying in from the outside;
- the degree to which a particular component – or its cost – is critical to the overall performance or cost of the final product;
- the requirement of securing 100 per cent certainty of supply;
- the degree to which the firm can get manufacturers and sub-contractors to take their requirements seriously – this is a particular problem for smaller firms;
- finally, the complexity associated with managing a range of outside suppliers.

But in making appropriate choices the firm needs to consider: 'what business are we really in (for example,

manufacturing *or* designing, assembling, testing and selling a
particular product)?' 'Which area of the business must we
control directly in order to succeed – production, marketing,
distribution?' 'Where do our particular skills lie and how can
we most effectively utilize our necessarily limited resources,
not least, managerial resources?' New firms inevitably en-
counter these dilemmas early on, but their resolution is not a
once-and-for-all affair. Successful strategy is built around a
willingness to re-address continually the question, 'what
should we make and what should we buy – or sub-contract?'

Substitution. Narrowly defined, close substitutes are products
with a high cross-elasticity of demand. For example, the use
of saccharin in place of sugar as a sweetener. Substitution
occurs most direcly when one product is chosen to replace
another where both products fulfil approximately the same
function. To illustrate: imagine two products, both of which
can be used for the same purpose. If the price of product A
rises, close substitutability implies that demand will shift
from product A to product B. Hence demand for a product
will be determined, in large part, by the price and performance of related substitute products. Thus substitution and the
associated threat of it exert considerable influence upon the
profitability of an industry. If we define an industry in terms
of a group of firms that offer products or services that *are*
close substitutes for each other it becomes immediately
obvious that the threat, and the ease with which consumers
can switch between products, will impact upon the margins
and therefore profits that firms are able to earn. In textiles for
example, the advent of man-made fibres depressed the prices
charged and margins earned by producers of natural fibres.

Substitution is more likely to occur where consumers have
low SWITCHING COSTS or where the producers of substitutes
aggressively encourage substitution – for example, by offering higher discounts, lower prices and enhanced product
performance.

Understanding the threat of substitutes is therefore a
critical part of strategic analysis. At one level this is relatively

straightforward; the firm can look for and identify products that perform essentially the same functions as its own. However, restricting the analysis in this manner is risky. Substitution may be both direct, as in the case of saccharin and sugar; or indirect, for example deciding to forego a holiday so as to be able to buy a new car. Holidays and cars have nothing in common except that they both compete for a share of disposable income and, to that extent, represent potential substitutes. Strategic analysis needs to work, therefore, with a broad definition of the substitution process; a process that will be driven by technological change (as in the demise of the slide-rule and the ascendance of the calculator), by changing consumer preferences (like the switch from investment in equities to bank deposits), and by improvements in the relative price and performance of comparable products (witness the switch from large mainframe to minicomputers). Understanding fully how the dynamics of substitution work is a prerequisite to positioning the firm and its products in such a way as to resist the squeeze in profitability imposed by the threat (*see also* FIVE FORCES).

Sunrise and sunset industry. The terms often used to describe EMERGENT and MATURE or DECLINING INDUSTRIES respectively connote inevitability, implying that businesses are part of a natural INDUSTRY LIFE CYCLE. This has often led to companies writing premature death certificates for their sunset divisions. Because of the demotivating impact on management and the tendency for the centre to starve these businesses of cash, they can make decline a self-fulfilling prophecy.

Industries like steel or textiles, for example, have often been termed sunset industries, with the implication that those who could should exit before it became too late. In fact, speciality steel-makers in high-cost locations such as Europe and the US have re-emerged as highly profitable businesses. Demand for textiles, meanwhile, has increased some 40 per cent in real terms in the developed world over the past decade with demand for personal wardrobes of greater variety and shorter fashion cycles. Companies like Benetton, with innovative approaches, have grown dramatically in the setting sun. Nike and Reebok have each built $1.8b businesses from a standing start in the shoe industry that many saw as fading.

The facts show that the extent of COMPETITIVE ADVANTAGE attained by a firm in its industry is a far more important determinant of profitability than the general 'attractiveness' of its industrial environment. Blanket descriptions like sunrise and sunset, therefore, prove of little use in identifying opportunities in the quest for profit and growth.

Supplier power. All who provide resources or services to an organization have an impact and may exert influence on it. As one of the FIVE FORCES that determine the profitability of an industry, supplier power forms a central part of any strategic analysis. Careful assessment of this variable, and of the way in which it has changed and may change over time, should begin with an examination of the conditions that favour suppliers. For example, they are likely to be in a strong position when their number is relatively small, thereby concentrating the sources of supply available to a firm; when the costs of switching from one supplier to another are high – as for instance where a particular production process relies heavily on specialized products that are not widely available; where a firm's purchases represent a small proportion of the supplier's total output, thereby making it difficult for the firm to ensure that its requirements are taken sufficiently seriously. Finally, being able to threaten credibly to move into the producer's business will enhance supplier power (*see* INTEGRATION).

When the obverse of these conditions applies suppliers find themselves in a relatively weak position; for instance, concentrated producers, credible threats of backward integration, numerous, fragmented suppliers, purchasing biased towards commodity products, and the ready availability of substitute inputs, all strengthen the relative power of buyers over suppliers. Understanding how the dynamics of supplier relationships operate is an integral part of understanding what makes an industry tick and what a firm needs to do in order to succeed in that industry. More specifically, strategic analysis should concern itself with the impact that suppliers have upon operating margins, the consequences for profitability of an increase in input costs, and the ways in which supplier relationships can be manipulated – for example, by diversifying suppliers – to create advantage.

Evolving effective strategies in relation to suppliers therefore entails stepping outside the perspective of your own organization and understanding fully how a supplier's business actually works. Doing this, and by identifying ways in which you can create value for suppliers without incurring costs, will leave a firm better placed to exert power over its suppliers, rather than vice versa. (*See* PURCHASING STRATEGY.)

Supply-side strategy and strategic staircases. Most organizations, like individuals, have an inherent preference for continuing to do what they do well. The lowest-risk option often appears to consist of repeating the business formulae which have worked well in the past. Their facilities, networks, procedures, information systems, supplier and distributor relationships, job descriptions and organizational structures are set up to do just this. The multitude of unquestioned assumptions they apply to daily activities ensure that they do so.

There is a degree of fundamental conservatism in most companies. It is not surprising, therefore, that they are most comfortable with planning systems which project the status quo forward. This process, depicted in figure 30, projects the firm along its current trajectory (A) and then makes some adjustments to this base case designed to take account of the predicted environmental developments, often with a healthy dose of optimism (B). Given the basic lack of predictability of events which directly or indirectly impact on our market environment (recent developments in eastern Europe and German re-unification being good examples) we end up at (C). All things considered, the planning process hasn't done at all badly; after all, (C) is considerably better than our

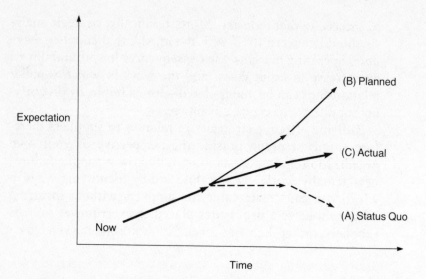

Figure 30   Projecting the Status Quo Forward

rudderless fate at (A). On the other hand, it has missed its target (B) by a wide margin.

The essence of supply-side strategy is that, rather than projecting today forward, it must start from a clear statement of mission or aim and derive key milestones by working back towards the present. Such an approach can have far-reaching implications for the structure of planning systems and their success in supporting real change if properly implemented. Figure 31 depicts this process of working back. The first implication concerns the specification of the mission itself. If my company is to become 'the best and most successful company in the airline industry', the mission recently announced by British Airways, it must form an identikit of what success in achieving this mission might look like. Does this imply that it must be significant in the US domestic market and intra-regional markets within Asia? Which are the target customer segments which must define BA as 'the best'? What are the key parameters used to define 'most successful'? Safety record? Size and growth? Financial return? Customer satisfaction? Employee loyalty?

The second stage would be to ask what the airline capable

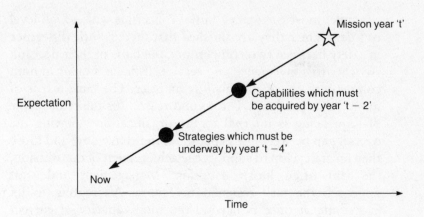

Figure 31   Working Backwards

of delivering that picture of success would itself need to look like in terms of capacity, resources, staff skills, route configuration, organizational structure, brand image and so forth. Rather than forecasting demand and sales, this approach emphasizes prediction of the capabilities necessary to deliver a future definition of success.

Stage three involves projecting our supply-side prediction back in time to ask the question, 'employing realistic lead times, what milestones must we have reached, say, two years prior if we are going to be on track to get the resources, skills, capacity, brand preference, structure and so on we need to achieve this supply-side goal?'

Successive application of this planning procedure allows us to work back to what actions must be taken now to build the future capabilities required. This amounts to defining our mission in terms of the supply-side imperatives to achieve it and planning the critical paths to constructing these. Behind supply-side strategic planning lies the concept of the *sequential* development of capabilities, skills, and hard and soft assets (such as plants and brands) in a deliberate way. Just as in any construction project, the sequence is important for two reasons.

Firstly, the customer's buying behaviour often dictates the ability to supply certain attributes of a product or service *before* others are even considered. Take the air transport

example: most customers' initial concern is with a high level
of safety. Once they are satisfied that there is little difference
in safety between two competitors, the basis of their decision
switches to convenience and service. If this is similar in both
competitors, they probably buy on price. The same is true of
many other products. The second reason for the critical role
of sequencing is internal to the organization. Viewing the
overall gap between the capabilities they have now and those
they must develop to support the achievement of our mission,
the gulf often looks daunting. Management and staff
approach the task resigned to failure. Attempting to fix
everything at once is beyond the total capacity of current
resources. Moreover, the successful development and exploitation of some capabilities must build on the base of
other skills. Excellent marketing skills which stoke up customer expectations are a definite liability if deployed before
we have the capabilities to deliver.

The answer to these problems lies in breaking up the
overall requirement to close a capabilities gap into 'bite-sized
pieces': tasks which employees can focus on, which they can
believe are realistic rather than overwhelming. These can
then be sequenced to take account of the complementarity
between the capabilities and the order in which they must be
deployed in the market.

The earth-moving equipment industry provides a good
illustration of the importance of sequencing in supply-side
strategy. The costs of equipment breakdown on a construction site are high: scheduled labour must be laid off, idle
materials incur interest costs, resulting delays to progress and
final completion often attract the expense of penalty clauses.
Equipment reliability, readily available maintenance and
rapid supply of parts and service traditionally dominated
buyers' decision-making and earned a price premium for
those with the capabilities to provide them. Where the buyers
could obtain these from a number of suppliers, however,
their attention turned to price. Once competitors were able to
offer high reliability at very similar prices, the buyers chose
equipment with additional features relevant to the needs of
their particular applications. Eventually, as their market

matures, it may be necessary to have the capability to follow major customers into new, diversified business areas.

Starting from a long way behind, the Japanese manufacturer Komatsu set itself the mission of catching up with the world leader in the earth-moving equipment market, Caterpillar of the US. With a scale only one sixth of Caterpillar's, even in 1971, a small and undemanding home market, virtually no dealer network, little relevant technology, poor quality, a 'cheap and nasty' brand image, poor parts supply, lack of familiarity with world markets, few English-speaking staff and a narrow product range, it was clear that the problem lay not in forecasting demand, but in generating the necessary capabilities to compete in the market and match its ambitious mission. Even to the most committed Japanese team, however, the gap must have looked daunting.

Working backwards from Caterpillar's strengths, it was clear that Komatsu would need a broad product line and possibly the ability to match future diversification by Caterpillar. An excellent service and dealer network was also essential. Yet, no dealer would touch a product he didn't believe he could sell. With low labour costs and subsidized steel prices, Komatsu could market on price alone. Facing the operating cost penalties of 'downtime' when their equipment failed, however, few customers were prepared to take the risk. To deal with this risk aversion, the first step in Komatsu's strategic staircase (figure 32) would be to achieve close parity with Caterpillar on quality and reliability. The strategic plan thus focused on LICENSING to improve technology from key component suppliers and companies in related industries as well as implementing total quality-control systems throughout the Komatsu organization (see QUALITY CIRCLE). This was then extended to key suppliers and subsequently to its dealers.

Quality was a 'bite-sized' objective on which employees could focus their energies, not for its own sake but as part of a sequence for building capabilities long term. Once achieved, customers would face minimum risk of downtime whether they bought Komatsu or Caterpillar. Their attention would then turn to relative prices. Komatsu's next step in the

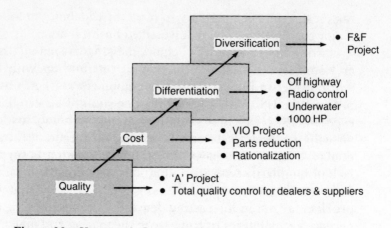

Figure 32   Komatsu's Strategic Staircase

supply-side staircase was therefore to whittle away Caterpillar's cost advantage. Looking to minimize the disadvantage of its smaller scale, Komatsu set about reducing the number of parts in its products, maintaining variety through combining different base modules, and rationalizing its product and supply networks to reduce costs for any given level of volume.

With quality and basic functionality at competitive costs, further market share would have to be won through the ability to differentiate the product for specialist requirements and innovate to meet the needs of new applications. The challenge of taking this next step forward into DIFFERENTIATION, without adding unnecessary costs involved 'efficient production-orientated choice specification' ('EPOCHS') a system designed to make Komatsu capable of broadening its product line while maintaining production efficiencies.

Having matched and sometimes bettered Caterpillar's capabilities, coming a close second on worldwide market share during the early 1980s, Komatsu re-examined its mission. It defined a new set of capabilities required to carry it into the 1990s, and with it a new staircase based on sequenced development of the resources and skills necessary to make it competitive in the manufacture and supply of robotics.

The strategic staircase in practice

Extrapolating from the past and projecting observed trends into the future makes good intuitive sense; working forward from the present to the future feels 'natural'. Working backwards from the future to the present, extrapolating the implications of our future aim back to the here and now feels unnatural; it is counter-intuitive. Applying the strategic-staircase framework successfully entails breaking down this inhibition. It also requires that attention is given to the following key principles:

- The mission – the aim to which the staircase ascends has to be defined clearly, concisely and in terms that are motivating. Time should be devoted, therefore, to distilling a statement of aim that provides a clear context within which to evolve an appropriate sequence of strategic initiatives (*see* MISSION STATEMENT).
- The sequence – this supply-side approach to strategy is about the deliberate, *sequential* development of capabilities, skills and resources. Specifying the precise order or sequence of steps, as well as the rationale behind one particular sequence rather than another, is therefore critical. Moreover, the link between adjacent steps must be explicit. Moving from step 1 to step 2 is precisely that: a step, not a leap. It must be made clear, therefore, exactly how one set of strategic initiatives prepares the way for undertaking a second set of such initiatives. (*See also* CRITICAL-PATH ANALYSIS.)
- The trade-offs – choosing one step in preference to another necessarily entails making choices and trade-offs; saying 'no' to one thing in favour of another, at least for the moment. Developing strategy from the supply side, and embodying this in a strategic staircase, ensures that choices and trade-offs are forced out into the open. In developing a strategic staircase beware, therefore, of the danger of eliding or fudging the trade-offs.
- The timetable – although the final aim itself may have no firm date attached to its accomplishment, timetables must be agreed for the building of the initial steps, and specifically the

putting in place of each particular step. However, beware that the time that each step is expected to take and the time the company can afford in taking it may be two quite different things.

● The initiatives and measures – 'step 1 is to improve the quality of our products'. Of itself, this objective is not particularly helpful. For it to have a real impact two things must happen. First, the specific initiatives to be taken to improve quality must be spelled out in detail. Secondly, there needs to be a definition of the measures by which progress on these initiatives will be judged, measures that answer the question, 'how do we know that we are making good progress in relation to our chosen targets?'

Communicating supply-side strategy

The strategic staircase is a powerful organizing idea around which the strategy-development process can be undertaken. But it has another, vital function. As a device for presenting, communicating and, indeed, 'selling' strategy within an organization. Using the strategic staircase provides a way of giving a clear answer to that perennial question so often asked at the end of a strategy presentation: 'what does this mean for me and how I do my job?' It answers it for two very good reasons.

First, defining an aim, and working *backwards* from that aim to the present, provides a clear context within which a strategy can be elaborated. The intuitive simplicity and accessibility of the framework, the way in which it graphically presents the sequence of initiatives required to accomplish an aim, enables people to visualize the point of the whole strategy exercise and believe it to be achievable.

Secondly, the staircase, with its emphasis upon the deliberate, sequential acquisition of skills and resources, breaks the overall aim down into readily digestible pieces. It provides a simple – but not simplistic – method of representing in manageable stages an organization's priorities, the choice between competing priorities, and the specific initiatives required to accomplish each of these. As a means of representing and communicating strategy, and its consequences, the strategic staircase is therefore both powerful and motivating.

Supply-side strategy constitutes, therefore, a fundamentally different approach to strategy development. One in which forecasting still has a role to play, but where what we are forecasting is not demand or sales, but rather those skills, capabilities and resources required to compete successfully in the future. The strategic challenge then becomes the generation and creation of an adequate *supply* of these essential skills and capabilities. The task of strategy is to guide the specification, selection and supply of those capabilities. Developing strategy from the supply side is an essentially creative process that leaves a company properly supplied with the skills and resources essential to continuing its competitive success. Using the strategic staircase facilitates the translation of that strategy into action.

Switching costs. Most firms incur costs or face barriers when they switch from one supplier to another. These might include the cost of testing and certifying a new supplier's product; adjusting their process to conform to slight differences in specifications; running down stocks of the old supplier's material or components; the cost of downtime in the transition; re-establishing logistics; and employee or management resistance or disenchantment associated with severing the relationship with an established supplier and its people. Final consumers may also incur costs which discourage them from switching, including the cost of searching for an alternative or the discomfort associated with the risk that the new product might prove unsatisfactory; think about the resistance consumers would have to switching from one home dry-cleaning agent to another, when they face the risk of discolouring their favourite outfits. There will be a strong preference for sticking to the brand they know.

Switching costs enable a supplier to increase the price of the product to established customers without having them desert to a competitor. The higher the switching cost the higher the potential for premium pricing because the higher is the barrier an alternative supplier faces in inducing customers to switch. Building up switching costs is therefore an important objective of many strategies. Indeed, in consumer goods, much of the rationale for BRANDING (the 'Don't your friends deserve Smirnoff?' campaign is a good example) lies in its ability to signal to the customer that the costs of switching (in this case 'social death') are potentially high.

In producer-goods markets, suppliers can build up switching costs by encouraging their customers to design products around the unique features of their components or materials. Suppliers who provide a replenishment system to their customers have found this also can act as a powerful deterrent from switching if the customer's alternative is to establish a system in-house in order to use a competing supplier who is unable to offer the facility. Other firms have offered discounts on maintenance of existing equipment for every pound spent on new equipment and 'upgrade deals' to discourage switching. The sale of brand-specific displays and shelving or dispensers to customers can also discourage switching since, having made the investment, they are loathe to make it obsolete by changing to an incompatible supplier. *See also* BUYER POWER, SUPPLIER POWER.

SWOT analysis. 'SWOT' stands for 'strengths, weaknesses, opportunities and threats'. It has become a popular checklist for assessing the strategic position of a particular business, highlighting the need to consider not only the current position, but also how this is likely to change in the future.

Determining strengths and weaknesses looks deceptively simple. Many businessmen are likely to rate these in absolute terms. However, the concept of COMPETITIVE ADVANTAGE alerts us to the fact that it is the position relative to competitors which counts at the end of the day. Phillip Morris Inc. saw itself as having strengths in consumer marketing based on its long experience in tobacco. It successfully applied these to the packaged-beer market when it acquired Miller Breweries. When it entered the soft-drink

industry with the acquisition of 7-UP, however, it found the
going very tough. Those same consumer-marketing strengths
were a relative weakness compared with the highly sophisticated and specific skills of Coca-Cola and Pepsi in that
market.

Similar arguments can be made for 'opportunities'. Technological advance offering potential cost reductions is only a
profit opportunity if market prices hold up. If it also causes a
rapid fall of competitors' costs, and prices tumble as a result,
the same technological potential becomes a threat.

Synergy. This deceptively simple idea is that by combining or in
some way linking different businesses, processes or activities,
the whole will be worth more than the sum of the parts. By
sharing fixed-cost facilities, spreading overhead, transferring
skills or technology, merging product lines, redistributing
cash and investment, and applying other mercurial sciences,
synergy will ensure that 2 + 2 will become five.

Synergy, often in the form of a concept rather than the
result of a realistic set of action plans, has been invoked to
justify the execution of innumerable acquisitions, mergers,
restructurings, co-ordinating committees, centralizations,
product introductions and diversifications. It is also a word
many managers wish they had never heard, either because the
costs of achieving these benefits far outweighed the value of
the gains achieved, or because 2 + 2 turned out to be 3 after
all.

The first problem encountered in achieving synergy lies in
the fact that the opportunity for linking two businesses
becomes confused with the potential for generating additional value by making the link. Certainly it is possible to
integrate a cement business with a ready-mixed concrete
business: the output of one is an input for the other. The real
question, however, is why would the two businesses be more
profitable if integrated in some way, rather than let a market
manage the relationship between them? In other words,
where is the synergy?

One might argue that the cement business suffers the

vagaries of the BUSINESS CYCLE which undermines its ability to run a smooth volume through its plants and avoid costly EXCESS CAPACITY. Now if the two were put together, the cement business would have an assured customer and could better plan its production: a prize of synergy there for the taking. What has been found in practice, however, is that the cement business is apt to offload a higher volume of cement onto its ready-mixed concrete sister than its internal customer requires when the market becomes weak. Compared with an arm's-length market arrangement, the supply line is difficult to cut back. With rising stocks of cement the ready-mixed concrete company strives to offload a higher volume onto the market. Since its product is perishable, it is forced to cut prices, and profitability is undermined. This illustrates the second problem which can arise in the pursuit of synergy benefits: the undesirable side-effects of the link can swamp the benefits to be gained.

The third problem is that in combining two businesses, often related but somewhat different, each is forced to compromise its free-standing choice. In a joint warehouse introduced to spread the costs, for example, the eventual design may reflect a common denominator which is sub-optimal for both parties.

A fourth problem with synergies in practice is that while the *potential* may be there, insufficient incentive exists for one party to ensure it is achieved. If both parties have profit responsibility for their own businesses, yet the gains are one-sided, for example, the 'giver' may have little incentive to co-operate.

Finally, combining two operations may result in a business which is very difficult to manage and suffers high COSTS OF COMPLEXITY or DISECONOMIES OF SCALE. Alternatively, centralizing certain functions may lead to them becoming divorced from the market and mute their customer responsiveness.

Despite the difficulties of achieving synergy, however, the potential gains can be large if the nature of the benefits stand up to critical analysis and the means by which they can be achieved are thoroughly specified. Asea Brown Boveri, a major supplier of turbine generators and other heavy equipment, benefited from synergy across a wide range of areas, from more effective R&D without unnecessary duplication, to cost improvements and a stronger sales and service-support network, following their merger.

To reap the benefits of synergy it is essential to get beyond vague notions of 'compatibility' and analyse both the costs and benefits of potential links and develop a clear plan and timetable for how and when they are to be achieved. Most successes have involved the inclusion of synergy benefits in the annual budgets of those involved as a way of keeping the opportunities on the 'front burner' of management's concern, or some other clear link to the incentive system. In other cases the appointment of a 'champion' with clear accountability for forcing through the changes required to achieve the synergy has made the difference between success and failure. Also important, although seemingly obvious, is the necessity for geographic proximity of the businesses to be linked or an organizational structure which generates frequent interaction between the individuals who are impacted. It is surprising how many planned synergies implicitly rely on telepathy. There may be magic in the $2 + 2$ making 5, but behind it lies realistic weighing of costs and benefits, down-to-earth planning and clear management of motivation and accountability.

T

Tactics. In military terms, tactics (for example, the movement of troops) are the means whereby a strategy (securing a bridge-head) is accomplished. The same distinction applies in management. Strategy defines what is to be achieved, tactics translate the 'what' into 'how': tactics are therefore typically of short duration, relatively narrow in focus and, of necessity, adaptable.

To illustrate: a firm's strategy may be to grow via acquisition, in pursuit of which it will identify and evaluate a number of potential targets, certain of which it will acquire. Within this strategic framework the choice of target is essentially tactical and each acquisition, irrespective of its size, represents the tactical translation of the strategy into action. Acquiring a company twice one's own size may appear to merit the label 'strategy' but it is, in essence, a tactic – albeit a large one.

But drawing the boundary between tactics and strategy is not always easy since the difference is largely a matter of perspective. One person's tactics may be another's strategy; for example, from the point of view of the CEO the specific steps taken by the marketing director to implement the firm's strategy are, in a sense, tactics. But to the marketing director these tactics, possibly embodied in a detailed plan of action, represent his department's strategy.

There is no need to become bogged down in drawing such fine distinctions. Rather, the essential point to remember is that tactics, like strategies, need to be adapted in the light of experience. In trying to translate your strategy into a set of precise actions, and in taking these actions to accomplish your strategy, do not be afraid of adapting what you do to meet changing circumstances. Tactics that are cast in concrete are a liability. Applying strategy affords an opportunity to 'learn' about it and to adapt your tactics to apply it in the light of what you learn (*see* EMERGENT STRATEGY).

Technological change. Three key sets of issues for strategy are raised by technological change: whether it pays to be the FIRST MOVER or a FOLLOWER; how the technological change will influence the basis of competition; and how to manage the shift from one technological generation to the next?

Being a technological first mover has some major advantages: it provides opportunities to define the standards; to pre-empt control of scarce resources, distributor relationships or retail locations; to sell on the basis of filling a need rather than displacing an existing product (compare the first versus the second cheque account); it allows lead time to build SWITCHING COSTS and BARRIERS TO ENTRY, and the chance to make early profits out of an innovation which may be short-lived. On the downside, however, early exploitation of a technology often lumbers the pioneer with the high costs of gaining the initial regulatory approval; educating the buyer to create generic demand; developing infrastructure, and investing in ancillary services which late comers can buy-in. These things expose a first mover to low-cost imitation by those who follow and to becoming stuck with heavy investment in early, sub-optimal technology.

Technological change not only alters cost level but also COST STRUCTURE. In so doing the basis of competition can change dramatically. The level of purchased inputs, for example, may rise significantly, eliminating the benefits of scale or skill in component manufacture. The required level of knowledge and skill among employees, from the salesforce to production operatives, may require improved training in some areas while other jobs become less skilled. Incumbent suppliers may therefore be left with the wrong mix of staff and an entrenched wage structure which restricts their adjustment. The basis of competition may also change as a given technology matures: from basic technology in the early stages, through a battle for standards, followed by a struggle for COST ADVANTAGE, only to shift towards DIFFERENTIATION as specialist customer requirements emerge. Volatile technology therefore places flexibility as a high strategic priority, making sure that BARRIERS TO EXIT and BARRIERS TO MOBILITY are kept low.

Sustained success in an environment of technological change also requires an ability to manage the transition between successive generations of a product or service. Many of the most profitable high-technology companies avoid the heavy marketing and sales investment in recruiting a new customer base when the technology changes by establishing a clear migration strategy. By close and continuous interaction with the customer, by upgrade schemes, leasing and retrofitting, they maximise their influence over the process of technological change within the customer, leaving few opportunities for competitors to enter and divert the business.

Time-based competition. We all know the old adage that 'time is money', yet in many companies costly time has been squandered in long product-development cycles, production queues, work-in-progress inventory, and batching of orders for data-processing or to provide longer production runs. Before its turnaround, Harley Davidson motorcycles, for example, found its lead time for assembly was 73 days. After painstaking analysis, which only followed near bankruptcy, it was found that the motorcycle was worked on for only 11 hours! It spent 72 days and 13 hours of its time in the system sitting in queues of every conceivable description.

Such queues create a vicious cycle. The long lead times which result from queues require sales forecasts. The longer the lead times, the more forecasts are relied upon but the less accurate they become. The greater the errors in forecasting, the higher the 'safety stocks' required. Burdened down with stock, product variations are delayed to avoid write-offs. A recipe for spiralling costs and dissatisfied customers.

The root cause of this problem has been that the costs of time are generally hidden. They show up in the budget only partially through the interest costs on stock. Even then, these interest costs of working capital are often not charged down from the corporate to operating-unit levels. The crippling costs avoid the gaze of management. Indeed, many of the initiatives to reduce processing costs, such as increasing batch sizes or run lengths, actually aggravate the unreported costs of time.

Now enter a company who sees time as a key competitive weapon. It concentrates effort on reducing the product-development cycle. It systematically squeezes out every source of delay between customer order and delivery. Real-time order entry replaces batching. Flexible manufacturing and reduced set-up times cut the minimum run-length down to a single unit (Toyota now assembles its cars with a batch size of one). Deliveries are made every few hours, not when a 'full load' is accumulated.

Initially, the accountants are horrified. Yet to everyone's surprise large amounts of cost disappear. There is little or no stock, nor obsolescence, since everything is made to order. Armies of planners, schedulers and reschedulers become redundant. Computer systems can actually be simplified. Expensive warehouses are unnecessary and plant floor spaces can be reduced. Customers find their own planning easier and their stockholding reduced as lead times drop. Satisfaction increases. The introduction of wave after wave of new variety is now possible without the drag of plant inflexibility and fear of stock obsolescence to slow it down. The score: time-based competition, one; rivals, nil.

Top down. See BOTTOM UP/TOP DOWN.

Transaction cost. Any completed exchange between a buyer and a seller constitutes a transaction; in effecting this transaction one or both parties will incur costs. For example, the newly established beer wholesaler might well be confronted with a range of possible suppliers (brewers) about whom he will need to acquire information and, having selected a preferred supplier, with whom he will enter into negotiations intended to produce an agreement or contract for the purchase of beer. The management time spent in acquiring reliable informa-tion, meeting the prospective suppliers, conducting negotia-tions and subsequently settling bills, all constitute the wholesaler's transaction costs. That is, the costs associated with completing the transaction or exchange.

Similarly, the holder of shares in company X, who, wishing to diversify his/her portfolio, begins investigating other companies in which s/he might invest, incurs costs, the level of which may in fact deter him/her from diversifying the portfolio at all. Transaction costs are only eliminated in the hypothetical situation in which all buyers and all sellers have equal, 'cost-less' access to all the relevant information. There are, however, ways of reducing transaction costs.

To return to the beer wholesaler. After five years successful trading the wholesaler might decide to go into beer production, thereby creating his own, independent source of supply. One rationale for this decision may be that the cost of making and selling beer within a single firm – and agreeing a TRANSFER PRICE from the department responsible for brewing to that responsible for selling – will be less than the costs incurred in negotiating the supply contract between two independent firms – the wholesaler and the brewer. This rationale lies at the heart of the strategy of vertical INTEGRATION, the traditional justification for which is that by effectively replacing transaction costs in the market by a series of transactions within the firm – in other words by replacing market exchange with internal planning and co-ordination – the firm will be able to reduce its costs. Similarly, the logic behind many mergers is that the merged firm will have access to better information and lower costs, since it is in principle easier and therefore cheaper to monitor what is happening within a firm, and to co-ordinate activities internally, than it is to obtain information about, and to co-ordinate activities with, other firms.

The implications of this for strategy are twofold. First, a buyer who can credibly threaten a supplier with the prospect of backward integration (that is, taking over the supplier's activity) may substantially improve his bargaining position and thereby reduce his transaction costs (*see* BUYER POWER). Secondly, the cost savings derived from integration are notoriously difficult to pin down. Although there is little empirical evidence of the cost savings associated with integration, it is nonetheless clear that integration may mask the real costs of internal transactions, thereby creating a false picture of just how profitable – or unprofitable – a particular activity really is. It is precisely because internal transaction costs are so often hidden and somewhat intangible (for example, what is the 'cost' of obtaining relevant information?) that particular attention should be paid to them in developing strategy, especially one based upon the assumption that making something is cheaper than buying it in the marketplace: often the reverse is true.

Transfer price. Prices charged for goods or services transferred internally from one part of a company – typically a PROFIT CENTRE – to another are transfer prices. Ideally a transfer-pricing system should meet two, sometimes conflicting, conditions. First, transfer prices should avoid distorting the reported profits of a particular division and enable the managers of that division to retain a sound basis for their decision-making. Secondly, the system should simultaneously improve the firm's overall performance (for example, by exploiting the interrelationships between its constituent parts), and at the same time provide profit-centre managers with the right degree of incentive.

Transfer prices are either market-based or cost-based. Market-based prices, which may have to be estimated in the absence of an actual market price, give no advantage to either the buyer or the seller. However, the administrative simplicity of such a system, in which individual business units trade with each other on an arm's length basis, may actually impede the exploitation of those interrelationships between units upon which a firm's overall success depends. Cost-based systems can work from actual or standard, marginal or full costs. Using standard rather than actual costs guards against the possibility of one part of the firm passing on its own inefficiencies to another. The problem with a system based on marginal costs is that it is unlikely to provide sufficient motivation for the regional managers.

In practice transfer prices are rarely set on the basis of such clear-cut market-based or cost-based guidelines. The price at which internal transfers are made is usually the outcome of internal negotiations and, with multinational businesses in particular, of an assessment of the political, taxation and currency consequences of charging those prices.

Transfer pricing is becoming an increasingly important issue as new interdependent strategies become more common, built on plant specialization; the formation of a global network of business units taking advantage of local conditions but exchanging products and information; or the sharing of skills and assets such as distribution facilities. An inappropriate transfer-pricing system can drive a wedge between the strategic imperatives and the incentives faced by 'front line' managers. Such an inconsistency will consign the strategy to become a failed dream.

Trend analysis. Any set of data – for example, annual sales figures – which contains a consistent pattern or movement is said to exhibit a trend; that is, an observable movement or pattern across time. Data analysis may immediately reveal a trend which provides a basis for forecasting likely future trends. In other words the historic value of a variable (say, sales data) is used as a guide to forecasting its future value by extrapolating – or projecting forward – a trend into the future. The simplicity and intuitive appeal of this method makes it highly popular. Indeed, a recent survey of the world's five hundred largest corporations revealed that trend analysis is one of the most widely used forms of forecasting, being employed by more than 70 per cent of all companies surveyed.

But the method must be used with care. For example, any collection of data may well contain 'rogue' figures – abnormally high or low sales in a particular month, for instance – which will distort the underlying trend. In such instances the data will have to be 'smoothed', for example, by according less weight to aberrant items. Underpinning all trend analysis is an assumption – often tacit – that the world is reasonably consistent and only changes slowly in the short run. The past therefore provides a reasonable guide to the future which can be seen in a sense as a continuation of the past. In the late twentieth century such an assumption is, for an increasing number of industries, becoming wholly untenable as accelerating changes and dramatic discontinuities render the past an unreliable guide to the future. However historically well-grounded a trend forecast is, rapid unanticipated change in any significant variable may invalidate it. Using historical trends as a platform on which to build a strategy can be akin, therefore, to erecting a building on quicksand. Moreover, over-reliance on forecasting trends limits the strategy in two fundamental respects.

First, the forecast may act as a constraint or, alternatively, as a set of blinkers where the basis of performance measurement is how well the firm is doing in relation to the forecast (and by implication in relation to last year's actual performance). There is a danger of ignoring or underplaying what is happening in the market, what competitors are doing, or how customer needs are changing. Doing well in relation to the forecast – or maintaining an established trend – is not necessarily the same thing as doing well in competitive terms (*see* BENCHMARKING). Moreover, the forecast, by its very nature, presents the firm with a limited number of options – those encompassed within its range.

The second limitation is equally serious. The detection of historical trends and extrapolation of these into the future, entails taking the present and the observable past as a starting point for strategy. Intuitively this makes sense. But this approach to strategy does not encourage the derivation of strategies and initiatives from a clear sense of where the firm is aiming at or what its mission is. The real challenge of strategy is to start with the future – that is, with the firm's ambition, aim or strategic intent – and then work backwards towards the present. Proceeding this way poses the following strategic question, 'what strategies must be put in place now, next year and the year after if our mission is to be accomplished?' In contrast, the question posed by trend analysts takes the following form: 'where will we get to if previously observed trends continue?' Such an intrinsically passive approach to strategy is becoming increasingly ill-suited to a

world characterized by shortening trends, massive uncertainties and sharp discontinuities.
See also REGRESSION ANALYSIS.

Turnround. Narrowly defined, a business confronting an acute cash crisis constitutes a turnround situation. More broadly, any business requiring corrective action to arrest steady decline and avoid eventual failure represents a potential turnround. In such instances a business may exhibit symptoms of failure well before experiencing a full-blown crisis.

If there is one golden rule about the process of restoring a business to financial and competitive health it is that gaining control takes absolute precedence over everything else. A US survey of 81 turnround CEOs produced the following ranking of critical factors in turnround management:

1 initiating tight controls;
2 changing people's attitudes;
3 understanding the business fully;
4 providing visible leadership;
5 having a strong financial executive;
6 giving control to management.

The priorities for control will vary, reflecting in part the underlying causes of the firm's difficulties, but they will typically encompass: costs, purchasing and suppliers, sales and marketing, product range and development, head count, cash management and debt restructuring. But the selection of the right control priorities will play a key role in determining the success of the turnround. In making the selection it is essential to recognize that tackling all of the problems at once will only dilute the effort and its effectiveness – many problems can wait. That initial effort should focus on those areas that are critical to survival, those which offer greatest turnround leverage and scope for achieving quick – and visible – results. In turnround situations speed is often of the essence, and it usually pays dividends therefore to adopt a solution that is 80 per cent effective rather than wait say three months for a remedy that will be 90 to 100 per cent effective.

Whatever strategy is adopted, whether it entails a wholesale change of management (as is the case in over 90 per cent of successful turnrounds), instituting tight financial controls, cutting costs or financial restructuring, a sustainable turnround requires a fundamental change in the beliefs and attitudes of all who work in the business. To turn a business round you have to turn round the people who work within it. Hence an integral part of the role of the turnround CEO is to provide a clear vision of where the business is going, what the future holds and what is required from all staff to realize that future.

One final point: turnrounds are often associated with cost-cutting and containment, with retrenchment and withdrawal. This is not necessarily the case. Achieving a successful turnround may entail new investment, even at a time when the company is losing money. For example, in 1980, when Jan Carlzon took over the ailing Scandinavian Airlines System, the business was heading for a $20m loss. The expectation was that he would increase traffic by slashing fares, and improve margins by cutting costs. Instead, Carlzon, having redefined SAS's mission to become the preferred airline of the European business traveller, presented a recovery plan which called for new, additional investment of $45m and an increase in operating costs of $12m per annum. This money was to be spent on 147 different projects, such as a comprehensive punctuality campaign and major improvements to airport facilities that were intended to support SAS's chosen strategy. In parallel with these initiatives Carlzon initiated a huge project called 'Trim' which generated $40m worth of savings. In determining what to cut, the key criterion was 'does this area of expenditure support the goal of serving the business traveller?' By 1985 SAS was voted 'Airline of the Year' for business people and profitability had been restored. The story neatly illustrates an essential ingredient of turnround management. Defining a clear vision for the business, gaining control and identifying the *right* costs to be eliminated, while at the same time selecting appropriate areas for new investment, lie at the heart of any successful turnround.

U

U curve.   *See* DISECONOMIES OF SCALE.

U-form organization.   *See* FUNCTIONAL STRUCTURE.

Unbundling.   *See* BUNDLING.

Upstream.   *See* DOWNSTREAM.

V

Value added. The concept of value added has become infamous through its close association with that ever present business companion: the value added tax or VAT. It is the difference between the total revenue of a firm and the cost of bought-in raw materials, services and components. Hence it measures the total value which the firm has 'added' to these bought-in supplies through its own efforts. Value added therefore represents the total cake from which all of those who lay claim to the fruits of the firm's internal activities, including shareholders, employees and the government, must take their share.

Thinking in terms of value added can be helpful in focusing on the strategic question: 'what business are we in?'. Strategy might ask, for example, 'what is the value added of a wholesale distributor?'. The answer probably lies in some combination of breaking bulk, transportation, providing information to retailers, increasing the speed of replenishment by holding stocks, managing credit risks and sales relationships. Therefore, the concept helps a business in separating out the value already inherent in what it buys in, allowing it to concentrate on where it really adds value for its consumers.

What, then, determines the amount of value added generated by a business? The answer lies in its ability to do what its suppliers or customers either cannot do or don't wish to undertake. This puts an interesting perspective on the strategies of successful firms: they will be those who make a business out of undertaking those activities which their suppliers and customers think of as a nuisance. As the old adage goes: 'your problem is our business'.

Mathematically, value added is often written as follows:

value added = operating costs + profits

The implication, however, that value added is determined by costs and profits, is obviously flawed. It is the customer, after all, who determines how much value added the firm has created. Perhaps, then, we might rewrite the equation this way:

profit = value added − operating costs

This is one step closer to the truth, but any manager who is held responsible for a profit target will recognise that profit cannot act as a passive leftover of the value added cake. In Japan they sometimes like to rearrange the equation like this:

operating costs = value added − profit

The customers and suppliers set the value added, the shareholders the profit. The job of the manager is to make the costs fit.

Value capture. Successful DIFFERENTIATION creates additional value for the buyer, almost always at some extra cost. To benefit at the 'bottom line', part of this extra value must be captured by the business in the form of a sustainable pre-

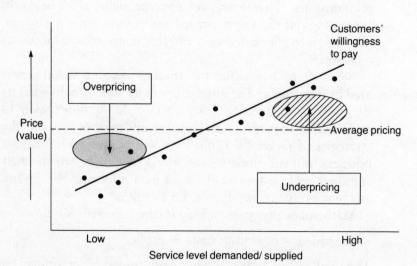

Figure 33   Value Capture

mium above the price which would have been obtained without it. (See figure 33.)

Many firms' 'average out' the price across different varieties or specifications in their product line or in a bundle of goods and services provided to the customer. This makes it difficult to capture the value of differentiation within a product portfolio. The result is CROSS-SUBSIDIZATION between varieties, products and services. This represents a LOOSE BRICK in the competitive wall and an open invitation to competitors to cherry-pick the products that are overpriced relative to their level of differentiation or to 'unbundle' the product offering (*see* CHERRY PICKING). An important co-requisite of differentiation is therefore a price structure which parallels the true value to customers and reflects the product- or variety-specific costs involved.

Value chain. Overall COMPETITIVE ADVANTAGE must derive from better design, execution or resources applied in the specific individual activities which make up a business. The more numerous the activities where a firm enjoys advantage and the more diverse the sources of this lead, generally the more difficult competitors find it to copy the successful formula. Building a complex web of advantage across the whole spectrum of a firm's activities is the key to sustainability.

The so-called 'value chain' is a useful framework for exploring how each activity might contribute to competitive advantage. The consistency (or lack of it) of the individual policies which make up the strategy also becomes obvious when laid out in the value-chain structure.

The roots of this methodology are to be found in MCKINSEY & CO.'s 'business system' concept which emphasized that all businesses were a sequence of activities from input purchasing through to after-sales service. Each link had to play its role in exploiting potential sources of advantage over competitors. Professor Michael Porter refined this into the basic structure shown in figure 34.

Along the base is a set of 'line' or 'primary' activities from

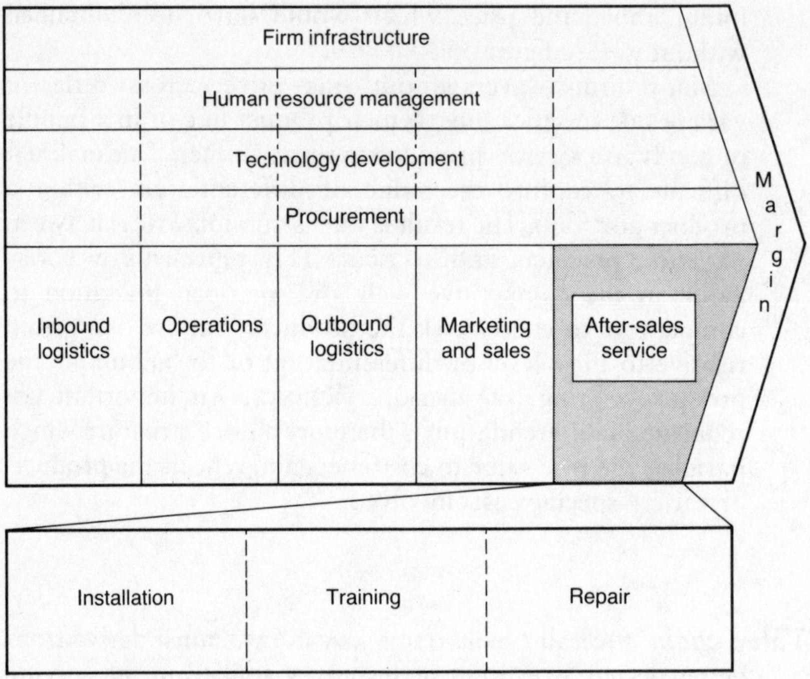

Figure 34   Michael Porter's Value Chain

physically handling the flow of required inputs ('inbound logistics') through 'operations', distribution ('outbound logistics'), 'marketing and sales', and 'after-sales service'. Each of these may be further subdivided into a set of more specific activities – the after-sales service, for example, can be seen as comprising its own three-stage value chain. Across the top of the figure is a set of support activities: the 'general firm infrastructure' (including such things as its capital resources or borrowing capacity), 'human resource management', 'technology' and 'procurement'.

An important point highlighted by this structure is that each primary activity involves its own procurement, technology and human-resource issues which may require different approaches from those appropriate to other activities. The greatest financial advantage of better technology, for example, may come from developing superior servicing equipment rather than from trying directly to improve the product itself. After-sales service may also have its own procurement problems and opportunities which may be dealt with differently.

Another key lesson is that every activity within the firm should be considered as a potential source of advantage, even those which are considered purely routine. For example, clear, well-coded and reliable invoices which can be easily checked against the goods received by the customer can simplify his own procedures, cutting his costs and improving your attractiveness as a supplier compared with a competitor who send wads of unintelligible computer print-out. Use of bar-coded documents might offer an extra edge. Even the accounts department can therefore be a direct source of competitive advantage.

Advantage comes from COST LEADERSHIP or DIFFERENTIA- TION in each individual activity in the chain. There is a need, therefore, to understand costs and value creation pertaining to each activity. We need to go on subdividing until each activity which has either its own impact on the customer or a substantial and independent cost structure has been separated and analysed.

Once operating policies for each of these activities have been decided upon in isolation, consistency throughout the chain needs to be checked. It is almost inevitable that conflicts will arise: reducing costs in one activity might increase costs or reduce differentiation elsewhere. Trade-offs may be necessary. Conversely, proper strategy based on the value chain can generate an advantage in one activity which reinforces advantage elsewhere. Canon undertook careful market research into the needs of those using small photocopiers aimed at eliminating rarely used features. The object was to keep size and price down and to simplify selling and training. Yet this also allowed engineers to reduce dramatically the complexity of internal machine components with the bonus of improved reliability.

The value chain has therefore a variety of uses, two of which should be particularly noted. First, as a conceptual tool that helps managers to analyse the costs of different activities, to understand where costs are being incurred, where the margin is being made, and where the firm might be better off making what it cannot buy rather than buying what it cannot make. Using the framework properly also directs attention to the interrelationships between activities, functions, customers and products, and the costs of co-ordinating activities across this broad spectrum.

Secondly, the value chain is a useful presentational tool that enables managers to explain to those working in a specific functional area exactly where their functional group fits in, what precisely is its contribution to the firm's overall strategy, and how it can perform its activities in such a way as to sustain and support the strategy, imbuing it with the degree of consistency necessary to succeed.

But as with many frameworks in strategy the utility of the value chain lies not so much in filling in the various boxes but rather in thinking systematically through the entire set of activities which make up the firm. The real benefit of the framework is derived from thinking about the firm as a series of interlinked activities, each of which offers scope for building competitive advantage. It is a framework that a manager should, in effect, carry in his head; it is not simply about filling in boxes on a piece of paper.

See also BUYER VALUE CHAIN.

Value line. The choice of quality level at which to compete can be an important element of strategy. Two basic relationships dominate this decision: how the quality level affects the sustainable price premium and how much this quality costs to supply. The value line is the theoretical relationship between price and quality which appears to exist in the market. Therefore, in figure 35, it seems that brand D is able to achieve the same share of the market as the private-label brand, P, while sustaining a substantial price premium because this properly reflects its quality differential. Brand B on the other hand, is pitched at a price far above that consistent with its quality. In consequence it has a very small market share, comprising those buyers who are 'fooled' about its real quality. As those buyers gain more information, we might

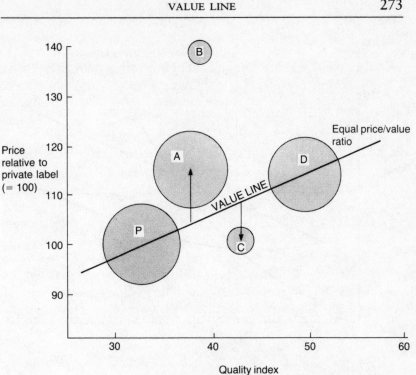

Figure 35 Branding and a Price-quality Value Line for Paper Towels

expect brand B to lose even more share. Brand A, meanwhile, appears to command a moderate price premium above that warranted by its quality without surrendering share. This may reflect the successful use of advertising to establish an image among buyers which makes it more popular than its price or objective quality would lead us to expect.

The converse is true for brand C. It is actually underpriced compared with its true quality, yet it currently has a small share. It may be in the early stages of a new pricing policy designed to grow the brand. Alternatively, its poor performance might reflect an inadequate distribution and shelf-space allocation.

The value-line framework is a useful way of laying out the different competitive options regarding quality positioning, pricing and market share as growth objectives. It can also be

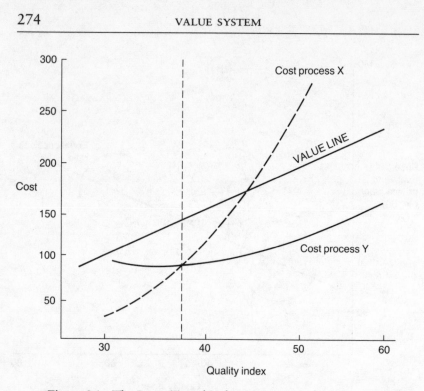

Figure 36   The Paper Towel Value Line versus the Cost to Produce

an aid to deciding where to compete given the cost structure of existing technology. In figure 36, for example, it is clear that a firm with technological process X is only likely to be competitive at the lower-quality end of the market. This is because the costs of producing a higher quality rapidly become greater than the price premium achievable. Conversely, the high-quality end of the market offers greatest profit potential for firms with process Y. Here the available price premiums cover the extra costs of improved quality plus a healthy boost to profits.

Value system. Michael Porter's VALUE CHAIN framework provides a tool for analysing how overall COMPETITIVE ADVANTAGE can be built up on the basis of COST LEADERSHIP or DIFFERENTIATION in each of the individual activities which comprise a business.

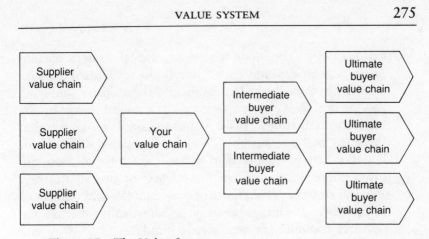

Figure 37   The Value System

Potential sources of cost reduction or differentiation, however, very often depend on the structure of buyers' and suppliers' own businesses. Forms of differentiation which reduce the buyers' own operating costs, for example, will be valuable to them. Fibreglass roofing is a good case in point; it is faster to lay compared with traditional roofing materials and therefore much cheaper for contractors to handle. Some suppliers' products command a substantial premium because they are considerably cheaper to lay. Likewise, a differentiated component, such as a 'Swiss movement' in watches, may have value to a watch assembler above its inherent accuracy because it is a recognized label which helps encourage customers to pay a price premium for his final watch.

Given the importance of the economics of suppliers' and buyers' own businesses in deciding how to create advantage it is often useful specifically to analyse each of them as separate value chains. The firm's own value chain may therefore be thought of as part of a larger sequence of chains which comprise the complete value system from basic raw materials to the end user as illustrated in figure 37.

Policies to build advantage then are explicitly based on the interactions between each of your activities and those of others in the system. To the extent that your firm can reduce the costs or improve the performance of others, a profit potential is created. Capturing that profit is then an issue of VERTICAL STRATEGY.

Vertical strategy. The modern view of vertical strategy encompasses a great deal more than simply the traditional decision of whether to backward integrate into the industry supplying raw materials key components or forward integrate by buying into distributors (*see* INTEGRATION). It recognizes that there are 'make versus buy' decisions associated with virtually every activity involved in a business and that these are often important choices in the context of overall strategy. Vertical strategy can enhance or constrain the achievement of competitive advantage as well as drastically altering the resource commitment necessary to build it.

Increasingly we are seeing some very successful firms like Benetton and Sulzer who concentrate their resources at each end of the VALUE CHAIN of activities required for their product and sub-contract out the intermediate stages. More than 50 per cent of the actual knitting activities required by Benetton's products are undertaken by small outworker firms. Benetton purchases the yarn and controls the design, dyeing, marketing and distribution through its own retail outlets. Sulzer is solely involved in the detailed design of its marine engines, as well as the marketing and spare-parts supply. The actual engines are built, sold, and spare parts installed by third-party licencees (*see* LICENSING). Vertical strategy therefore not only involves a choice of which activities I want to be in, but also which ones I need to control.

From the strategic standpoint, performing activities in-house has a number of advantages. There may be cost economies in continuous flow: hot rolling of steel or direct application of protective coatings without reheating are standard examples. The co-ordination of changes in specifications or volume fluctuations may be easier and having purchasing or selling functions within the firm may improve planning and help to reduce in-process inventory.

Having direct control of the customer relationship may help a firm to develop better product DIFFERENTIATION through the direct experience of customers' needs or the ability to support the sales effort with specialized technical staff from other parts of the organization. It may also be a way to side-step strong BUYER or SUPPLIER POWER which would squeeze profits. It may raise BARRIERS TO ENTRY by keeping the markets for the intermediate products thin. It is argued, for example, that one of the main difficulties in entering aluminium smelting is that the dominant firms control such a high percentage of the downstream distribution and fabrication that there is virtually no reliable free market for the output of an independent company of any size.

Yet for all this it is surprising how many businesses claim that in-house buyers, suppliers or support functions are the worst to deal with. They are charged with lack of service orientation or failure to focus on cost improvements because the protection of secure 'markets' within the firm removes the pressure to improve.

There are other disadvantages. Often the economic scales of different activities are a poor match. This can mean that a vertically integrated operation runs with excess capacity at some stages and scale disadvantages at others. There is also a loss of strategic flexibility; owning upstream component or materials manufacture may increase the difficulty of switching to substitutes if they become more attractive on price or improved technology. Firms who were integrated back into packaging materials have often been reluctant to change at discovering their cost in lost sales. Owning a distribution channel may be an impediment if new, more competitive channels emerge. A wide span of ownership along the chain tends to increase BARRIER TO EXIT from a business. Some stages may also absorb large amounts of scarce capital at a relatively low return.

In order to gain control of the key stages for capturing profit along the chain and minimizing exposure to powerful buyers or suppliers without carrying some of the costs and constraints of full ownership and in-house involvement, many firms are taking other approaches to vertical strategy. These have been based on licensing designs or technologies for particular stages, JOINT VENTURES or acquiring minority interests in certain activities, FRANCHISING or using sub-contractors are all becoming more common. Perhaps even more importantly, innovative businesses are becoming more selective about the activities within the value chain which they undertake. Like Benetton, they now recognize the possibility of certain stages within their vertical span being best left to others.

Vision. It is tempting to develop a vision by asking the question, 'where do we want to take the company in the future?' This can lead to comforting, but damaging, ignorance of the changing demands of the market. It is often more useful to develop a vision of the future around 'what the successful competitors will look like in tomorrow's competitive environment'. This would include a view of the relative size of existing and prospective market segments, the state of future competition, and the new RULES OF THE GAME, and might require consideration of whether vertical integration would be an advantage or a disadvantage, the future importance of brands, whether competition would be local, regional or global, or how the optimal scale of production or distribution would change.

Developing such a vision is the first stage in identifying viable market options for a business in the future. It informs as to what capabilities and resources a firm will need to amass in order to be able to survive and prosper. It points to actions necessary now to open up opportunities for the company in its future environment and to avoid becoming trapped in a declining position without the flexibility to respond.

The essence of the vision process is the generation of a view about what future options exist. Forecasts, by contrast, often narrow options by asking 'where will the firm be in the future' as if there is inevitability about its future position. *See also* SCENARIO ANALYSIS, LEVELS OF STRATEGY.

W

Walled city. Some businesses will be protected from competitive attack at almost all costs by their owners, often beyond the bounds of economic rationality. This often occurs when a large group has grown and diversified around the base of a core business. It may make sense to leave that business in which it now lacks competitive advantage. Corporate cultural and psychological commitment to the business, however, may lead them to defend the business aggressively. Losses may be accepted or cross-subsidized using cash flow from other businesses to keep the 'grandfather' alive.

It is important for strategy to recognize, before attack, that it may be facing walled cities among some of the competitors. Clearly it will be a long and often costly siege if the attack is head-on with a ME-TOO STRATEGY. The most effective response to potential walled cities is to change the RULES OF THE GAME by bypassing existing distribution channels or changing the product specifications, for example, so that the incumbent is forced to fight on new ground.

See also BARRIERS TO EXIT.

Wheel of strategy. An early device used to emphasize the critical relationships between the firm's goals (growth, profitability and so on), its target competitive strategy (like cost leadership in particular segments) and its operational policies, is shown in figure 38.

The 'spokes' highlight the need for each functional area to transmit the strategic objectives directly into actions in the market which turns the wheel forward. The 'rim' depicts the need for each set of functions to link smoothly with the others, avoiding jagged interface 'gaps' in the cover. The result is a consistent and defensible whole, capable of advancing through the market.

Figure 38   The Wheel of Strategy

X

X-inefficiency. A measure of the degree to which a firm uses its resources inefficiently and thereby fails to maximize its productive potential. Contrary to much economic and financial theory, which presumes strict economic rationality, Harvey Liebenstein argued that X-inefficiency should be expected as the norm in organizations. The psychological costs of removing X-inefficiency, such as disruption and employee discomfort entailed in changing work practices, results in inertia. X-inefficiency therefore tends to stick in the business system. An important role of strategy is to remove this inertia and help shake out X-inefficiency by promoting plans for change in line with market demands.

A build-up of X-inefficiency blunts the competitiveness of a business; it means both its tangible and *intangible* ASSETS are being poorly deployed. Failure of management to attack the problem exposes the firm to predatory ACQUISITION, where the new owner seeks to increase productivity by squeezing out X-inefficiency or redeploying the assets more productively through disposal.

Y

Year end. The day of reckoning for many strategists is often the year end: the time when the performance of the strategy is re-assessed and potential conflicts with the external capital market, as one of the firm's key CONSTITUENCIES, come to a head. Despite a certain inevitability, this approach to measuring the strategy has a number of inadequacies. Most importantly, the relationship between the achievement of strategic objectives and the year's annual budget is at best a tenuous one.

Stellar results on the year-end budget may mask the fact that the market is being HARVESTED for short-term profit when strategy requires signals of continued commitment to winning the END GAME. Progress on a key strategic move, such as initiating a shift in the mix of distribution channels between indirect and direct, may not show up in a budget review at all. The consequences of failure to track competitor moves this year may not emerge until two budgets down the road when a large reduction in sales occurs.

Strategy operates over a wide range of horizons. The time-scale of strategic costs and benefits is unlikely to be consistent with annual performance measurement. Nor do traditional budgeting procedures highlight whether or not strategy for the future is being implemented now. Specific systems for strategic monitoring are therefore required. These must attempt to assess both how well the strategy is being applied day-to-day – by the line 'are they managing strategically?' – as well as whether managers are making the necessary strategic investments for beyond the year end.

Z

Zero-sum game. One reason why a poker game is prone to generate emotion, and often ill-feeling, lies in the simple fact that what one player wins the others must have lost. Rather than generating a surplus of cash, it simply re-distributes the wealth around: the hallmark of a 'zero-sum game'.

Much business has been traditionally treated as a zero-sum game. This thinking lies behind the view that, for example, what a customer gains in a negotiation the supplier must have lost, or the assumption that the growth of one competitor implies a loss of sales for another. In fact there are cases when the game of business strategy is a zero sum; four competitors in a market all vying for increased market share is a situation where a gain for one means a loss for the others. The problem with approaching business as a zero-sum game, however, is that it often provokes violent retaliation; the business equivalent of poker's 'Colt 45'. The situation can rapidly degenerate into a 'negative-sum game' where the result is a net destruction of profit potential in the market as a whole.

Innovative strategy often works when it is successful in producing the conditions for transforming a zero-sum game into a positive-sum game. When the application of JUST IN TIME principles paved the way for eliminating unnecessary inventory between supplier and buyer, both had the opportunity to gain by the removal of dead-weight cost. The replacement of paper cheques by debit cards was a positive-sum game for banks, retailers and customers, by their eliminating excessive handling and errors which ultimately imposed costs on all three groups. Early computer manufacturers saw the battle for standards as a zero-sum game: increased sales of one meant less for another. The eventual agreement on common standards for disc-drives and printer interfaces, however, helped the PC market to grow more rapidly to the overall benefit of suppliers, hence creating a positive-sum game, even if some individual makers lost out.

Becoming locked into a zero-sum game is an important

cause of strategy failure. Recognizing this pathology is the first step in breaking out of an unprofitable loop where it is difficult for any of the players to win consistently.